Beyond the Quest to Become a Physician

Beyond the Quest to Become a Physician

INSIGHTFUL AND INSPIRATIONAL TALES OF

Parenting, Perseverance,

AND

Pediatrics

Robert E. Burke, MD, PhD

ARCHWAY
PUBLISHING

This book is a work of non-fiction. Unless otherwise noted, the author and the publisher make no explicit guarantees as to the accuracy of the information contained in this book and in some cases, names of people and places have been altered to protect their privacy.

Archway Publishing books may be ordered through booksellers or by contacting:

Archway Publishing
1663 Liberty Drive
Bloomington, IN 47403
www.archwaypublishing.com
1 (888) 242-5904

Because of the dynamic nature of the Internet, any web addresses or links contained in this book may have changed since publication and may no longer be valid. The views expressed in this work are solely those of the author and do not necessarily reflect the views of the publisher, and the publisher hereby disclaims any responsibility for them.

Any people depicted in stock imagery provided by Thinkstock are models, and such images are being used for illustrative purposes only. Certain stock imagery © Thinkstock.

ISBN: 978-1-4808-3984-7 (sc)
ISBN: 978-1-4808-3986-1 (hc)
ISBN: 978-1-4808-3985-4 (e)

Library of Congress Control Number: 2016920823

Print information available on the last page.

Archway Publishing rev. date: 12/21/2016

CONTENTS

IN MEMORY OF

This book is dedicated to the memory of my parents, Carl Gustave Burke and Catherine Elizabeth (Gallagher) Burke. I will be forever grateful for the inspiration and family they gave me. In particular, Dad's work ethic and Mom's inspiration and their love helped me to fulfill many dreams. My resolve to become a physician was strengthened by the tragic death of my brother, Billy (William Frederick Burke), and so this is also in loving memory of him, my closest teen idol.

ABOUT THE AUTHOR

As the middle son of an impoverished family, Dr. Burke blazed a trail through higher education and success in the field of medicine as never before in his family's history. The tortuous path he followed in his quest to become a physician began at Wilkes College, where he graduated magna cum laude with a bachelor of science degree in biology (1970). At the Pennsylvania State University, he earned a master of science in botany (1972) and the doctor of philosophy (PhD) in Biology (1976).

He pursued breast cancer research as an NIH-sponsored post-doctoral fellow, at the University of Texas Health Science Center at San Antonio (UTHSCSA) prior to medical school there. He published that research, continuing as cell culture lab consultant and researcher during the first two years of medical school for the late Dr. William L. McGuire. His long quest to become a physician was achieved in 1982. He then completed a three-year residency specializing in pediatrics at the UTHSCSA.

Dr. Burke earned and maintained board certification throughout his thirty-plus-year career as a fellow of the American Academy of Pediatrics, before retiring from clinical practice in 2015. He has touched thousands of lives in many ways. His career has focused on the clinical practice of general pediatrics, and thousands of children have identified him as their primary doctor. For nearly a decade, he was a solo pediatrician in a rural community in central Pennsylvania with Geisinger Healthcare System. Teaching medical students and resident physicians was an integral part of his longer career at Scott & White in Temple, Texas. He was an associate professor and served as vice chairman of Pediatrics there. Dr. Burke has lectured to medical students, other doctors, community groups, and schools. He has written newspaper articles and given interviews for television and community blogs on literacy, child and brain development, and attention deficit disorders. He has relentlessly promoted literacy and preventive healthcare regionally.

Previously, he wrote a parenting manual, *Caring for Kids*, which his healthcare institution copyrighted and distributed for more than a decade. Recently he wrote and self-published *Photo Journey, Baby's First Year*, as a visual aid and advice for new parents.

Dr. Burke met his soul mate, Bonnie L. (Rood) Burke, at Wilkes College. They have been blessed with four children and eleven grandchildren. His expertise is supported by thirty-three years as a pediatrician, tempered by his roles as a father and grandfather.

PART 1

Before the Quest

Like a knight-errant or quixotic visionary, he was relentless. Almost everyone he met encouraged his pursuit of someday being anointed "physician." Encouragement always pushed him onward but was never sufficient for meaningful direction. How he started on that quest is not known for sure. He can't remember when it became his *raison d'etre*, but he does know that his mother would always tell folks, "Bobby will be a good doctor someday. He has wanted to be a doctor ever since he was four years old."

Really? Four years was not enough time to have become knowledgeable about career options. In fact, he had not traveled anywhere outside of his small town. He had not known any doctors. He likely did not even know what doctors did except that they helped people. He was not exposed to physician role models at four, and he had not yet drunk from the chalice of imperfect knowledge known as a television. Nevertheless, he also told people who asked that he would become a physician. This is what his "queen mum" told him, so it must be true. This question usually came from teachers or curious relatives or family friends. Was it his quest, or was it chosen for him? Regardless, his quest began very early. He swore allegiance.

This is a true tale of that quest. The adventure brings challenges, knowledge, character changes, distractions, and revelations. At times it seemed he would never escape the home castle as the gates would close, the drawbridge would be raised, or the moat would fill with dragons and beasts of uncertain danger. But as he managed these first hurdles, the quest got underway. To be anointed as a physician, however, he had to earn the medical degree. He learned of the fortress that held the degree. But the goal remained elusive. He attempted to scale those hallowed walls, but he painfully fell, time and time again. The guardians of the fortress and its degree had created barriers that seemed impenetrable. His queen sent words of encouragement and emissaries, but to no avail. As he wandered away hopelessly, a new vision took hold of his life, but so did a new queen. He pursued that new vision with zest and fortitude, and just as he reconciled himself to this, his queen talked of how he could still become a physician. She had met a sage who sent direction and new information. Relentless but half-expecting to fail, he resumed the quest, hoping that this time it would be different.

The allegory above, about knights, castles, queens and quests, emulates the story of my life. Quest, the word most often associated with a medieval knight's pursuit, would be my best one-word description of what it was like to strive to become a physician.

There are many forces that drive our ambitions. Those forces are emotional, cognitive, social, religious, and perhaps fateful. Ambition often springs from ability and hope for change. Knowing that a goal is worthy, and knowing that one is capable of achieving that goal, can drive our actions and ambition. Multiple forces sustain us during difficult times, providing the ingenuity to overcome obstacles and the comfort to forge ahead. And so it was for me. At times, it seemed like chasing windmills, trying to find the Holy Grail, naively perhaps, but steadfast.

To become a physician—this is what I knew was my life's purpose. Seeking the real or symbolic Holy Grail for its special powers and the happiness it could bring has been the theme of much literature. So it is with the quest to become a physician. Special healing powers, knowledge, wealth, status, and happiness would be bestowed upon that person. Although people often think that becoming a physician is accompanied by the immediate transformation of self and the securing of one's destiny, it does not happen like that. Only in fantasy does that happen. Reality sets in. However, a portal to a new life opens. I wanted to enter through that portal.

Little did I know what a tortuous path it would be to seek and find that Holy Grail. Little did I know how my personality would change, what inner transformations would occur. How did it all happen? What experiences drove that transformation? Who was responsible, and what enabled it? Little did I know how enriched my life would become, taking those other paths.

CHAPTER 1

Just What They Needed—Another Boy

The Why of Whom We Become

There has been much written about how we have no control over our fate. There has been much written about how we control our fate. Where is the truth? Is there a master plan for every single human being? Do we live the life we earned in a prior life? Or is it all about chance? Do bad or good things simply happen, regardless of how we live our lives? Is it about opportunities and lack thereof, or is it about genetics? Is it like the song from Jesus Christ Superstar laments, "Everything is fixed and you can't change it"?[1]

Anyone can claim to know the answers to those questions, the why of whom we become. But no one really knows. It would be nice to have a "sorting hat" like that used on the fictional characters in a Harry Potter novel.[2] Place it on the newborn's head and put that child in the right house. A nano-version could sort out the unborn. Sorting could optimize every life. This one plays rugby, this one becomes a doctor, this one creates music, this one writes, and this

---

[1] *Jesus Christ Superstar*, MCA Records, Inc., 1970.
[2] J.K. Rowling, *Harry Potter and the Sorcerer's Stone* (New York: Scholastic Inc., 1998).

one leads the greatest nation on earth. Unfortunately, we have no such tool. But we do have the influence of family, friends, and faith. We can look to science, experience, and reason, as well as intrinsic and extrinsic motivation. Those are the hats we wear, not always separate, but they are determinative.

So, was I predetermined to be who I am? Early in life, I knew I wanted to be a physician. How would I get there? What would influence me? After all, no one in the history of our family on either side had ever been to college. In fact, my dad dropped out of the eighth grade, and Mom grew up in an abusive family. How did growing up with six brothers in poverty in a small town and facing all the challenges of everyday life mold me, or did it? Was being a middle child influential, determinative, or irrelevant? What were the defining milestones of my life, who were the other people in my life, and how did my decisions and the opportunities afforded or lack thereof affect it? What roles did love and tragedy play? How did they matter? These influences may all be immeasurable, but they are not irrelevant to achieving that niche.

Why am I me? Why do I do what I do? Perhaps I could have been someone else. The possibilities are endless and could have included singer, thief, actor, politician, athlete, entrepreneur, or bachelor. But I am not that someone else. I am a husband, father, and grandfather. Professionally I am a pediatrician, scientist, teacher, and author. Along the way I also became a nonprofessional but skilled carpenter, coach, gardener, martial artist, and photographer.

To understand the why requires understanding the how, who, when, and where. It requires insight as to how genetics, expression of those genes, and our experiences interact.[3] The interplay of nature, nurture, and niche results in who we become. Our brains

---

[3] David S. Moore, *The Developing Genome: An Introduction to Behavioral Epigenetics.* (Oxford, UK: Oxford University Press, 2015).

determine how we feel, who we love, how we act, and of what we are capable. Logic therefore dictates that whatever affects brain development affects who we become.

The most rapid and arguably most important years of brain growth are the preschool years. There is a certain inherited genetic potential already present at birth. However, the development of that potential is experience related. At birth, the brain is suited up for survival. The capability to regulate body temperature, heart rate, and blood pressure is quite well developed. However, it will take roughly a year for a newborn to develop growth in those brain areas that will enable some ambulation, speech, and social interaction. Over the next year, emotions will progress, as will coordination and cognitive-social development. This brain development depends on the establishment of connections (synapses) from one brain cell to another (neurons). It has been reported that the brain is made up of 100 billion-plus neurons that communicate via trillions of synapses.[4] Input to the brain is by way of our senses of sight, touch, taste, smell, and hearing. These environmental experiences lead to established neuronal pathways as a result of repetition. The brain is the ultimate use-it-or-lose-it organ, and neurons that are not used get discarded.

Fortunately, most of the areas that are critical for survival are present at birth or shortly thereafter. There is a caudal-cephalad (tail to head) and inside-to-outside directional development of the nervous system and brain. The highly developed neocortex is what separates us from animals. It is located in the front of the brain and develops rapidly over three years but continues for another two decades. This is where language development, concrete and abstract thinking, analysis, and executive decision-making all occur.

---

[4] <http://www.md-health.com/Parts-Of-The-Brain-And-Function.html> 2014 WebMD, LLC.

However, the brain remains capable of remodeling throughout life. This is known as neuroplasticity and is explained well in the book *The Brain That Changes Itself: Stories of Personal Triumph from the Frontiers of Brain Science.*[5] Some of this is remarkably demonstrated by areas of the brain being able to pick up functions done previously by areas of the brain that have been damaged say by stroke or trauma.

A key concept in understanding brain development and therefore individual development is that in the child, experiences drive that development.[6] Contrast that to the adult where our developed interests and capabilities drive our subsequent experiences. Constructing a new building is remarkably easier than re-modeling. Similarly, brain development is most rapid in the early years, proceeding slower as brain complexity increases. Witness the ability of any newborn to learn any language on earth, dependent upon that to which it is exposed. Contrastingly, for me to learn Mandarin at my age would be more difficult, and it would perhaps be impossible to sound like one whose native language is Mandarin.

Warm, nurturing interactions are beneficial if not critical to optimal human development. In contrast, stress elevates cortisol levels that impair neurogenesis and the migration of neurons essential for brain development. So what happens in the early years is critical to developing our capacities to learn and to whom we become. But remember, one's brain continues to remodel throughout one's life. Perhaps the earliest years are the most important, but the others count as well. Certain interventions and experiences and decisions can make a significant difference. Of course, the timing of these is all important, earlier being more effective.

---

[5] Norman Doidge, *The Brain That Changes Itself: Stories of Personal Triumph from the Frontiers of Brain Science.* (New York: Viking, 2007).
[6] developingchild.harvard.edu "Key Concepts Brain Architecture"

In order to understand my quest to become a physician, and the path to getting there and beyond, it is important to review my childhood, looking at specific experiences created by my parents, siblings, friends, and community. Their combined influence was greatest during my childhood. My acquired interests, decisions, changing social connectedness, and opportunities also contributed immensely to that path, but somewhat later.

Enjoy the tales of this not-so-famous pediatrician's life as I have. Feel the vast range of emotions of that tortuous quest and the journey beyond. Think about how our experiences help to shape who we become, quests we engage, and what we do thereafter. Think about how we impact each other's lives. Think about child-rearing strategies and their impact. Think about what is controllable and what is not. Think about what is important.

Fateful decisions

If only we could go back in time, we could discover when I first realized that my *raison d'etre* was to become a physician. Likely there was no specific moment. Likely there was no specific influence. But we could witness the evolution of the quest and the excitement and results of that pursuit. It would be a tale that would be more accurate, as it would not depend upon the memory and historical research of the author. Alas, there is no time machine as of yet. Besides, theorists believe the value of a time machine for travel into the past would be limited by the date of creation of that machine.[7] Those who read about this quest will have to depend upon the truthfulness of the teller, which is hereupon pledged. Agonizingly, even in timely witness of events, truth is often colored by one's

---

[7] *The Economist* 2015 (Sep 5): "The moving finger writes," 76–77.

perspective. In that sense, my apologies to those whose perspectives differ from mine. Although we like to think that events occur at specific times, they often develop along a spectrum of antecedent influences. Those influences lead to fateful decisions. Those decisions are not always our own. It is thus most accurate and truthful to state that my quest to become a physician had its foundation in early childhood.

What were those earliest years like? What are some of my earliest memories? Why did my parents sell the farm shortly after my birth? What were the consequences of that decision? How did we end up in what would become my hometown? What would be my place in the family? How would all this influence my development?

This journey begins on a farm in Dallas Township, Pennsylvania. Those must have been hard times as Dad worked the night shift for a company that provided steam heat for a city, with the stench of sulfur from the boiler room where he fired the coal furnaces. During the day he tended the farm. Mom was nine years younger than he and often recounted stories of how they lived there without indoor electricity or running water, while caring for his parents, who had emigrated from Sweden, and simultaneously raising three boys. These days, she would be referred to as a member of the sandwich generation, charged with the care of both younger and older family generations.

I was born but not bred there. Not long after my birth, we moved. I was just what they needed: another baby, another boy. Four boys in four years would be a challenge for anyone under the best of living conditions! At best, it takes a toll on the mother's physical health. Each of her deliveries had complications, so that added to the toll. Then there are the psychosocial stressors of four toddlers all thinking the world is centered on their needs. Bless her, Mom was rewarded with that first baby the day before her twenty-first birthday and got a similar present every year for the next three!

Even though Dad often joked that kids are cheaper by the dozen, he knew differently. Here came another mouth to feed. His worries must also have been for his young wife, who he had little opportunity to help with child-rearing, as he worked both day and night. Likely tired of waiting for the township to provide electricity and tired of the long hours and hardships, Dad impulsively sold the farm to a stranger who one day came by and asked if he ever thought about it. Perhaps he was also depressed, as his mom died that same year, six months before my birth. That sale was a decision that would haunt our family for years.

People are complex. That is what makes them fascinating. My parents were no exception. Certainly, as a youngster, they were really hard for me to understand. The saying, "The older I get, the smarter they become" seems to me to be somewhat true. Dad in fact encouraged me to become a psychiatrist so I could perhaps figure out what makes us tick. Well, that understanding may never be fully realized. Despite all my education, my understanding of human behavior, my experiences as a husband and father and grandfather, my experiences as a physician, and my extensive introspection, I will never figure them out completely. But I will always love them.

Experiencing life as their son and within their family helps somewhat in analyzing who they were and why they behaved the way they did. It also helps to think "like father, like son." But science teaches us that who we are is the result of our genetics and experiences. I am therefore not a clone of my father, although at times I may act or think like him. He and I also had different parents, so that adds other genetic and experiential influences. The experiences that each of us have and perceive are really unique. Our thought processes are unique. My parents' experiences are largely unknown to me, especially for their formative early years. They talked on occasion about their past and upbringing, and I witnessed some of their experiences, so that helps some in analysis. But I never knew his parents and only saw Mom's parents occasionally, often not at their best. So, sorry, Dad, I likely will never figure out exactly what makes us tick—but I do have some insight.

What I do know is that my arrival was not inconsequential. Just like the arrivals of the first, and second, and third, and fifth, and sixth, and seventh, and eighth sons, this life would impact theirs in ways unforeseen by anyone. Besides meeting my essential needs for food, clothing, and shelter, they would need to meet my emotional-cognitive-spiritual-social needs. They would be responsible for me for another two decades. Their own needs would become secondary. Or would they? And why should they? At this point, they were unaware of how their family would grow. But they were acutely aware of their responsibilities as parents, and always would be. They also understood their responsibilities to each other. How would they meet these?

Clearly, their education was limited, so they would have to rely on how they were raised and how they perceived what was good and what was bad. Their own experiences would help to define their parenting skills and how they performed in the other roles that were theirs. Eventually I would need to become independent of them—leave the nest, make my own way in the world. They could only hope to prepare me and that I would embrace some of their values.

Having digressed with purpose, let me return to why selling the farm would haunt us forever. Both Mom and Dad embraced the role of being loving adults in their kids' lives. Dad was very much the outdoors type, but nostalgic, melancholic, and introspective. He believed in self-determination—you reap what you sow. He was a workaholic. In retrospect, he treated his melancholy by delving into his "projects." Mom was more the sociable type and less obsessed with projects. She was more fatalistic. If it was meant to be, so be it. Although she shared his many goals, Mom also brought a sense of reality back to his reminiscences about how good the old days were. Their roles in the family were clear cut and typical for that time: he was the bread-winner; she was the bread-maker. His work was outside the house, hers was in the house. He was responsible for food, shelter, and clothing. She was responsible for emotional and social needs. He was the one who stressed over material things; she stressed over feelings. "Opposites attract," they would often say about their relationship. This, however, was the perfect setup for conflict.

Despite the appearance of being soul mates who had a loving and lifelong marriage, they were at times more like fire and gasoline. A word, an event, and sometimes no particular thing seemed to trigger an explosive confrontation. Fiery words of anger spewed forth from Dad's mouth. Mom retaliated. It was always the same. His job was killing him, and she didn't understand. He wanted to move back to the farm, and she didn't. Of course, there was no farm to move back to, but we looked. Sunday drives were a recurrent family event, to search out land and places to move to or farms to buy. In fact, we put our house up for sale several times, and even though there were potential buyers, our parents backed out of each potential sale. Blame would be cast repeatedly for their impoverished situation, for their intermittent unhappiness. Somehow, they would forget about all the blessings they repeatedly spoke of and lapse back into the arguments. They could not figure out how to break the cycle.

Some of the fights were horrific—usually verbal, but sometimes physical. Dad would tear the phone off the wall after his boss called, or out of anger at times he would break furniture. Only once did he hit Mom, after he had been drinking. It is still painful to recall how he threw the carpet at her and grabbed her by the neck. Fortunately, my brothers and I were able to subdue him. Then there was the time Mom threw a butter knife at him after he threw the spaghetti and meatballs at the wall. The wall stain remained as a sad reminder. He told the doctors that he walked into the knife, as they put a couple of sutures in his forehead. Mostly it was painful verbal abuse. Calling each other names, cursing, and wishing bad things on each other, they would blame circumstances for their uncivil behavior. Countless times I cried myself to sleep and prayed that the fights would stop.

After years of fighting and hoping to leave his job, Dad faced reality. There was a buyer for the house, and a farm was available. His dream was about to come true. However, his sense of responsibility as the bread-winner and lack of confidence would not allow him to quit his job. Mom and the rest of us could not believe it. He said his time had passed. He could not work two jobs again, and he was getting too old for farm work.

The fights continued, but the topics changed. It wasn't until Dad quit his job at age fifty-seven, following the devastating flood brought by Hurricane Agnes in 1972, that their lives got better. Stressed by upper management that would not give him the help needed to get the city heat boilers up and running for the soon-to-come cold weather, Dad was having chest pains and nervous tremors. Mom begged him to quit before he had a stroke or heart attack. So, he did. He asked my father-in-law for a job as a carpenter, which was his love in life, and got it. Thankfully, he enjoyed peace of mind for the next nine years, until his untimely death from mesothelioma. His exposure to asbestos occurred more than three decades earlier, while breathing in the dust from covering the boiler room pipes. He was right—his job would kill him.

Earliest Childhood Memories

So, selling the farm could not have been easy for Dad. But he did. He was ready to till new soil and reap whatever he sowed. They moved to a house on the main avenue, in Courtdale, Pennsylvania. Dad moved to dayshift at work. Being a workaholic and self-taught carpenter, though, he had purchased a condemned three-story building called the Junior Mechanics Hall, also in Courtdale. He alone and without power tools took it apart board by board, removed the nails, and saved all the materials to build what would become our home for the rest of our parents' lives.

Actually, he had help: me. I remember how hard it was to remove the old cut nails with their rectangular heads and tapering rusted iron shanks. Each one had to be hammered straight and saved. Besides that, I was allowed to help clean up the work areas. There was not much else a five-year-old could do. Dad demolished the building, built the house, and created a yard all in his spare time over a period of three years. But he spent a lifetime remodeling, repairing, and maintaining this residence. It became his castle, his work of love, his other mistress, his other family. Undoubtedly, helping Dad also helped me. At this impressionable age, I admired what he was doing and would often help him with future projects. The basis for my interest in and use of tools, my desires to construct and remodel things, and learning how to work hard were being set.

The year was 1954, when we moved into a rental house at the curve in the road on Rose Hill, Luzerne, Pennsylvania. Elvis Presley debuted on radio with "That's All Right, Mama." President Eisenhower was in office, communism was on everyone's minds, inoculations of children against polio began, and one of my baseball heroes, Hank Aaron, hit his first of 755 home runs. Incredibly, the Stanford Research Institute declared California's excessive sunshine as the cause of smog in Los Angeles, and the American College of Chest Physicians was not ready to declare cigarette smoking as a cause of lung cancer, as was being suggested by the American Cancer Society. Our move was temporary while Dad finished building the house. Like other houses in the area, I recall that this was an old two-story building with a basement and a lattice-enclosed foundation beneath the front porch. It was our house for only a year, but that year produced some very vivid memories for me.

Always impressionable, Billy taught us a lesson. At that time there were five boys in the family, and mom was pregnant with the sixth. Keeping us safe and preventing injury had to be a challenge. After viewing a situational comedy on television starring "Sid" Caesar, wherein the actor was swallowing pills to help him sleep, Billy ran to our parents' bathroom medicine cabinet, with his shadow, me, at his heels. A brief search gave him the treasure he sought. Swallowing some pills, he then feigned sleepiness. Fortuitously, I alerted our parents that Billy would not share. These were pills Dad used for soaking his feet! Everything would be okay, we were told, but the doctors had to use this *huge* stomach pump to get the poison out. Huge? Pump? How do they do that? Glad it wasn't me. Poor Billy—it must have hurt. A parental lecture about the consequences of helping ourselves to medicines interrupted my thoughts. Lesson learned.

Unfortunately, young children do not do well at applying lessons learned to new or different situations. They think literally, concretely. Sometime later, I found trouble all by myself.

This was not his habit, but one cold winter day Dad had taken a drink of some port wine before work for "medicinal purposes." That bottle of wine must have been inviting. Vaguely, I can remember difficulty walking, a white room spinning, feeling sick, and holding onto the doorway leading to the front room while a circumspect Mom gently held me up and looked into my eyes. Years later, Mom recounted how my brothers reported their concerns and how she quickly diagnosed drunken stupor when she found the "medicine" bottle from which I drank. Her treatment included a tincture of time and later another lecture.

I'm not sure about the timing of any of these, but there are other memorable events from that year. The very first day of kindergarten, I was kicked out. Honest, I did not do it on purpose, but the little girl next to me thought so. I had one of those old-time flat but somewhat tubular brown sticks of licorice. I bit off each end and used it like a straw to blow air at her. Unfortunately, saliva blew with it. Though it was less than a mile, the walk home seemed longer but gave me time to practice my proclamation of innocence.

Then there was the time my brothers and I were stupid enough to let an older neighborhood boy use us for target practice. Maybe it was abuse. Maybe we were willing. Four of us lined up with our navy-like pea coats, feeling invincible and laughing as he shot us repeatedly in the backs with his BB-gun. Those coats were warm and thick, dark blue or black, double-breasted, with large black buttons and large lapels. Perhaps the commotion drew Mom to the crime scene in our backyard. How it occurred and what happened afterward I do not remember. But our "friend" never came back, or at least never shot us again. Part of the lecture we received related to the inherent danger should he have missed the coats, but part of the lecture included how it could have ruined our new jackets.

Other fond (fondling?!) memories from that year related to playing with the girl next door under our porch, and at times exploring the difference between boys and girls. The scientist in me also enjoyed watching slugs make their sticky, windy paths as they moved along the back porch and walkways. Someone taught me how to make them shrivel or dissolve by coating them with salt. Back then, it seemed like a fun thing to do.

My Hometown

If you blink, you will miss it—this was how we often described my hometown. Although I went to kindergarten and had some memorable experiences in Luzerne, the Borough of Courtdale will always be considered where my brothers and I grew up. This small town lies west and north of Wyoming Valley in northeastern Pennsylvania, just at the beginning of the road (309N) to the "back mountain" area that includes Dallas and surrounding small towns. Some folks in the boundary towns of Luzerne, Trucksville, Pringle, and Larksville drove through it daily but did not know the town's name. To this day, the town[8] remains 99 percent white and poor, with the median household income now around $38,000. Back in 1960, it was less than $5,000. The land area is one square mile, and mostly woods. There has been a slight downward trend, but today's population is around 750. One focal point of my childhood, the Courtdale Grade School, is now just a playground. Our nuclear family was about 1 percent of the population. Details of what it was like to grow up in a small town will follow.

Becoming the Middle Child

Our family grew large, with all boys. A familiar sound when some-one did something wrong was our dad yelling, "Carl, Lenny, Billy,

---

[8] <http://en.m.Wikipedia.org> Courtdale, Pennsylvania-Wikipedia

Bobby, Kevin, Ronny, or whatever your name is, get over here!" Perhaps I had been the proverbial straw that broke the camel's back, as our parents waited three years after me for each successive sibling. They always hoped for a girl. So did we. After all, a sister could do the dishes and dust and all those inside "girlie things" that we had to do, and leave us to the outside "boys' chores"!

Just ten days after moving into 10 Center Street, Courtdale, my mother gave birth to the sixth son, Kevin. In another three years we would welcome Ronny. Tragically, in the spring of 1965, we would not get to welcome David. He was a term and healthy baby who died during a difficult delivery. Though I was a junior in high school, I had never before seen my dad cry. David did become a permanent member of the family as he was always counted in reference to how many boys there were. "What, eight boys and no girls?" was the familiar refrain to queries about our family size. By this time, Mom was forty-one, Dad was fifty, and there would be no more. They would have to wait for grandchildren to get a girl.

Thus, I became the middle child. There is much written about the significance of birth order and siblings. In *The Secret Power of Middle Children*,[9] the authors debunk myths about the middle child being negative, resentful, lacking in career focus, and of low creativity. Middle children are thought to be neglected and at a disadvantage in childhood. However, it is argued that this tends to give them attributes of empathy, independence, and creativity, which enables them to be more successful than their siblings. My brothers, by the way, would take issue with the comparative success part! And I would agree. Achievements and success in life are intertwined, but if success is defined as a productive life with happiness, then educational achievements alone could not be interpreted as

---

[9] Catherine Salmon and Katrina Schumann, *The Secret Power of Middle Children*. (New York: Plume: 2011).

more successful. People such as Bill Gates, Julia Roberts, Abraham Lincoln, and more than half of all presidents of the United States have been middle children. The authors argue that research supports that middle children are agents of change, diplomatic, team players, outgoing, flexible, deeply loyal, and more motivated by fairness than money.

Not just my brothers and me but others would also argue for and against this depiction of the middle child. Much of the discussion of the importance of birth order I suspect has merit, considering that interpersonal experiences would be different, despite being in the same family as each birth changes that family's dynamics. However, birth order is only one variable. Who we become, our niche in life, and finding that niche are largely dependent upon the totality of our individual experiences as well as genetics and expression of those genes. Each of us boys lived in the same house, with the same parents, in the same town, and shared most of our pre-adult lives together, in poverty. Yet, each of us has a distinct personality and life story because our experiences, although some were shared, could never be exactly the same. Our decision-making would also differ. Our perspectives on the same events similarly could be shared or different. The more siblings, though, the greater the difficulty of meeting each one's needs. The effects of poverty on development would be accentuated.

Community, not just family, shapes us. "It takes a village to raise a child," title of Hillary Clinton's book,[10] is an old African proverb that seems true to me. The size of that community, the opportunities or lack therein, the resources, the demographics, and the time spent help create individual experiences. As noted, those experiences drive brain development, which in turn drives

---

[10] Hillary Clinton, *It Takes A Village*. (New York: Simon & Schuster, 2006).

personality development. Our cognitive-emotional-social behaviors are thus bred in a specific milieu of other personalities.

Mostly, the earliest years are spent at home. Interestingly, these are the years during which brain growth is most rapid. This is when we develop the capacity to learn. Long before we enter a formal educational system, our learning template is being forged. Parents and siblings, then, are among the most influential early drivers of who we become. By age six or so, we have already established how to filter and direct information that comes our way through all of our senses. Although abstract thinking comes much later, a foundation for learning is set earlier. The details of those years may not be known, but inferences can be made by understanding family dynamics and the socioeconomic milieu.

How then did my parents and siblings deal with "another baby, another boy"? Could they really afford another child? What impact would even more children have? What experiences would be positive, and what would be negative? Would the positive outweigh the negative? How would this new boy impact his brothers' relationships with each other and with each parent? I have already noted some of the stressors known about my early childhood and some of those that persisted into adolescence. Stress elevates cortisol, which impairs neurogenesis and neuronal migration and therefore impairs brain development. However, loving and nurturing bidirectional interactions foster brain development and learning. How aware they were of the relative importance of these is not known, but my parents and siblings certainly provided both stressful and nurturing experiences.

Colin Powell founded America's Promise,[11] an alliance to help children of all socioeconomic sectors to succeed. They contend

---

[11] www.americaspromise.org

that this requires: a caring adult in every child's life; safe neighborhoods; healthy nutrition, exercise, clothing, shelter, and appropriate healthcare; education that gives them the tools to succeed; and opportunities to give back to the community. Which of these factors were available to me? What was missing, and how did that impact my quest? As you will see, I certainly had caring adults in my life. Our neighborhoods were relatively safe. Opportunities for team sports were limited, but exercise was a part of my daily life. Although my parents provided adequate shelter and clothing, our nutrition was suboptimal, our healthcare was reactive, and there were behavioral patterns within the family that put us all at risk. There were also barriers to educational opportunities. There would, however, always be opportunities for me to be a part of the community at large, and to give back to others in meaningful ways.

What were the effects of our poverty? Eric Jensen defines poverty as "a chronic and debilitating condition that results from multiple adverse synergistic risk factors and affects the mind, body, and soul."[12] Poverty, he contends, is complex, having different meanings for different folks. He identifies and explains six types: situational, generational, absolute, relative, urban, and rural. The mnemonic he uses to explain the potential consequences to families living in poverty is EACH: emotional and social challenges, acute and chronic stressors, cognitive lags, and health and safety issues. Many of these are evident in my story. How did the risks manifest themselves, and what were their relative impacts? Were children really "cheaper by the dozen," as Dad contended, or were they more consequential? Although I am understandably biased and happy that they had me, was another baby really what they needed?

---

[12] Eric Jensen, *Teaching with Poverty in Mind,* ASCD, 2009.

CHAPTER 2

A Free-Range Childhood

Childhood is complex. The interconnectedness of life events and experiences and who we become begins in early childhood. Many believe that the preschool years are critical to how we gather information, process it, and react to it. Those experiences we have literally drive brain development, which in turn determines who we become. Once that personality develops, with its socio-emotional-cognitive structure, then we begin to make choices based on what interests us or what we need. It is what drives us. Interestingly, what drives us can change as our experiences change. How change occurs is sometimes apparent and sometimes not so. When and where change occurs may be recognized, but the why is often never clear.

Unfortunately, or fortunately, there is little memory of our earliest years. Those things that contributed to our individual emotions and intellect can only be surmised. However, there is much data to support that negative and/or traumatic experiences inhibit brain development, whereas positive and nurturing experiences enhance brain development. Thus, reading, talking, and singing to an infant in a loving manner promote language development and early literacy skills that better prepare a child for the school years and success. Spanking, other abusive and negligent behaviors, negativity, and indifference to a child's needs are detrimental.

Words are concepts, so the more words a child hears, the better that child conceptualizes. The 1995 Hart-Risley research study[13] demonstrated that the child not so stimulated may have a 30 million–word deficit at four years of age compared to one who had very involved parents/caretakers. They estimated that children of professional parents heard 48 million words by age four, whereas the average child heard an estimated 30 million words, but children in welfare families may hear as few as thirteen million words by that age. The good news is that we can continue to learn and change throughout life, although it gets more difficult as time passes.

By the time I started school, I was cognitively ahead of most of my peers. As a result, I was allowed to start elementary school early. I can only surmise that my early experiences were positive and helped to lay a foundation for my later success in life. Since most of my preschool experiences occurred within the family environs, then my parents and young siblings deserve credit for helping to shape who I am. Of course, throughout my life there would be others who gave unconditional love or encouraged me to learn. There were those who taught me right from wrong and others who were or were not good role models. Peers, teachers, acquaintances, and countless others played parts in my experiences. The foundation for my success was set early and involved experiences with family as well as others, but decisions throughout my life would make a significant difference. Some of those decisions and actions and experiences delayed my quest and even threatened my life at times. Other decisions, actions, and experiences were more fateful.

[13] Betty Hart and Todd R. Risley, *Meaningful Differences in the Everyday Experiences of Young American Children.* (Baltimore, MD: Brookes, 1995).

Unsupervised Childhood Experiences

Being a free-range kid gave me a lot of time to experience perhaps the right things at the right times. My daily interests were being forged by my experiences and vice versa. There was time to be me, to become me. It was not someone else's control of my time giving me those experiences, as may happen when an overly involved parent shuttles a child from school to soccer practice to piano lessons and then the library. These have affectionately been called "helicopter parents," as they hover over their child's every movement and moment.[14]

One lesson learned from brain research[15] is that the brain develops sequentially. It forms in a caudal-cephalad manner, from the brainstem toward the cerebral cortex. The brain also forms from inside to outside. The development of neurogenesis and neural pathways is dependent upon what precedes it. The same occurs with learning. The child must be exposed to the right information in the right amounts at the right time to be most effective. For example, a toddler will not benefit much from a quantum physics lecture, and an adolescent can be consoled in ways other than by rocking. Some structured time, though, is important.

To be great as a musician, you must have a certain genetic inheritance. You also must have the right experiences early in life. There are windows of opportunity that close early in life. A great example of this is the problem of amblyopia. Amblyopia is blindness in an otherwise perfectly normal eye. It is due to the failure to develop a significant portion of the visual cortex, due to strabismus,

---

[14] Lindsay Hutton, "Your Parenting Style: Are You an Extreme Parent?" life. familyeducation.com.

[15] National Research Council and Institute of Medicine *from Neurons to Neighborhoods: The Science of Early Childhood Development.* (Washington, DC: National Academy Press, 2000).

or crossing of the eyes, by age five. The strabismus causes two images to appear on the brain. To make sense of this visual input, the brain area responsible for vision suppresses input from one eye. That prevents diplopia, or double vision. Because of chronic suppression, that eye becomes nonfunctional. To prevent amblyopia, strabismus must be corrected before age five, and the sooner the better. A future brain surgeon certainly needs stereoscopic or binocular vision, the capacity for which would not occur if this window of opportunity to correct strabismus is closed.

Organized experiences can be as important as that from unstructured time. This would be in providing age-related and educational experiences that may otherwise not be timely or ever occur. In my hometown, school was perhaps the most structured experience. For me, in further descending importance, church, family events, employment, and organized sports would also structure my time. The rest of my time with friends and family was mostly unstructured.

Not everyone learns at the same pace or in the same manner. Studies done with twins document that although they may arrive intellectually at the same place in generally the same time, how they get there can be totally different.[16] For example, all students may be on the same page as the teacher discusses a story. However, one student may be thinking of certain aspects of the story, another may be focused on the font or the pictures, another may be generalizing information to his or her experiences, and another may be daydreaming. It is not possible to know exactly what a particular student needs at a particular moment, but it is necessary to provide

---

[16] Marie M. Clay, *By Different Paths to Common Outcomes* (London, UK: Heinemann, 2014). (Note: she coined the term *emergent literacy* in her doctoral thesis.)

opportunities for that student to access information that his or her brain needs at the moment.

The teacher also has to follow how a student gets to a particular result, in order to understand that student's progress and needs. For example, a student who appears unable to print her name may actually know all the letters and the correct sequence but may be superimposing the letters. Thus, her name would appear as an unintelligible scribble. However, the teacher monitoring how that student wrote her name would understand that instruction on how to space those letters is what is needed.

Discussions of what is best for child development often center on what should be the balance between structured and free time. Is it better to present information in a didactic manner, or is it better to teach the student how to access the information needed? Is it better to allow students to progress at their own pace, or should time expectations be set for them? Is it more important to structure a child's time and activities, or is it better to allow self-directed activities? Is "free-range" parenting better than "helicopter" parenting? If both styles of parenting are important, how do you determine the approach for any particular child? Is there a choice for most parents, or is parenting style related more to available resources?

Although school was required, and we each had our daily chores to do, we were encouraged to find things to do on our own. We would play pick-up sports with whomever we could find. We would play army in the woods, or play kick the can, duck on a rock, or steal the bacon in the streets. Romp through neighborhood yards, climb trees, go pick wild berries or the fruit on neighbors' trees, sit around and do nothing but talk, or walk to adjacent towns to swim in a creek or fish with a freshly cut branch pole-string-hook-worm setup were the ways we would bide our time. Depending on the time of year, we would sleigh ride or ice skate or build igloos, ride bikes, play in the rain building dams with sticks and stones in the street gutters, play sock-ball tag (a form of ball tag with the ball made of old rags stuffed inside a large sock), and do endless other things during daylight hours.

After dark, we would play board games or cards or read comics or adventure stories. Rarely, we would watch television, which could only get one or two clear stations and a snowy third. Often we would chase lightning bugs and make homes for them in mason jars with grass and put holes in the cap to give them air. Sometimes we wrote our names with them on white T-shirts to watch the name glow in the dark! It was not unusual to play one-on-one or two-on-two football in the front yard in the moonlight, or to play hide-n-seek or 1-2-3 relivio or tag or king of the mountain in the backyard with our friends.

Free-range kids—yes, that is what we truly were. Our activities were not limited to our town. We would walk to the pool or ball fields in Pringle, or go swimming or fishing in the creeks in Luzerne. Occasionally my brothers and I walked unsupervised to the Luzerne movie theatre. Sometimes Mormons we did not even know would drive us to a ball field in Kingston, delivering a pre-game sermon. We would hitchhike rides to Harvey's Lake, or to places to work such as the golf course in Dallas or the farms in Kingston and the Back Mountain area. Once I even went selling magazines in surrounding towns with a complete stranger who offered me a job. He sent me door-to-door to pitch the sale, while he played the pinball machines in a local diner. He would then finalize the sale when I returned with the name and address of a potential client. Some of these activities were not without consequence, as we would become involved in fights or dangerous rides, or we would be at risk of dog bites or witness and participate in undesirable behavior, such as smoking cigarettes or vandalism. Unsupervised play or work also makes one more prone to accidents or injuries.

Childhood Injuries and Medical Experiences

Small-town friendships are easy to make, as there are shared and limited resources. Most of my friends were my age or also friends of my brother Billy, who was a year older. But even the older kids engaged us, especially for pick-up sports. In fact, the young teenager across the street, Richard, took an interest in teaching me how to play baseball, football, and basketball. It did not matter that I was more than half a decade younger than he. We talked sports and exchanged baseball cards that came with bubble gum purchases. There was not a famous baseball player for whom I did not know their stats. Richard was a star athlete in the catholic school he attended and planned on being a priest. Eventually he became a psychologist and married. His brother was a year older than me and was a close friend to me and Billy.

Richard was my idol, for good reasons. No one else ever took such genuine interest in teaching me how to hit or catch a ball, shoot hoops, or run low to the ground with a football and evade tacklers. We shared the same sports heroes: Mickey Mantle, Hank Aaron, Ted Williams, Don Larsen, Yogi Berra, Willie Mays. We liked the Yankees and the Chicago Bears. It was not unusual for the "older kids" to come and ask me to play sports because they needed another body on the field. Richard was the one asking me to play and looking out for my safety. In my mind, he was the best at whatever sport we played. Another of my childhood idols was John, a couple of years younger than Richard, but a star wrestler and runner.

It was my trust in Richard and John that encouraged me to

join them in a dare. There were about thirteen narrow concrete steps leading down from John's front porch to the sidewalk below. Someone challenged us to climb onto each other's shoulders and then to climb down the steps. I was a lightweight six-year-old and was given the top position. Well, we made it safely down all those steps but tripped on a slightly raised sidewalk. Tumbling from atop, I landed on my outstretched left hand and broke both the radius and ulna. I remember how they apologized all while they helped me home, two houses over. Mom came running to meet us as she could hear what must have been blood-curdling screams. I did not calm down until she reassured me that the doctor would fix it and not have to cut it off, as I had worried. The pain is not as vivid a memory as the fear.

Those greenstick fractures of my left forearm were my first broken bones. That injury introduced me to Dr. Klem, our family doctor. He smiled and talked to me all while he wrapped my arm with layers of plaster after pulling hard to line up the bones. It would be six weeks before I could get the cast off. "Just don't get it wet," he warned, "and you can play as you wish." The memory of cast removal is just as vivid. The scare of the saw, pliers, and scissors used to remove it was quickly followed by the shock of seeing a dirty, dead skin–covered, skinny, and wasted arm that could not be moved well and that stunk! Mom made faces all while she gently cleaned it off and reassured me that it would be back to normal soon.

Dr. Klem was a regular at our house and we at his. It was in part due to the size of our family, frequent injuries, and the ever-present childhood diseases that spread easily, especially among close contacts. He came with his little black bag of tools and medicines, visiting us for the chickenpox, measles, mumps, whooping cough, colds, staph infections, skin rashes, and other acute febrile illnesses.

If we were not too sick or did not have a suspected and dreaded contagious childhood disease, we would go to his office when we could get a ride. There were no scheduled preventive checkups for any reason, and there were no regular immunizations. However, we did receive the oral polio vaccine when it became available at the Luzerne Community Center, where we waited in long lines for the sugar cube they promised! My brothers and I were excited about that vaccine, because we lamented the Pringle community swimming pool being closed frequently when polio was in the area.

As was common practice, our family physician's office was in his house. It consisted of a small waiting room and then his exam and treatment room. He lived in Kingston, about two to three miles from our house in Courtdale. There were no appointments, as you called to see if he was there or just walked in. Often the room was full, and we waited for a long time. No one seemed unpleasant for the wait, and all seemed to smile when he appeared at the door to release one patient and to ask the next to come in. Everyone, though, was keenly aware of whose turn was next, as they memorized who had been in the waiting room upon their arrival. Sometimes he took patients out of turn, out of necessity for how ill or injured they were. He would explain and apologize, and it seemed that folks were always understanding. They knew that he would do the same for them when needed. Once I had to leave his exam room as my oldest brother's screams, from getting an ingrown toenail resected, frightened me. Otherwise, we were always allowed in the room.

Our family doctor was awe-inspiring. How could he always figure out what was needed? How could he know all that, and how could he remember all those medicines and doses? Where did he learn all those skills? You have to study hard, do well in school, and spend years in training in a medical school after college, is what I was told. Dad always talked about the need for perseverance of character if we were to succeed at anything. He also often told us that he heard that very few people survive medical school. It was not for the faint of heart. The mental and physical stresses were demanding. He heard that many students committed suicide by jumping from windows, just like those investors who lost everything during the Great Depression. If it were just physical stress, learning how to work hard would get you through. However, someone calculated that one hour of mental work was as tough on a person as eight hours of physical work. So, you better be mentally ready for what most people are not.

Where Dad got that information is not known. Who would want to become a physician, if it was that hard? Where were the words of encouragement? Knowing Dad, it was his way of challenging and preparing me for the quest. Both he and Mom had a love-hate relationship with doctors. Their experiences with them were not always positive. But it was always their hope that at least one of their sons would become a doctor or lawyer or famous musician. It was always their despair that they had no resources with which to help us. They also did not know where to begin. No one in their families had gone to college, and Dad had not attended school beyond the eighth grade. They wanted us to succeed at whatever would make us happy and move us out of poverty. They always admonished us to do something worthwhile with our lives. Perhaps they felt that it would help validate their parenting.

One challenge to my thoughts of becoming a physician came with another injury. John's sister was playing football with us in the backyard between her house and mine. She was quite heavy and fell on top of me when she pushed me. My nose skidded along the ground, and suddenly there was blood everywhere. I ran to my dad, who was raking leaves in the backyard, screaming that my nose was split off. He calmly told me it was just a bloody nose and to have Mom take a look at it. Well, moments later she could see that indeed my nose had been split and the nasal ala on the left was just hanging there. The ala is the wing of the nose that forms the outer part of the nostril. Quickly she placed a dish towel on my nose and told me to place pressure on it and not to let go until we got to the doctor. Mom ran to Dad, shouting that my nose was off and we needed to get to the emergency room quickly. His remark was something like, "Why didn't he say so? I thought it was just a bloody nose!"

The emergency doctor had difficulty "numbing" my nose. His nurses had to restrain me as I struggled to get away, screaming that my nose would be okay and for them to leave it alone. I can still see the needles approaching my nose and feel the burning pain of the local injections. They made multiple injections, then decided they would have to proceed suturing even if the local anesthesia was not working. In total, they placed eight sutures externally and four internally per Mom's account. After it was over, Mom smiled and asked me if I still wanted to be a doctor after all that. "You bet," was my response. "I will get back at those nurses and that doctor!" Later I turned a vengeful motive into one to become a "good" doctor, as in more capable.

There may have been something about Dad working in the backyard that affected me. I would get hurt or in trouble. Of course, it could have been coincidental, since he was always working to beautify our home and yard, and to maintain them in excellent condition. "In Sweden," he would say, "the houses and yards are always immaculate." No unwanted weeds or high grass, no faded or peeling paint, no trash, no deteriorating structures and no lazy people would be found there. He had never been there, but his parents told him about the old country. He also saw pictures of those things. So, they were standards that he held for himself and set for us. Never put off until tomorrow what you could do today. In fact, he told us this so many times that I still remember the refrain: "Be a job great or small, do it right or don't do it at all." When he wanted to be dramatic, it would be: "Be a job great or small, do it right or *leave the goddamn thing alone.*"

Besides the nose injury, one time I went temporarily (less than a half hour) blind. Curiosity made me look directly into an old small purple bottle that I had found in the woods adjacent to our yard. Some unknown liquid went directly into my eye and stung. Suddenly everything was black, and I could not see even when the stinging sensation stopped. Once again, I ran to Dad, crying that I could not see. Once again, he sent me into the house to have Mom wash out the affected eye.

Another time, I was playing in the same place and decided to clean up the trash I found. Dad had raked leaves and now was burning them. That's what everyone did back then. The leaves from the tree-lined streets and yards would be raked into piles, and there would be dozens of these burning and smoking around town, clearly reminding everyone that fall was here and a cold winter not far behind. So, like Dad, I set fire to the papers in the trash that I had found. Unlike Dad's, my fire got out of control and started to spread through the grass, twigs, and leaves on the hill. Dad looked skeptically at me as I ran to him for help, having "found" a fire in the woods!

There would be many times during childhood that Dad would remind me of this whenever he doubted the veracity of what I was telling him. Childhood lying was not common in our family, but my brothers and I used it to avoid those harsh spankings with his belt that paradoxically were meant to keep us honest and responsible. Our loving mom, just like her parents had done to her, also would teach us not to steal by burning our fingers on the stove!

The punishments were worse if we were found to be lying, so often my brothers and I colluded on our stories. Their physical reprimands were often accompanied with admonishments that as liars or stealers we would never get good jobs or be trusted individuals. So we learned to think twice before stealing or lying. Eventually, we learned not to steal or lie. That is what bad people do. I wanted to do good and to be trusted. I wanted to become a doctor.

Certainly I had decided to become a physician sometime before the eighth Christmas of my life. Just think of how you could help the sick and injured, and how people would admire you. Perhaps I also thought about making money, as I repeatedly asked for a cash register for Christmas. I never got the cash register, but I did get a Junior Doctor Kit for Christmas of 1957. Evidently I had shown no talent in terms of earning or saving or handling money.

Perhaps my parents preferred that I become a physician, as they were held in high esteem and made enough money. They must have been also impressed by my interests and diagnostic skills. Len, my second-oldest brother, had fallen out of our neighbor's apple tree where we had been playing. His sagging forearm and pain had reminded me of my first broken arm, so I helped him home. Taking some cloth diapers, I wrapped his arm and then placed it in the sling that had been mine. When Mom and Dad arrived home to find us waiting on the porch stoop, they were skeptical of our story. "Oh, have you been playing doctor again, Bobby?" That cynicism turned into surprise as they confirmed the diagnosis, looking at the sagging, painful arm inside the sling.

One time, I ran away from home. Why? I can't remember. Before leaving I prepared a peanut butter sandwich, packed a can of pork and beans and water into a lunch box, and emptied my piggy bank of its entire sixty-eight cents. Halfway down the driveway, I returned for my doctor kit. Mom must have had to restrain the laughter as I told her in anger that I was leaving. She knew that I would be back. But I was determined not to return, or so I thought. There was this big rock on the "mountain" behind our house that was a favorite place for me to play and just to hike to and meditate. So, that is where I went. After eating all my supplies and spending a few hours there, I started to worry about where I would sleep for the night. Swallowing my pride, I returned home. Something sarcastic like, "Well, the hobo returns," is how I was greeted! That Junior Doctor Kit was my best friend that day.

Childhood School Experiences

Although the free time that was unsupervised sometimes got us into trouble, we learned from it. It also gave us opportunities to make decisions and to suffer the consequences or reap the benefits of those decisions. Such freedom helped to spawn a sense of independence. Unsupervised time with friends enabled us to learn about others' feelings and behaviors. Free time provided much opportunity for introspection.

Childhood life was not always that chaotic. There was structure in school, church, employment, and organized sports. Perhaps the greatest structured activity back then was public school. There were only two houses between our house and the Courtdale Elementary School, so getting to school was easy and did not require parental assistance. The schoolyard was also easily accessed and was where we spent a lot of time playing throughout the year. Center Street ran perpendicular to Academy Street and to the lower half of the schoolyard. For many years the schoolyard was dirt and grass and surrounded by maple trees. These trees in summer were filled with so many birds that we would all cover our heads when they flew in or out. It was not infrequent to get pasted white! There was a short, two-foot concrete wall along most of the sidewalk, but it reached a maximum of six feet on the lower end that was along the steep downhill side of Academy Street. There was a flagpole in the middle of the lower yard, centered and across from the opening to the janitor's room where the large coal-fired furnaces were. Several steps led into the school from the front, but students usually entered from the schoolyard by separate side doors for girls and boys. Eventually the schoolyard was paved and enclosed on three sides by chain-link fencing. Our parents were upset when that happened because we more quickly wore out our blue jeans and shoes.

The schoolyard was where we would play baseball, basketball, touch football, and other competitions, such as running and marbles. For tackle football, we played at different sites such as behind Carlson's backyard or Elks Field near the volunteer fire station. Although we played baseball in this same field, we often had to walk to our neighboring town of Pringle, where there were dedicated baseball fields near the community swimming pool. The schoolyard wall was useful for testing our jumping skills, and the chain-link fence gave us opportunities for climbing. This was also a central place for socializing. The building itself had a wooden siding exterior except for the concrete walls of the basement, wherein there were the janitor's room and restrooms.

Often we used those outside walls for play. Individuals would play catch by bouncing golf balls or rubber balls or even hard baseballs onto the paved yard and rebounding off the wall. Sometimes teams of two or more would compete, similar to tennis. Bucketybuck was another of my favorite games, using the school foundation. One person standing against the wall served as a cushion for one or more who bent over like horses in tandem. The opposing team would run and jump onto the backs, trying to collapse the "horses." If not, then the last person on would hold up a few fingers and yell, "Buckety-buck, how many fingers up?" A correct guess was needed to change horses and riders. Of course the player against the wall often tried to cheat and signal how many fingers he could see.

The schoolyard was also the setting for fights and injuries. Arguments and insults often were settled by agreeing to meet in the schoolyard for a fistfight. There would always be onlookers cheering for their favorite person. Who was on your side varied depending on your popularity at the time. Since almost every boy fought at one time or another, it was easy to rank each other in terms of physical prowess. It was also easy to predict the outcomes. Some surprises occurred, though, as certain boys progressed through puberty sooner than others. The paved playground gave more than one child skin abrasions, goose-egg head injuries, concussions, and fractures. Once I nearly broke my neck, as I tripped in the ditch between the road and sidewalk in a running attempt to jump onto the school wall. Evidently I was small enough to fit between the ditch and wall, which I hit head on. Two weeks in the hospital with sand bags around my head and required immobility taught me never to try that again!

In general, our class size was usually less than twenty. However, one half of the room was dedicated to each of two classes taught by the same teacher. While teaching one class, the other had assigned study time. The combination wooden seat-desks were individual and had an ink well. For special assignments, we used those wood pens that had sharp metal tips with a hole in the center for dipping into blue writer's ink. Other times we used number-two pencils or crayons or chalk. At least two walls had those large chalkboards with trays, with a cork board above them for hanging artwork or notices. The other two walls had large windows that moved with a weight system. The very top windows could only be opened partly with a long pole with a hook to grab a metal loop. The lower windows were usually decorated by the teacher and students with a holiday or seasonal theme. The floors were wooden and highly polished and creaked a lot. As I recall, the ceilings were covered with painted tin and had incandescent light fixtures suspended from them.

Entering through the front doors required climbing several steps, and getting to the first floor involved some more. There were wooden handrails along the interior steps and no elevators. The corridors had open cloak closets, where we would hang our jackets, hats, boots, and gloves. It was also where we were sent for misbehaving in class. The first- and-second grade classroom was on the first floor, and across from that was an all-purpose play room. In that room, we often rehearsed Thanksgiving plays or minstrels. It is also where I often tutored students in reading and math. Those were the students who passed only because of age and who needed extra help. The school assembly room with a stage was also on the first floor and is where we met every Friday morning for an hour of activities that started with the Pledge of Allegiance and prayer, before we sang hymns and a few popular old songs such as "Santa Lucia." That was also our theater for minstrels, seasonal plays, and graduations.

Unless my recollection is inaccurate, the second floor is where the other classrooms were. By far my favorite floor was the school attic. It was musty and dusty and housed books, old class banners, broken desks, play props, and other items. Whenever I completed my assignments early, the teacher would let me go there to get a book that I could check out for reading at home. That privilege was only for a few who belonged to the "book club" and competed for praise or bragging rights, for reading extensively outside of the classroom. It is where I fell in love with the Hardy Boys adventure series.[17] As the sons of a famous detective, they found and searched for clues to solve their own mysterious cases during their school-free time. Somehow I managed to get a hold of numerous books in that series, and I enjoyed cuddling next to the forced hot air vent in our house behind a heavily upholstered chair to join them on those adventures.

Each teacher had only one classroom, within which she taught two different grade levels. Although I clearly remember their names, faces, and demeanors, I have elected not to use their names, except for Mrs. Nicholas, who had an extraordinarily positive effect on my self-esteem and life.

One of the most pleasant teachers was my first and second grade teacher. She was strict but nice. There were two incidences though that got me angry with her. The first was in first grade when she was busy teaching the second graders and did not see my raised hand. We were standing in front of the class and writing on the chalkboards. I really had to pee. That was one of the earliest, most humiliating events of my life. Suddenly my pants became soaked, a puddle formed on the floor, and the teacher finally looked when there was this sudden laughing and taunting from my classmates. She did apologize, chastised the class, and told me if ever she did not see my raised hand for me to just go to the restroom as needed.

The other event was during my mom's visit on parent-teacher night. She told my mom that she got a good laugh when I told her about one of our neighbor's behavior. Back then, there were multiple families connected to the same telephone line. The party lines were indicated by distinct ring tones. It was common courtesy not

---

[17] Franklin W. Dixon, *The Hardy Boys Series: While The Clock Ticked*. (New York: Dunlap, 1932).
(Note: The characters created by Edward Stratemeyer in 1927 evolved over the years and were published under collective pseudonym Franklin W. Dixon for ghostwriters.)

to pick up the phone unless it was your ringtone. You also could not use the phone if some other party was. Think about this: small town, gossip, and you could listen in to your neighbor's conversations. Privacy? Not on the phone. Well, our class discussion had been about being good neighbors. When asked to give an example, I could not think of one, but I did tell on a well-known town gossiper who always listened in on our phone calls and would only hang up when confronted. Mom was embarrassed and verbally reprimanded me later for telling the teacher such personal stuff. "Bobby, you just don't say those things to your teacher."

By the time I reached third grade, word was out that I was an A student. Mrs. Nicholas always made me feel that I was special. There was always praise and special attention to my abilities and needs. I enjoyed the privilege of being her helper while others were finishing their work. She would send me downstairs and outside to clean the chalk erasers. I would help stack supplies for her. I was allowed to bring in the students' half-pint milk bottles when delivered so they would not freeze outside. If anyone needed extra help with reading or writing, she would call on me to help tutor. She would put her arm around me and say how proud she was of whatever it was I did. If anyone inspired me to love school, it was she. Perhaps this is what inspired my dad to nickname me "teacher's pet." My brothers also had derogatory nicknames, labeled and used by Dad whenever he was angry or upset about our behavior or inability to do something to meet his expectations. Dad set the example for how we could antagonize each other in more ways than one: call a sibling by his nickname and watch the fun!

The least-liked teacher and most feared was our fifth- and sixth-grade teacher. Perhaps her life as a spinster caused that behavior, was what most parents said. Or the conjecture was also that her behavior explained why she was a spinster. She played her favorites and was regularly nasty to others. We disagreed about her nicety but agreed about her halitosis, notable when she would hold you tightly to show her joy in your behavior or to scold you. She had a way of keeping the class in order, using or displaying her *shillelagh*. This was a thick stick that she would use for public spankings. There were two particular intellectually challenged students in our class who regularly felt that stick across their backs or knuckles.

One time, she used it on my brother Billy for talking with those kids while she was trying to teach. To this day, I can feel my fear as she beat my brother's legs repeatedly in front of the class. By the time we got home, there were bruises everywhere.

"Gus, don't do it," I remember Mom saying to Dad. He was so angry that he threatened to go to the parent-teacher meeting that night, which he never did previously, and use that stick on that teacher. All of us believed he would, as he had quite a temper. He went. The story is that she proudly showed my Dad her *shillelagh* when he asked to see what she used to maintain classroom order. With that cudgel gripped tightly in both hands and staring angrily at her, Dad swung it past her and broke it in two on her desk. Mom also reported that our teacher turned pale as Dad told her that if she ever hit any of his boys again, then she would be on the receiving end just like that desk. As I recall, she never bought or used another *shillelagh*. After that, she would not be able to count on me to defend her reputation.

By the time I graduated from eighth grade, one of the teachers I had most admired for teaching us about civility also lost her halo. Civics class was one of my favorite classes. She told us how important it was to be nice to others. By example, she discussed how her husband would never pass by anyone, even perfect strangers, without smiling and saying hello. That lesson inspired me such that to this day, I do the same. However, as the end of eighth grade and selection for valedictorian drew near, she displayed a favoritism for a particular student, the son of her near neighbor. Actually, he lived in our old house. He was always seen as her favorite, but now she was working to change the rules to improve his chances for selection as valedictorian. She wanted the basis to be solely how the student performed in her classes the last two years of elementary school, rather than the best cumulative average for eight years. Fortunately, she did not get her way. This was brought to my mom's attention, and I believe she did some networking to prevent the change, as it seemed unfair to inexplicably change what had been an expectation for the students for eight years. Besides, her son's performance for the eight years had no close competition. But the change would place this teacher's favorite student in contention for the honor.

Always, I was the youngest student in the class. At the time I started, the age requirement for entry to first grade had to be six years old by December 31 of that year. Because my birthday was less than a week later, Mom talked the school into granting an exception for me to start at age five. Evidently she never told them about the trouble that I had on my first day in kindergarten in Luzerne! She claimed that I was too bright to be held back another year. The fact that she had two other kids at home likely had no influence on her motive! Having three brothers precede you in such a small school could prejudice the teachers for better or worse. To that end, they were in for a surprise!

Learning always came easy for me during those childhood years. It was not unusual for me to be sent out of the room for yelling out answers to questions the teacher posed to the students in the grade ahead of me. They tried to ignore me, but I would raise my hand and come at least partway out of my seat, hoping to get recognized. Intermittently, the teachers would default to me, likely out of frustration with the other students. Getting their praise, that intermittent reward, is likely why that behavior persisted. Perhaps it was that middle child syndrome that made me thrive on praise. The downside is that my parents quickly learned that a little praise went a long way with getting me to do chores around the house. In fact, I would wake up early on a Saturday morning and pull all the weeds out front or cut the grass, looking for that praise.

One of my favorite classroom competitions, which I excelled at, was to see how many words we could make out of a short phrase or sentence that the teacher would place on the chalkboard. Learning everyone's lines in our plays and skits was easy, fun, and an opportunity to show off or get in trouble for preempting others. Mrs. Nicholas once told my mom that I was the most brilliant child she had ever seen and that she hoped to live long enough to see what I would become. No wonder she was my favorite teacher forever thereafter.

Proudly, I or my parents would recount to others when school performance was discussed that I had all A's from first through eighth grade. It was no surprise, then, that I would become the valedictorian of our class. These had been formative years. By that age, I knew for sure that my quest to become a physician was on track. I felt confident that I would achieve that honorable and worthy position in life. However, what seemed to be an almost insurmountable barrier or threat to that accomplishment came just before that graduation.

Purportedly for financial reasons, the Courtdale School Board decided that starting with my class, we would have to go to Luzerne High School. Prior to that, students had their choice of either Luzerne or Kingston High. The tuition at Kingston was higher than Luzerne, but so was the value of the education. Almost no one interested in college went to Luzerne. The school was known for its high attrition rate and dismal preparation of students for college. On the other hand, serious students did well at Kingston and moved along to college. That was our bias. My hope to become a physician was thus threatened. My usually outspoken mother, however, decided things would be okay if she went to the school board and requested an exception for me, their valedictorian. Unfortunately, they refused. I told Mom that I would be willing to work all summer to earn enough money to pay the difference in tuition, just so I could get the better education. Mom looked into it, found out that it would be $90 a year, and approached the board again with that offer. They refused again, stating this was the new policy and they would make no exceptions.

"Stop him, stop him," yelled my eighth grade teacher to her husband, who was on the school board, during my valedictorian speech. Others saw it differently and began clapping and cheering for me. I remember my Aunt Peggy standing up and proudly clapping. She lived in Luzerne and just knew that attending that school would not prepare me for college. Aunt Peggy was not a blood relative but my mom's best friend since high school. She always told me that I would be a wonderful doctor and probably a surgeon because of my small hands. So the speech continued. My written speech was delivered, and then in an ad lib fashion, I voiced my fears of never becoming a physician because of the school board's unreasonable actions. After all, they did not have a high school, others before us were always given a choice, and I was even willing to pay the difference in costs between the schools. It would not be just an exception for me, they could let the offer stand for any other student wanting the same. This was my future, for which I protested.

Panic set in for our administration, and we were marched off the stage immediately after the speech. In the small playroom, our class was interrogated as to who put me up to such a thing. Was this

Mrs. Burke's doing? My teacher just knew it had to be. How could we disrespect the decisions of her husband and the rest of the school board? Didn't we learn anything from her civics class lessons? Just as I was tearfully trying to convince her that the speech was mine, heartfelt, and approved by my mother, we were rescued. Mom and Dad, Aunt Peggy, and others came in and scolded the teachers for how they ruined our graduation ceremony. They promised it would not end there.

It worked. The speech and happenings became the talk of the town, and community pressure got the board to agree that any student could pay the difference in tuition if he or she wanted to attend Kingston instead of Luzerne. Yes, the quest was back on track! My future looked bright.

Childhood work experiences

Fortunately, I was no stranger to work. Dad's own work ethic, and his insistence that we persevere through hard work or hard times, helped to develop a character attribute in me that would serve me well the rest of my life. There were many opportunities for me to work at chores around the house, and I often went out looking for work to make money for personal wants. Now I would have to earn enough money to meet those wants and to help with needs such as new clothes for school (although I mostly had hand-me-downs from my three older brothers) and to pay the tuition fee. My brothers and I peddled newspapers, but that did not pay much. Intermittently, I would hitchhike with my brother to the country club and sit around all day hoping to get at least one round as a golf caddy. That usually paid $1.25 for a single bag or double that and possibly a small tip for double bags. Sometimes my neighbors would pay fifty cents or a dollar for me to cut their grass. Also, I would sell mail-order vegetable and flower seeds. However, I would need much more money than those ventures would bring. What could I do?

Some of the older kids in our town worked on the farms, but you had to be at least sixteen years old, we were told. Desperate, a couple of my brothers and I ride-shared to Kingston, where we would seek work suckering tomato plants, pulling weeds, and later harvesting tomatoes, corn, and cabbage. All the way there, I kept practicing, "Yes sir, I'm sixteen, or will soon be." Actually, I was thirteen. Skeptical, the foreman hired me anyway. I was ecstatic. So, I made $3.50 a day, working ten hours. By the end of the summer, I had saved enough money for tuition and was quite proud of it.

Supervised Sports and Cub Scouts

Most sports were high school-related. Our only school was first through eighth grades. The only community sport that I recall was the Luzerne-Courtdale-Pringle baseball league. Both my brother Billy and I played in the little league and the teen's league. I was usually a pitcher and he the catcher, although we rotated to other positions as needed. It was strictly recreational. We played for fun. No one expected to gain college scholarships or to use this to prepare for professional sports. There were no baseball camps. There were no organized football, basketball, swimming, or other community sports. Soccer was not even heard of and was one of those sports that even avid athletes knew little about, kind of like lacrosse or rugby. Wrestling was popular in high schools, but not in the community.

The Luzerne community center did host boxing classes. Billy became quite good at it, inspiring him to go on to the golden gloves. I did not like competing but took pride in being his sparring partner. In fact, I would organize practice fights by roping off a ring in our carport and getting our friends over for some fun rounds. Billy probably did not pursue that dream because our family had no discretionary money, transportation, or time to be committed. Our parents were too busy raising and providing for all those kids' essential needs. The only other readily available organized activities in our town were found in our church and the Boy Scouts.

Although I was never involved much in the Boy Scouts after childhood, I did participate in the Cub Scouts, earning my badges from Tiger to Webelos. Our "aunt" Peggy was my den mother, and I remember going to her house in Luzerne for our regular meetings and projects. I have only positive memories of those years, where I learned the importance of physical fitness and competition, as well as socialization and specific scouting skills. Specifically, I remember sack races, tug of war, picnics, camping, and making game items out of wood. Creations of art and gifts from Popsicle sticks were also fun. By contrast, my interest in Boy Scouts faded within a few months, likely because of dysfunctional leadership and a troop structure that focused on only a few individuals.

Childhood and Adolescent Church Experiences

Church or religion is often central to structure in the lives of many, and so it was for me. Although my brothers had some peripheral interests in church activities, much of my childhood and adolescence centered around church activities and the friendships I developed therein. Dad never went to church, and Mom only did on occasion. However, both were proud to see us perform in Christmas pageants or participate in choir.

There was only one church in our town, the Courtdale United Methodist Church. There I participated in Sunday school as a student, teacher, and secretary-treasurer. Our choir leader and or-ganist, Mrs. Hattie Giovannis, was an inspiration to all. She ex-hibited a genuine interest in each child's well-being and provided sage advice. She also made the best brownies and banana cake. We counted on her to help organize our Christmas caroling and to provide hot chocolate and treats afterward. My interest in choir lessened, though, as a few of my attempts at solo singing failed. However, I did stay on because of my friends and would lip sync any difficult notes or unfamiliar tunes.

Every year I would participate in Bible school, memorizing doz-ens of Bible verses and enjoying the social activities. Throughout the year, we held ice cream socials, fund-raising dinners, and other fund-raisers such as selling seeds, magazine subscriptions, and needle-threaders. In fact, one of our most laughed-about "old-busi-ness" items during our youth meetings was needle-threaders, since it seemed that for years we could not sell them all. Other social events centered around being a member as well as president of our United Methodist youth group. We sometimes went to summer camp in New York and attended local evangelical meetings, where we would routinely be emotionally swayed to walk forward and to accept Jesus as our Savior. Christmas and Easter were special events for us, and we would decorate the church with pride. There was a core of us who routinely did things together, such as ice-skate, sleigh-ride, visit shut-ins, go to dances, or just hang out.

Once a year, I would participate in Layman's Day Sunday Service and deliver the sermon. That always made me feel special. My most memorable sermon was entitled "The Evolution of Adam and Eve." As part of a biology seminar college course, we were re-quired to give a speech to a public group. My best friend at college agreed to share the sermon with me and would present what was known about evolution. I would link evolution with religion as

God's master plan. Well, it went off better than we expected, and church members met us at the back of the church at the end of service to thank us for the inspirational words. Evidently our message got lost on some. This I found out when I accidentally entered upon a conversation in a local store, where two elderly ladies looked at me with contempt and said that I should be ashamed of myself, for "throwing out the Bible" in our sermon. That confused me, but in retrospect, I believe they were referring to the biblical version of creation, which they interpreted literally.

There are many other anecdotes to be told, but the potpourri of experiences presented provide a brief description and personal view of what it was like to grow up in a small town. The opportunities for socialization were greater than those for education, employment, and organized sports. Perhaps one of the greatest advantages to living there was to gain insight to human behavior and poverty. It was like having an extensive family, where every birth, success story, death, or tragic event had a personal impact. Gossip flourished, and everyone's personal business was everyone's business.

Unfortunately, a "free-range childhood" the way I experienced it is not available to many children these days. Besides, now there would be concerns about neglectful supervision. Fences separate yards, and collecting apples, plums, or pears from your neighbor's trees could now be considered criminal acts. Overzealous helicopter parenting, while providing safety and greater opportunities for career development, could deprive some of time for self-directed development and introspection.

CHAPTER 3

Family Life

Arguably, the most important influences on one's brain development and success come from experiences within the family. The impact is likely greater than that of the external social milieu, because of the intimacy and extent of interpersonal interactions. The parent-child relationships, parenting style and discipline, effects of poverty on day-to-day activities as well as on health and nutrition, and sibling bonds are all consequential.

Intuitive Parenting and Discipline

"You are either a devil abroad and angel at home, or vice versa," Mom often said. There are no studies that I am aware of that would substantiate her claim. Preconceived notions such as this one are often the prisms through which we view people and events or ideas. However, it was well known who in town behaved differently outside of their immediate family. "If only his mother knew how he acted, then perhaps he would be better disciplined and behaved." Indeed, people are complex and may not be as they appear to others. It is not unusual for people to judge others based on appearances,

trivial information, or preconceived notions. Praise or condemna-
tion may thus be given where it is not deserved. Characteristics of
an individual may be more broadly ascribed to classes of people.
We may become believers or not, faster than we can analyze why.
Becoming a good judge of character takes experience, appropriate
data gathering, and skilled analysis. For some, this is an innate skill.
For others, it is never learned. Mom and Dad had intuitive abilities
in this regard. However, at times, they relied on intuition too much.

There is merit to rapid, intuitive decision-making. Psychologists
talk about the "adaptive unconscious" as a survival mechanism
that frees a person from extensive decision-making based on gathering data and allows split-second actions. Part of our brain auto-
matically jumps to conclusions about people, places, things, ideas,
and situations. Some call it a *gestalt*. Others call it a *feeling*. Some
call it *foolhardy*. Malcolm Gladwell discusses this with extensively
researched reporting in his book *Blink*.[18] He states that decisions
made quickly can be every bit as good as those made deliberatively.
But he cautions, "*Blink* is not just a celebration of the power of the
glance …." It is also about why our instincts betray us. How can we
know when to trust our instincts? He argues well for the position
that we can teach ourselves how to make better snap judgments,
and that doctors and others owe part of their success to this ability
to "shape and manage and educate their unconscious reactions."

To say that my parents were opinionated would be an understatement. Indeed, they effectively passed this trait on to their children! However, there was little one could do to change their minds.
Perhaps having learned through the "school of hard knocks," they
relied on experience more than reason to form their opinions. They

---

[18] Malcolm Gladwell, *Blink*. (New York: Bach Bay Books/Little, Brown and
Company, 2005).

also seemed to think that people rarely change. How you were first defined by them is how you would be perceived, almost forever.

They would judge groups of people based on what they knew about a particular person. So, a neighbor whose only income was based on public welfare once asked my dad why he worked so hard, when he could get almost as much food, shelter, healthcare, and more from the government. Dad's resentment was clear, and he often referred to this when talking about welfare recipients. "They are all lazy. They *all* have generations who live off welfare." Politics and religion are typical areas wherein people simply have faith that something is true. My parents always voted straight Republican, because "Democrats always start wars to boost the economy." Besides, everyone they knew on welfare, including relatives, voted for Democrats. If their opinions changed, it would be only slowly and over time and likely out of frustration. As she got much older, Mom put it this way: "It doesn't matter which bastard you vote for, they are all still bastards."

One should never say "never" or "always," as there are always exceptions. That is true also about the statement I just made. Stereotypes may be positive or negative, and they are incomplete. However, they are useful. It is unlikely that any one person can fully understand another, as we are all individuals with different experiences and unique thought processes. Also, the same person can be viewed completely differently by two different observers. Thus, despite some of the anecdotes that I present, my parents and siblings are much more complex than those stories would indicate. Also, I loved them unconditionally. Having said that, a stereotype of my dad would be Archie Bunker from the television series *All in the Family*. He and mom even laughed and noted that whoever wrote the show must have lived with Dad! Perhaps a stereotype for Mom would be Judge Judy, the main character of a show she loved to watch. Certainly Mom was unlike Archie's wife Edith; she would give back as tough as she got. Mom was also all about fairness, an attribute she exhibited throughout her life.

Brain research supports that how we perceive the world is set very early in life. Our capacities to learn are also established early in life. That does not mean that we can't change as we get older. It just means that it becomes much more difficult. There is much known about the roles of the right and left sides of the brain. In fact, people are often stereotyped as being a "right brain" or "left brain" person. Very few people use both sides well. The left hemisphere is more analytical, the right more intuitive. The left focuses on details, the right on the whole. The left is more action-oriented, the right is more nurturing. The left is the scientist, the right the artist. Dr. Leonard Shlain has written extensively about this. In his final book, *Leonardo's Brain*,[19] it is his hypothesis that Leonardo was perhaps one of a very few people throughout history to use both sides of his brain equally. That is why, he contends, that Leonardo was both one of the greatest scientists and artists that ever lived.

People can and do change. The brain has a great degree of "plasticity" and can continue to learn throughout life. Experiences change people. People also choose experiences to get better at specific abilities, and to gain knew knowledge and abilities. No two people have the exact same experiences or abilities, including identical twins, and so generalizations about families, races, gender, nations, politicians, or other groups are highly prone to error and bias. To shed preconceived ideas based on new information is the core of scientific inquiry. So it is difficult for the primarily right-brained person to accept change and for the left not to expect it. However, both sides of the brain are connected, and experience can

---

[19] Leonard Schlain, *Leonardo's Brain: Understanding da Vinci's Creative Genius.* (Guilford, CT: Lyons Press, 2014).

lead us to use one side more than previously. Change may be more difficult for the non-inquisitive and/or the non-analytical person.

What does it take for change to occur? Several forces are at work here. First of all, new information has to be gathered or at least perceived. Second, some analysis has to occur that sheds new light on the person or situation being analyzed, based on the new information. Third, change may require motivation, internal or external or both. Thus, expanding our experiences will expand our information and perhaps our perceptions. Advanced or continued education, exposure to diverse peoples and cultures, and willingness to hear and/or embrace different ideas all contribute to how one may change throughout life. Similarly, the absence of exposure to new or different people, cultures, ideas, or experiences will slow and inhibit change.

"Why is it that when you go to college, you then discard religious teachings and your parents' values?" Mom's assertions startled me. I do not recall the exact setting in which she said this, but I do remember that I was having a discussion with someone about religion and science. Mom had been listening closely and could no longer contain her emotion.

"What do you mean?" I queried. How could Mom think that I would discard my values, many of which were influenced by her, our family, and my religious and other experiences? Why did she blame college? This was her perception. She was basing it on the transformation she saw in her two sons who were the first ever to go to college in our extended family. She mistook discussion and the free exchange of ideas for dissent, and dissent for disrespect. There was no way that Mom would be familiar with studies that show that it is a natural part of development and important for adolescents to embrace their own ideas of work, relationships, values, and understanding of life in general. Such information was not readily available. There were few experts explaining the developmental milestones and challenges for children, especially since the field of pediatrics was in its infancy and adolescent medicine was not yet born.

"Children are to be seen, and not heard." "Don't do as I do, but do as I say." "Why? Just because." "It is because I say it is." "I'm the parent, you are the child, so you do as I say." "Spare the rod, spoil the child." "Mind your own business." Those were quotes we often got from our parents. That is how things were back then, or at least in our family and town. Although some passive parenting was obvious in some families, children generally had no rights. Parents were omniscient and all powerful. Any query or dissent could and often was interpreted as a sign of disrespect. "Eat your food or go to bed hungry." "Do your chores, or you are grounded." Often we were spanked and grounded and got no privileges until those chores were done. Any argument about the chores or when to get them done was disrespectful and would be met with additional punishment.

That is how our parents were raised, and that is how we were raised. Our parents must have mellowed over time, as my older siblings and I accused them of being soft and favoring the youngest. They got away with things that we would never have! There is some general belief that this is not uncommon. Perhaps parents learn what is and what is not important as they age, or maybe they just get tired of "parenting."

Perhaps one of their most important attributes as parents was their focus on teaching us to be responsible. We had daily and weekly chores that rotated. Dad hung a chart with our chores and names, and we had to check those we completed. We had to wash, dry, and put away the dishes. The beds were to be made before school. The furnace was to be tended. That included stacking firewood, shoveling coal, regulating the fire and heat, and removing the ashes. Of course, a wood- and coal-fired furnace created lots of dust, so we had to dust and vacuum weekly. Cutting grass, raking leaves, pulling weeds, trimming hedges, cleaning the basement, scraping and painting siding, helping with remodeling projects, keeping our rooms clutter-free, doing homework, and finding jobs to earn personal spending money was expected. Some of those jobs included a regular newspaper route that we ran, delivering newspapers daily, and collecting the money every two weeks and submitting that to the publisher. We were encouraged to put some of our earnings into a savings account and only withdraw it for special needs or wants.

All of us had chores, but they were not fairly distributed. For example, an older brother was often exempted from tough manual work, as he needed "delicate hands" to be a pianist as he aspired. However, he was expected to practice his piano lessons. Personally, I always felt a sense of accomplishment from manual labor and would get up early on the weekends to get my outside chores done. This allowed the rest of the day for play and was met with parental praise in setting an example for my brothers, who liked to sleep longer. I also loved to learn new skills such as car repairs, carpentry, and landscaping, so they tended to give me more tasks.

Although Dr. Benjamin Spock, pediatrician, came out with his first book on parenting in 1946,[20] it was heretical to think that one should not raise children in such a strictly authoritative manner. Even today, the ill-informed argue for the benefits of spanking. Spanking, now considered a euphemism for child abuse, is still practiced in some public schools as a disciplinary measure.

---

[20] Benjamin Spock, *The Common Sense Book of Baby and Child Care*. (New York: Duell, Sloan and Pearce, 1946).

Extensive research[21] to date concludes there is no advantage to physical discipline (spanking), and there are many complications, such as lowered self-esteem, impaired development and socialization, resentment and long-term mental health issues, inappropriate approaches to conflict resolution, and significant physical morbidity and death. At best, spanking gets a brief cooperation. Most of the time, spankings are done out of anger and frustration. Dr. Spock raised awareness of the developmental needs of children, and his cogent advice was embraced by many. He did emphasize the importance of "intuitive" parenting but aimed to help parents to manage that intuition better.

The classic poem "Children Learn What They Live," by Dorothy Nolte, came out in 1954.[22] This book[23] is one of my favorite references for parents, as it emphasizes key parenting attributes in a brief, intuitive, and easy-to-understand manner. Over the next half century, the American Academy of Pediatrics and others would advocate for children by making information widely available concerning the emotional and health needs of children. This has come to define a much better, more positive parenting style nationwide. Sadly, there are interest groups that are ill-informed regarding the behavioral and preventive health needs of children, and they continue to advocate inappropriate disciplinary and healthcare measures. During my childhood, information was much more difficult to access. There was no Internet. Television was strictly entertainment, and there were few if any community groups dedicated to promoting optimal child-rearing practices. Parents would have to be less sure of their parenting philosophy and highly motivated

[21] www.apa.org, "The Case Against Spanking."
[22] Dorothy Law Nolte, "Children Learn What They Live," column for *The Torrance Herald*, 1954.
[23] Dorothy Law Nolte and Rachel Harris, *Children Learn What They Live: Parenting to Inspire Values*. (New York: Workman Publishing, 1998).

to obtain books and research information about discipline. Some of what was deemed appropriate then would surely be considered child abuse or neglect now.

Now it is better understood that we should look at the causes of behavior and direct discipline appropriately to change the behavior. The student who appears to be purposefully disruptive, indifferent, and disrespectful may be so because of a condition called ADD, attention deficit disorder, with or without hyperactivity. Discipline does not and usually cannot become effective until this problem that relates to neurotransmitter deficits in the brain is chemically treated. The same behaviors may alternatively be due to oppositional defiant disorder, learning disorders, bullying, abuse, other mental health disorders, dysfunctional families or classrooms, lead intoxication, substance abuse, and so forth. Unless a correct diagnosis as to the cause of the behavior is made, the treatment strategy is likely to fail.

Some would argue that I became successful and have made a positive contribution to society because of the physical discipline and excessive punishments my parents inflicted. I would argue that it was in spite of that. Their unconditional love, encouragement, nurturing, and other positive parenting skills were much more important. The latter were embraced, the former resented.

Praise motivated me, but punishment made me resentful. In fact, I would sometimes do naïve and stupid things to get praise. For example, one time I found a short wooden stick with nine leather straps on it and brought it home for Dad to use on us instead of his belt or hand. I knew that he would be delighted, since he often talked of making one. Why did I do that! After the first beating, I realized that it wasn't worth the praise, and I regretted having given him that stick. Eventually my brothers and I made the straps and stick disappear. But Dad resorted back to his belt.

Punishments also included verbal reprimands that were de-
grading, such as name calling. For example, I was "teacher's pet,"
and each of my brothers had a label such as "wooden head," "stupid," "girl scout," "Gallagher" (a reference to behavior he detested in
his in-laws), "loud mouth," etc. Nonphysical punishments such as
being grounded or other restrictions became ineffective because of
excessive application of those restrictions. So, if I were grounded for
two weeks (the usual), it became four weeks or indefinitely if I protested or violated the restriction. Eventually he or my mom would
give in to my whining or counter-strategies, such as not talking to
them and ignoring them for days at a time. Their methods were
briefly effective but caused much resentment, fear of authority, and
disrespect because the angrier they were, the harsher the punishment. Punishment out of proportion to the "crime" conflicted with
a sense of fairness, as did punishing all for the misdeed of one. It
was easier than figuring out what happened. "It takes two to fight,"
they would say, and they would punish both, regardless of who
started the fight. The rules were also not applied uniformly, and
we learned to lie to evade the punishment, rather than to recognize
that what we had done was wrong.

"Really, you want to test our son for the Talented and Gifted
(TAG) program?" I asked in disbelief. Our first son was very difficult to "manage." He was ornery and seemed to be slow at everything he did. Once we learned of his high IQ and enrollment in the
TAG program, I began to look at his behavior differently. What I
had been interpreting as slow was really his efforts to do his assignments perfectly, such as spacing his letters exactly one finger-width
apart. His ornery behavior mostly centered around his frustration
that he would be interrupted at completing a task. So, once I understood his temperament, life and discipline became better. Instead
of spanking and forcing my will on him, as my parents had done

with us, I anticipated his reaction and worked to prevent the undesired behavior. For example, if we were planning to go somewhere within half an hour, I would alert him to that and suggest he work at putting a smaller puzzle together, one that could be completed within a half hour. Subsequently, all of our children benefitted from our change to only positive parenting strategies. Today they use the same positive strategies with their children. Styles of discipline are often embraced by children who later become parents. Thus, abusive parents often create abusive parents.

Now it is generally recognized that consistency in parenting is perhaps more important than whether the style is authoritative or permissive. Children need to have boundaries, and it is in their nature to test those boundaries. Consistency enables the child to learn more readily what is expected and what the consequences of misbehavior are. If Grandma and Grandpa always allow a behavior at their house that is not allowed at home, then the parents' job is more difficult. Firm, but loving, consistent, and timely discipline works best. The purpose of discipline is to teach, not to punish.

Family Relationships

"Family" has multiple connotations. For me, family consisted mostly of my parents and brothers. As noted, our family grew such that each of my three older brothers were one year apart, and the younger three were each three years apart. So, who comprised the family differed during different parts of my childhood and adolescence. Our extended family was so intermittently involved with us that they rarely came to mind when someone asked about our family. My dad's parents died before I was born, and his only sibling lived in Maryland on a farm with her large family. His sister was such an outgoing, affable person that we all loved her despite only seeing her on rare occasions. Our cousins on both sides of the family rarely visited, but we considered it a special treat when they did. My maternal grandparents lived in a neighboring town, but we seldom visited. They lived a life of poverty. Grandma was a very dependent type person, so we got to visit mostly when Mom went there to help her. Occasionally we would sleep over, but we didn't like that because we would always get bedbug bites. Grandpa became an alcoholic and visited only during a drunken state.

Despite his drunkenness, Grandpa Gallagher was charming. He had lost several fingers and parts of fingers in the mines. Playfully, he would try to scare us with those hands and recount the horrors of mining. I always felt empathy for how tragic it seemed, and I wondered how his life could have been different. Dad felt that Grandpa was a poor example for us and complained about any visits. He would use Grandpa as an example of what would happen to us if we drank and smoked and lived off welfare. It was his fear that Mom's family would move in, should something happen to him.

Grandma had a sense of humor that showed through her life of despair. I recall visiting with her, sitting in her kitchen, bored. "Let's go for an airplane ride," she said in a wistful manner. We talked about what it must be like to fly like a bird, and to go above the clouds and view the earth from on high. It would be joyful but scary as well, but worth the risk. Sadly, I realized that there were so many things that she would never experience in her life because of her poverty and lifestyle. Alcohol and tobacco hastened the death of both maternal grandparents, with Grandpa also suffering from black lung disease as a result of his years of work in the coal mines. The stereotypes I have presented certainly do not give an adequate overview of their lives and who they were. However, this is the side of their personalities that impacted me the most. By contrast, Mom's two sisters and four brothers each had their own families, and we got to know them much better, as they would visit on holidays and special occasions.

A couple of my parents' closest friends were considered part of our family and referred to as uncles or aunts. There were Uncle Ron and Aunt Peggy and their two sons and Uncle Fred and Aunt Becky and their son. Mom established many friends in town, and many of them visited frequently for coffee and gossip. We got to know them as though they were family.

Some folks consider pets a part of the family, but we never had that relationship with ours. There was a cat we once adopted, who we did not keep for long. Each dog we owned was kept on a leash attached to a dog coop or clothesline. Dad often lamented that they would be so much happier if we lived on a farm where they could roam at will. However, in town we had to keep them restrained. We never took them for walks, and they were not allowed in the house. Later in life, Mom did fill her empty nest with a cocker spaniel I believe she inherited from my brother and his wife when they moved.

Most of my memories of our dogs are tragic, although I do recall the joy of feeding them, and petting or playing with them. When I was around four years old, our dog was hit by a car as I chased after him to get him back into our yard. He survived long enough to scare me as he came yelping and bleeding toward me. Unfortunately, my other most vivid dog memory persists to this day. Crying, holding my mom's hand, and standing with my brother, we watched out the bedroom window as Dad shot our dog. "He has to put him out of his misery," mom consoled us as she wept. Our beautiful boxer, named Cesar, had a mortal neck wound inflicted by a large neighbor's dog who escaped and attacked Cesar while he was chained to his coop. There were no local veterinarians, and besides, we could not afford one. Dad chose to shoot him, after an unsuccessful club to his head, which broke my new baseball bat.

Poverty, Health, and Nutrition

How poor were we? Certainly we were in the lower socioeconomic status. Our poverty was relative. It was not absolute, as we always had adequate food, clothing, and shelter. It was perhaps generational but certainly not just situational. There were many families in our community that were better off financially, but we were not as poor as those on welfare. We lived paycheck to paycheck. Fortunately, Dad was never unemployed. His only other source of income related to doing rare specific projects for the borough or for neighbors.

"Waste not, want not," was another familiar refrain from Dad. He was not a pathological hoarder, but he saved everything and anything that could be useful. No matter the size of wood, if not rotten, it was saved for possible future use. Dad would bring home items that were discarded at work. Most of the materials he used to make our patio and to finish our basement had been salvaged from elsewhere. Despite our objections of embarrassment, we were told to bring home the discarded furniture that neighbors put out as garbage. We also saved metal scraps and rags to sell to the "rag man" or "junk man," who periodically came through the neighborhood. Once I was severely scolded and caused a fight between Dad and Mom for having sold a transmission for fifty cents. "You did what!" Dad yelled, as I proudly reported how generous the junk man was. Dutifully, I sold all the metal junk that was in the area behind our carport as Dad had instructed me before he left for work. Evidently, I had been conned into selling what the dealer must have known was a transmission but that looked like metal junk to me. That "junk man" never came around again.

Clothes were useful until they could no longer be patched or sewn or functional. Shoes were worn until they could no longer be re-soled. In fact, we often used the cardboard that separated shredded wheat cereal biscuits to line the inside of our shoes until we could afford to get the holes in the soles repaired. This was problematic in the winter when the cardboard got wet from the snow or ice. Metal cleats were placed to prolong the life of the soles, despite the teachers' complaints of how noisy they were. Everything that was still useable was passed on from sibling to sibling. Laughingly, Dad suggested that a particular "perfectly good" sweater that shrunk with each wash be passed onto the dog once it no longer fit our youngest brother! Mostly my only new clothes were Christmas or birthday gifts. Fights often erupted among my brothers and me over whose socks or underwear or other clothing it was that we were wearing.

Our house was a small, two-bedroom, one-bath, sixteen hundred–square-foot ranch-style house with a basement, which Dad had built with materials salvaged from a three-story building that was previously on that lot. He constantly worked to keep it nice, and that made all of us proud. He insisted on our participation in projects, and we had regular chores to do, both inside and outside of the house. There was a wood- and coal-fired furnace, with forced hot air system. Our basement was constantly humid and cold, because of the three-foot-thick stone wall foundation. We added a bomb shelter by making a doorway in the wall near an outside stoop, which also had the thick stone walls for support. My brothers and I would load five-gallon paint buckets with the dirt, carry them outside, and dump the dirt on the distant area of our backyard. Our bomb shelter was also used to store canned goods and vegetables. Eventually we plastered and painted the walls of the shelter, put in a concrete floor, paneled the other walls in the basement, and turned it into a family play and party room, as well as a workshop area for Dad.

On three different occasions, we dug out areas of the backyard next to the house to add bedrooms. The first two times, we had to refill that area as Dad cancelled his remodeling plans. The two bedrooms were finally built after I had started college and a couple of older brothers had moved out. Before adding the bedrooms, Mom and Dad had a queen bed and shared their bedroom across from the kitchen with my three youngest brothers. I slept with my brother Billy, and the two oldest brothers slept together, with our side-by-side beds and a dresser filling the small room. Needless to say, we got to know each other well. We pulled tricks on each other, fought over pillows and bed position, complained about body odors, and shared scary night-time stories that were usually narrated by our oldest brother. Often we talked about things that were happening in our lives and agonized over Mom and Dad's arguments that sometimes kept us awake.

There was no access to sewers in our town until the 1970s. Instead, we had a septic system known as a "standard gravity" soil treatment system. Solids would settle into an underground tank in the backyard, and liquids would filter by gravity into the surrounding soil. Unfortunately, drainage slowed in the winter, and problems resulted if the tank was too full to hold some of the liquid effluent. We could not afford to have the tank emptied until there were problems. We certainly had problems. The effluent would back up into the basement. This worsened after building the two bedrooms in the back of the house, as the basement under them flooded more frequently because of greater proximity to the septic field. The problem then became persistent throughout the year. Rains would saturate the yard and make this worse. Our short-term treatment, for years, was to cover the soil in the basement beneath those two bedrooms with lye as a disinfectant until the effluent drained away. Eventually, we were able to have a better septic tank installed and scheduled tank maintenance. After that, we finished that part of the basement.

Not only did we not waste food, clothing, or other materials, we were self-sufficient for most home and car repairs. Others were only hired if there was something Dad could not fix, and there were very few things he could not do. My mother's brother-in-law was a television repairman and would service our second-hand television set that frequently needed tube replacements. Occasionally car repairs were beyond Dad's expertise, and he had a mechanic friend who discounted service for him. Electrical work sometimes was performed by another neighbor, as cheap as possible. These folks always allowed extended payment plans that were personalized. We did have credit extended to us at the local grocery store, which would be paid as soon as Dad received his paycheck. We also had one "revolving charge account" at the "Boston" store in Wilkes-Barre.

Healthcare focused on treatment, not prevention. No one was ever turned away from the hospital or the family doctor. Sometimes hospital bills were not covered by our insurance, but my parents would pay whatever they could until those bills got paid. Oftentimes our family doctors would tell Mom not to worry about their fees and to pay them only when we could.

"Betty, do you have money today?" her doctor would say when she asked how much she owed. Mom usually did not, so he would say, "Well then, you owe me nothing."

Mom felt embarrassed and never took advantage of his generosity. She would always try to round up a few dollars to take with her to her appointments. Sometimes she "borrowed" this money from the community organizations for which she was treasurer, or from the money we collected for newspaper deliveries that had not yet been sent to the news company. On paydays, she would replenish the source from which she borrowed. On occasion I would see her crying, as the money was due before she could repay it. Somehow she managed to borrow from a friend or only pay part of a bill that was due. My parents constantly were borrowing from Peter to pay Paul, and financial problems were daily stressors and the source of many of their arguments.

In those days, there was very little healthcare education or preventive medicine. Communities provided the polio vaccine, but there was no such thing as well-child checkups. With all of us boys, there was always someone with an injury or illness. When one of us got sick, the others all followed. How to prevent the spread of illness within a household and the infectious basis of disease was not well understood in our family. Consequently, my brothers and I experienced most childhood illnesses, including whooping cough, chickenpox, measles, mumps, and rubella. Skin staph infections, athlete's foot, conjunctivitis, gastroenteritis, and respiratory infections were common. Little did I realize then that these experiences would help with my education as a pediatrician.

Dad smoked cigars, Mom smoked cigarettes, their friends smoked, and all of mom's siblings smoked. No wonder we took up that habit. Our oldest brother didn't smoke, but the rest of us did. Many of our friends smoked. Most of us got hooked as children. I remember starting after finding out that my two older brothers were smoking. They were stealing my mom's cigarettes, bumming them off friends, and searching the streets for partly smoked cigarettes and butts. Mom often rolled her own, as it was much cheaper that way. We also did that. Cigarettes then were twenty-five cents a pack, and sometimes less than two dollars for a carton of ten. Dad smoked factory rejects, five cents a cigar. By recall, I experimented with smoking around age eleven or twelve and smoked regularly by mid-teens. It was very socially acceptable, and the clear dangers of smoking were not well-known or believed.

Unfortunately, that addiction was extremely difficult to break. Every time I tried to quit, I eventually resumed and actually increased how many I smoked each day. So I went from a half pack a day in high school to a pack a day in college. Before I finally quit in 1975, I was smoking two-plus packs a day. I also sometimes smoked a pipe. Our first child was my inspiration to quit, plus I could not afford the habit. She would cough every time she saw me. I thought then that surely my kids would smoke, if I did. After all, kids want to be like those who they love and admire.

To be successful at quitting, I would pretend to be smoking at times I normally smoked and when I felt the urge for a cigarette. Breaking the habits of inhaling and pretending to blow smoke rings and to flick off ashes were important. Kojak, the television series (1973–78) detective who sucked on lollipops, was popular at that time, so I would eat suckers in lieu of smoking. The first month was extremely difficult, but after that it became easier. There would be times when I would have a cigarette or two at a party or during times of stress, but I never restarted the habit. It would be decades, though, before the desire to have a cigarette would finally be gone. However, there was an immediate improvement in my breathing, sense of smell, and sense of taste. This encouraged me; I became a runner and more focused on healthy lifestyles thereafter.

Poverty certainly limited our food selections and nutrition. Most of our food was bought on payday, which was every second Friday. Cases of canned vegetables, cases of evaporated canned milk, dozens of eggs, a fifty-pound bag of potatoes, a couple of half gallons of ice cream, non-homogenized peanut butter, day-old bread, and a couple of packs of sandwich cookies and fig bars were staples. The cookies and ice cream would be gone in a day or two.

No other treats except some penny candies and Kool-Aid powder or an occasional soda could be bought until the next payday, or with money that we earned personally from shoveling snow or delivering newspapers or other work. On occasion, one of our neighbors who had a trucking business would stop by with unopened stale bread and pastries that he was supposed to take to the dumps for the manufacturers. We would salvage what we could, some for immediate use and some to be frozen. My dad hunted when he could, and deer or other game would help to fill the freezer. He did his own cleaning and processing.

Our typical meals included cereal or eggs and toast for breakfast. Soup, peanut butter and jelly sandwiches, canned sardines and crackers, or canned pork and beans were for lunch. Supper almost always included potatoes and canned vegetables and hamburger in various forms, such as meatloaf, meatballs, or casserole. Occasionally we would have homemade vegetable soup or liver and onions. Milk was prepared by adding equal amounts of water to the canned milk and karo to sweeten it. Mom was never successful at breast feeding, so even as babies, this milk was our "formula." Solids were introduced to babies as soon as possible at that time, usually by two weeks of age. We also had chocolate or strawberry flavored powder to mix with the milk. Occasionally we had homegrown rhubarb or other vegetables. Deserts were infrequent but would include homemade cakes, pies, fudge, bread pudding, or rice pudding.

Whatever was served, we ate or went hungry. On one occasion when Mom was in the hospital, Dad made some homemade vegetable soup that had everything in it except the cat's tail, as he put it. There were large lima beans, lentils, corn, peas, carrots, stewed tomatoes, and other canned goods. The pot was huge and would be enough for a couple of days, and by then Mom should be home.

Unfortunately, he burned it. Nevertheless, that was what we had. I could not tolerate it but could not tell Dad. He was suspicious, as I took my soup to the bathroom with me. Of course, I planned on dumping it down the toilet. "I just don't want my brothers to take it on me," I replied to his question as to why. My deceit worked, or so I thought. When I got back to the table, smiling at my brothers who were suffering through it, Dad refilled my bowl! He said I deserved a second helping for liking it so much. Laughter ensued. To this day, I cannot stand the smell of vegetable soup.

Another time that he was chief cook and bottle washer for the day, Dad decided to cook calf's liver and onions. As I entered the house, something smelled awful. He did not appreciate my asking what he burned this time. My response was that liver and onions never smelled that bad before, when Mom cooked them. So, I searched through the garbage and found the answer. Dad was cooking kidneys! Evidently he picked up the wrong package at the grocery store. "You will eat it or go to bed hungry." I went to bed hungry. To his credit, Dad made the best Swedish meatballs, and we encouraged him to do so thereafter when he had to play Mr. Mom.

Perhaps the most significant consequence of poverty for us was poor dental care. Unfortunately, professional dental care was not affordable. It was always a last resort, because of pain. Often we self-treated the pain by packing carious teeth with cloves or teabags or applying Anbesol and taking aspirin. There was no public fluoridation of water supplies, and we had no oral fluoride available. Several of my brothers and I had an inheritable soft enamel and yellowing of the teeth that was prone to caries. Although we brushed and practiced good oral hygiene at bedtime, we had little knowledge of what was appropriate. If a tooth failed to hold a filling once or twice, we would have our teeth extracted. Consequently, several of us had partial or full dentures by mid to late adolescence. Those dentures were made by a local handyman and were poorly fit.

Dental pain often came at inconvenient times. I remember trying desperately to finish my college board exams, while suffering from incredible tooth pain. Similarly, there were many times that my school concentration and performance were adversely affected. Not only did extensive dental caries adversely impact cognition, but being toothless with loose-fitting dentures during adolescence had a significant psychosocial impact. The damage to my self-esteem, confidence in public speaking, and underlying bony structures has had a lifetime effect. Fear of damaging or losing the dentures affected my participation in sports and other activities, such as riding a roller coaster and having to keep my mouth shut. Some of that confidence was regained, but it took decades. Mandibular dental implants have helped, but the maxillary bones were too thin for implants. Poorly fitting and long-term denture wearing contributed to the maxillary erosion. To this day I am embarrassed, but I feel it is important to discuss the impact that poverty and poor dental or health care can have on our cognitive, social, and emotional well-being.

Family Activities and Holiday Celebrations

Our family almost never went on vacation, as Dad would use his two weeks off to complete or start projects around the house. I only remember two trips to the Siperko's farm, to visit our dad's sister and her family in Maryland. However, we did go on picnics or weekend day getaways several times a year. Most of these centered around Memorial Day, Independence Day, and Labor Day holidays. These marked the beginning, middle, and end of our summers off from school. Our choices were usually Bowman's Creek, Perrin's Marsh, Rocky Glen, Harvey's Lake, or Barbacci's Grove.

The typical "outing" for us was with the Isaac, Simpson, West, and Ostrum families, all of whom were our parents' close friends. They all had children we knew well. Occasionally some of Mom's siblings and their families would join us. Typically, we would swim, hike, play badminton, play ball, or other activities. Most of the adults would smoke and drink beer, tell stories, play cards, rest in hammocks, and play horseshoes. It seemed that the beer drinking was competitive, and Dad often had to "sleep it off" before heading home. Dad would often drive, racing Mr. West all the way home, as we lived only a few houses away from each other. The parties started early morning and ended at dark. The next day we would all reminisce about those events.

Back then our cars had no seatbelts, and turn signals were not required. Mom and a kid or two would be in front with Dad, and the rest of us packed liked sardines in the backseat. The car had no air conditioning, so we most often rode with the windows down. That also helped to lessen the noise for our parents, as we were often fighting over room in the back or complaining about each other for some reason or other. Sunday afternoons we often went for drives into the country, in search of farms and just to enjoy the scenery. We would unload, then run and look around farmers' fields wherever there seemed to be a beautiful setting or potential sale. En route home, we stopped at the Twin Kiss for chocolate-vanilla twist ice cream cones, unless we were bad. When our parents had no money, Dad would accidently "miss the turn" into the ice cream place and promise to stop the next time.

Birthdays were always celebrated at home, with just us. Occasionally a friend or two would be present. Mom would make a cake of choice for the birthday person. After supper, the candles on the cake were lit, we all sang happy birthday, and cake and chocolate milk were served. A single small gift would be presented, while everyone looked on. My favorite cake was a spice cake with peanut butter icing. Oftentimes I complained that one of my Christmas presents was just held back, as my birthday was only a couple of weeks later. More than once, I received a jar of peanut butter as my present, as requested.

Easter was welcomed as a break from school, a joyous holiday, and as a harbinger of winter's end. Sometimes Mom joined us, but mostly my brothers and I went to the local church. We were proud to get dressed in our Sunday suits, slick back our hair, and behave, at least through the church service. Occasionally, some of us would get to go to the outdoor sunrise service in Kingston.

The night before, it was always fun to help Mom hard boil eggs, then dip them through differently colored water solutions and decorate them. We would do several dozens, and the prettiest would be placed in our baskets. Typically, jelly beans, malted balls, hard-coated candies, and chocolate eggs with fruit or peanut butter would be placed in each basket on top of fake green grass. Some marshmallow candies, and one solid or hollow milk chocolate egg, would be placed there along with an Easter card. Of course, Mom (a.k.a., the Easter Bunny) would fill each basket after we went to bed. By the time Mom and Dad got up, we had already been awake and eaten a large portion of the goodies. Although the hard-boiled eggs sat at room temperature for several days thereafter, we never seemed to get sick from them.

Thanksgiving was another big event, as Mom would create a large feast for us. Ham, sweet potatoes, red beats, a stuffed Turkey usually over twenty-five pounds, corn, white potatoes, cole slaw, cranberry sauce, green beans, and pies for dessert. Usually she made a couple of pumpkin and apple pies, one minced meat raisin pie, and one or two lemon meringue pies. Even though we ate until we almost passed out, there would be leftovers for an evening snack and sometimes for next-day sandwiches. Depending on the weather, we would play board games inside or play outdoors. Occasionally, my brother Billy's birthday coincided with the Thanksgiving holiday. and that would also be celebrated, usually in the evening.

As is true for many families, Christmas was our favorite holiday of the year. We got off school the week before and did not have to go back until after Russian Christmas, January 7. We also kept our decorations up until then. Always, we hoped for snow. Our church group would go around the town, knock on doors, and then sing Christmas carols. Folks would either look out windows and wave to us or step out into the cold to listen. Oftentimes they would give us money for our youth activities. We also sang all while we walked along the roads. Back at the church or at someone's house, we would warm up with hot chocolate and some of Mrs. Giovannis's brownies and cookies. Every year, our youth fellowship group would pick out the Christmas tree for the church sanctuary and decorate both. Spontaneous singing and fellowship made those special experiences.

In our family, each of us seemed to have special roles. Dad would drive me and another brother or two into the country to cut down a tree and bring it home. Usually we visited my godmother's place, Mrs. Spencer, as she had some land and lots of pine trees on it. She would often recount how she met Dad one cold winter morning, as he drove down to her place on his tractor with a snow plow and cleared her driveway, just being neighborly. I loved visiting with her, as she was fun to talk with and often made bread on her coal-fired cast iron oven. It was close to our farm, and I would ask Dad to drive out there so I could see it. However, the property and drive was private, and I could only see the fields from there.

Mrs. Spencer lived to be a centenarian and remained witty as ever, remembering all of our names and special events.

Usually it was my job and pride to care for the tree. I placed it in a large bucket of coal, watered it as needed, and secured it with twine to the corner of the room next to our fake fireplace and mantle, just as I had seen Dad do it when I was younger. For some reason or other, I claimed the right to decorate the back of the tree. Dad would put up the lights, passing the string to me in the back to continue it in spiral fashion. Next we would run garland parallel to that. Since there was little space behind the tree, and one would have to crawl out beneath the lowest branches, I would decorate the back before the front was started. For bragging rights, I resisted any arguments from my brothers to do that part of the decorations. They would later remind me that tree care was my job, when it came time to discard the tree and pick up all the pine needles that had fallen onto the carpet.

The rest of the family then joined in unwrapping the decorations that had been so carefully stored in newspaper the preceding year, and complete the decorations with the glass balls, handmade stars and other items, and tinsel as the final step. Electric candles would be placed in each of the windows facing the front of the house and driveway side. Some outdoor lights were also strung.

No one did as much as Mom. The tree was usually obtained and decorated a week or two before Christmas, although there were times when we put it up the day before Christmas. Usually this was when we had to buy a tree and waited until they were discounted or free. Mom did all the shopping at the one store in Wilkes-Barre, where they had a revolving charge account. The best sales were on Christmas Eve, so that is when she also did all of the shopping. Mostly it was for blue jeans, shoes, jackets, hats, gloves, or other clothes we needed. Every year we would get a new board game or two. Some of our favorites were Scrabble, Parcheesi, Chinese checkers, cards, and Monopoly. Many of our other gifts were shared, such as one sled, one bike, one basketball, one baseball glove, or one football. Some had to be personal, such as ice skates. Mostly we would get one special item each. After we went to bed, Mom did all the wrappings and placed them strategically around the tree and room. Our stockings were filled with an apple, an orange, a tangerine, a popcorn ball, candy canes, and hard candies. She also prepared the Christmas foods, cookies, pies, and ham that evening. By the time she got to bed, we were all rising to see if Santa had come. Despite the fatigue, she would get right up and act so surprised at what we got!

Seasonal affective disorder (SAD) is quite prominent in areas such as Pennsylvania where the winters can be exceptionally long, with overcast skies and cold from September through May. Some years it is much nicer and shorter, but the paucity of sunshine and the demands of the holidays and the cabin fever can cause melancholy or significant depression. Dad always was especially moody around the holidays and clearly experienced SAD. He participated as needed, but not with any enthusiasm, and often by watching us or getting lost in his work around the house. However, there was one Christmas that we talked about for years. Dad stayed up most of the night with us and celebrated in a way that he would never have otherwise allowed. He bought a dart board, placed it on the wall in our parlor, and challenged us all to play. None of us had played before, so there were a lot of misses, and we chipped the plastered walls, but Dad uncharacteristically took it in stride. He knew that he would have to repair and paint the wall, but that night he was determined to have fun with his kids! Dad had just a little too much port wine that Christmas, but it seemed to have treated his moodiness, at least for one memorable day.

Sibling Bonds

As a grandparent, I have noticed how each of our grandbabies would initially bond best with the youngest of their siblings or cousins. Perhaps it is related to size and/or common developmental interests, but I think there is an intuitive sense that drives this behavior. Similarly, special common bonds developed among us boys. Shared experiences also led to some unique bonds, which I will highlight. These bonds strengthened or weakened as our common interests or friendships overlapped. The nature of our grade school, where those who were one year apart were taught by the same teacher in the same classroom, likely added to those particular bonds because of the shared experiences. Regardless of how the bonds were formed, there is no doubt that there were unique relationships.

The following descriptions are not meant to stereotype anyone, or to talk about favorites, but are offered in perspective of how siblings can develop unique personalities, relationships, and lives, despite many common experiences and genetics. Those bonds of childhood did not remain unchanged as we progressed through life. Jeffrey Kluger's book *The Sibling Effect*[24] gives great insight to sibling relationships and what they reveal about personalities. This book is not about my siblings, as each is complex enough to devote an entire book to his life. However, I want to provide some insight to my bonds with each sibling. That in turn can put some of my life in perspective. One sibling requested that he not be mentioned.

Our personalities have been molded in a common factory (family), as well as by multiple workers there (siblings, parents) and nearby (community). However, our choices throughout our lives

---

[24] Jerry Klugar, *The Sibling Effect: What the Bonds Among Brothers and Sisters Reveal About Us.* (New York: Riverhead Books, Penguin Group, 2011).

have also created differences, in opportunities and experiences, and in the bonds that have been created. Undoubtedly, there are many similarities in our lives and relationships. Genetics and shared experiences account for some of that similarity. We take pride in each other's achievements and accept each other for who we are. We share concerns for each other's well-being. We have some physical, cognitive, and emotional similarities. Our mannerisms of speech, gait, and interactions with others, although unique, have similar qualities. Our social relationships and behaviors bear resemblance to our parents and each other, yet differ. Finally, the prisms through which we each view the world have similarities, but we also have unique perspectives shaped by our cultural and personal experiences.

Without a doubt, the brother with whom I had the most shared experiences was also the one closest in age. Billy was one year older than me. Thus, we shared each school year with the same teacher in the same classroom at the same time, four times throughout the Courtdale elementary school. We played together on the Courtdale-Luzerne-Pringle little league and teen baseball teams. Together, we went to boxing classes in Luzerne, and as teenagers we hung out together at the local pool halls and Flanagan's Danceland, USA. Our tastes in music, clothes, and activities were similar. We were close in size and therefore shared many clothes. Our friendships often overlapped, and we admired each other for different reasons. We worked together on the farms, newspaper routes, department stores, and the country club, and spent a summer together away from home at Lohican Camps in the Poconos as stable hands. Oftentimes we got into trouble together, as well as fights. Most importantly, we confided in each other a lot in terms of personal feelings, career goals, and interpersonal relationships. We looked out for each other and guided each other through those turbulent, risk-taking teen years. No one was closer than the two of us. In many ways, we were like twins. The impact of his tragic untimely death is discussed later.

The bonds with each of my brothers were special. I could tell hundreds of stories, as we had that degree of closeness. Previously, I mentioned many of our shared family experiences, which were perhaps the most influential. A brief description of my other siblings and bonds follows and in no way is comprehensive. Definitely, this is recounted as my perceptions, not necessarily theirs.

My oldest brother, Carl, and I were the most competitive. Perhaps it was because he was the first child, and the first to go to college. This gave him special status, until I followed. Likely, we vied for our parents' and siblings' attention and tried to prove who was smarter. He was the one we relied upon to read and interpret the rules of card games and board games. I would complain sometimes that he changed the rules to favor his chances of winning, and that led to a lot of arguments and abruptly ended games. He in turn accused me of cheating. After cooling off, we would go back to the games that we loved to play, being sure to clarify or adopt new rules at the start. Most of our other experiences were shared in church activities, as he participated in choir and caroling and often substituted as the organist. Some of his friends were ones with whom I played recreational sports, something that never seemed to interest him. His interests centered more on music and dancing, for which he took piano and dance lessons. For unknown reasons, he seemed to be obsessed and compulsive about sitting for hours and adding up columns of numbers. That always impressed our parents in a positive way. Interestingly, although he had a varied career, he eventually earned an MBA and was employed as a comptroller.

That competitive spirit seemed to follow us throughout the years and in certain ways persists today. He was very interested in languages and studied as well as taught in France for a couple of years. He also learned German, Spanish, and some Italian. Carl and I were in the same Latin classes in high school, and despite our competition, we supported each other. After college, he earned a master's degree in Romance languages. During my first year in college, Carl on occasion would advise me. I still remember with great appreciation the time that he helped me to finish a particularly stressful assignment. I believe my parents saw my frustration and encouraged him to help. Interestingly, he later went on to earn a dual MBA and master's degree in French business, after I had earned the master and doctoral degrees. Perhaps competition had nothing to do with it, but I teased him that it did. He remains a bachelor but continues to be the family worrywart and self-appointed center of communication for family crises or news.

Len and I also were particularly close, and I was best man at his wedding. He was always the rough and tough type of kid and shared a lot of experiences with Billy and me. We often held parties in our basement, decorating it and borrowing records (vinyl 45s) from our friends. In fact, one of these parties is where he met his future wife. He did not enjoy school. Early on, he showed an artistic talent that none of us had, but opportunities to develop this talent were not there. In high school, we shared a homeroom and some classes. Eventually he left school to enlist in the military. Initially he was in the navy but then transferred to the marine corps. I remember being so proud of how physically fit he became and noted how proud he was to be a marine. To this day, he is almost never seen without his Vietnam Veteran hat and Semper Fi truck sticker. Before deploying to Vietnam, he married Judy while on leave. Their beautiful ceremony and celebratory reception were planned in only a few days and went off without a problem. I cherished the '56 Ford that he sold to me for $100, just before his deployment. Years later, I sold it for $100, even though it needed a new engine and carburetor at that time.

Often we played one-on-one or two-on-two football in our yard at night, especially after returning from the high school football games. Of the many games we played, he particularly enjoyed king of the mountain, tag, and army. As teenagers, we also shared time at Flanagan's and working on the farms and as golf caddies. He was always the sentimental type, and we shared our love of songs performed by Elvis, Jim Reeves, and others. Saturday mornings we enjoyed the Lone Ranger, Sky King, cartoons, and other television shows. He and Billy and I would get into some trouble together, especially on mischief nights around Halloween. Carl also joined in some of that fun at Halloween. Soaping windows of houses and cars, throwing bags of manure on porches, ringing doorbells, tapping on windows, and other mischievous activities were commonly done for several nights before we would then go door-to-door for treats. In those days, we had to sing, do a skit, or tell a joke in order to get the treats. Those who gave nothing later found soap on their windows!

Leonard always had a good work ethic, and he became a tile specialist, working for decades in the casinos in Las Vegas. At a time when the minimum wage was less than five dollars, he was earning twenty dollars per hour there, making us all jealous. However, the exposure of dust from that, his exposure to Agent Orange in Vietnam, and other factors have led to some health issues that restrict his mobility. He is admired by our extended family and served as an inspiration for a nephew who had a successful career in the coast guard. He and Judy had four children, and their first daughter, Cathy, was the first girl born in the Burke family in more than half a century. Proudly, I accepted their request to be her godfather. Our close bonding has persisted through the years.

All of us have kept in touch over the years and feel that we have close family ties. My younger brothers and I have shared common family as well as some unique experiences. Kevin, who was six years my younger, had more energy than the rest of us put together. As a young child, he was quite acrobatic and would do two full flips from the top of the bed post to the bed. As Kevin got older, our bonding became closer. He graduated from technical school and became a carpenter. By that time, I had quite a bit of experience in remodeling and new house building. We worked with the same construction company as carpenters and later were joined there by Dad. Kevin and I also did remodeling jobs on our own, after hours and on some weekends.

He has always had a great sense of humor, and our shared work experiences have created a special bond as well. Kevin and I reminisce about those days. One story in particular gets repeated. We were remodeling a particular roof in Kingston, after the flood of 1972 caused by Hurricane Agnes. At break time, we were standing on the ridge, and I was bragging to another worker about how Kevin used to do flips off the bed post. Suddenly Kevin, with his nail apron on, did a full flip on the ridge! I couldn't believe it. He didn't lose a nail. As we resumed work and were laughing about that incident, he threw a piece of asphalt shingle off the roof but accidently hit me at close range with it. I bled profusely from an eyebrow laceration, and my face swelled. He looked quite pale but was able to get me off the roof and drive to the hospital. When the emergency room doctor asked what happened, I pointed to Kevin and said, "Him!"

We also shared a love for country music and Elvis. He married his high school sweetheart, and they had four children. Their house has always been a focal point for family celebrations. They took Mom into their house and diligently cared for her in her last years.

Prior to that, he used his skills to maintain and remodel her house after Dad died. His beautiful daughter, Shannon, family-oriented like her parents, organized a large family reunion at her place, just a year or so before she tragically died from a motorcycle accident. Kevin runs his own construction company and has passed his talent onto his two sons, who work with him.

Finally, there is Ron. Because there are nine years between us, we had fewer shared childhood experiences. However, we bonded in a different way than the others. He was the baby, so he taught me a lot about child development and parenting through my observations. I was his Sunday school teacher, so I take some credit for his better angels! Teaching him responsibility was a real challenge for my parents, as they had mellowed over the years and he was rambunctious to say the least. Nevertheless, they succeeded. He is a talented and gifted person, and those are often the toughest to raise.

Perhaps ours is a special bond because he, like me, has had a tortuous career path. Through the years, I watched with worry about some of the choices he made. He is brilliant. However, for adolescents especially, that is not sufficient for good decision-making. He was reckless with motorbikes and risk-taking. In school, he was an A-student until his peers started calling him "the brain." As his grades began to fall, Mom found out that he purposefully was trying to be an average student. Adolescents like to conform, even though they claim uniqueness, and they are often embarrassed to be noticed. Paradoxically, Ron now loves to be noticed!

Unfortunately, his high school experiences did not prepare him for immediate transfer to college or career. Personal experiences would do that, but much later. After high school, Ron worked several low-paying jobs before moving west to Las Vegas, where brother Len took him in until he could make it on his own as a black jack dealer in the casinos. Fortunately, his girlfriend and future wife moved out there and became employed as a nurse. I believe that it was her influence that encouraged him to return to college. Having had some real-life experience, Ron gained a focus on success. He returned and graduated magna cum laude from a local college in just three years, with a BS degree in computers and information systems. After a brief employment as a business systems analyst at a nuclear power plant, Ron joined one of the world's top consulting companies. Since then he has become recognized internationally by his peers as a thought leader and trusted advisor in the area of applying artificial intelligence to address very complex business issues for Fortune 500 companies across a wide range of industries.

Ron is still quite the attention seeker, plays a guitar and writes music, and entertains us all at family gatherings. He and Judy have been blessed with two wonderful children, and we have all maintained close ties over the years. We have enjoyed many intellectual discussions through the years, and we continue to share and discuss our often quite different perspectives and analyses of world affairs. Ron had also developed a special bond with Dad, as he was at home and helped to care for him during his last months of life.

As Cesare Pavese said, "We do not remember days, we remember moments." This thought is so true. I would add that those moments create the bonds of relationships. The memories of those moments create the bond with our past, our family.

CHAPTER 4

Preparing for the Quest

Experiences at Kingston High School

Nothing could stop me now, I thought as my freshman year at Kingston High School started. But history repeats itself. Just like kindergarten, I was expelled from school on the first day. This time it was not for spitting through licorice at the girl next to me. This was far more serious. My brother Billy and I were standing next to his friends in the hall when another student pushed his way past us. One of our friends made an anti-Semitic slur. Not understanding the slur, but trying to fit in, I laughed with them. Soon afterward we were called to the principal's office and expelled for two weeks. He would not listen to my involvement but said all of us had been accused. "This school has a large Jewish population and such slurs will not be tolerated."

It was a long, dreadful, and pensive two- or three-mile walk home. *How could this have happened? Didn't I earn the right to attend this school? Were all my efforts for naught? What will Mom and Dad think? How will they react? How will this affect my chances for college? How will this affect my quest to become a physician?* After she chastised us for our stupid behavior, Mom called the principal and apologized for our behavior. To our surprise, she then admonished him for not listening to our side of the story. She also got the suspension reduced to one day. If this happened again, though, my future high school days would be at Luzerne.

Reality would strike me like a sledgehammer at Kingston High. It would no longer be easy to get good grades. Teachers in jest made derogatory remarks about the town I came from, and one teacher would make jokes about my hairstyle (flat top). One even made comments about my brothers and his negative expectations for me.

Praise would be rare. Instead of looking forward to my mom's report after she met with teachers on parent-teacher night, I would dread it. The teacher for both my Latin and English classes told my mom that despite my test scores, he would not give me the A's I deserved. I would need to give him my "undivided attention" during class for that to happen. Mom's experience with my trigonometry teacher was also unforgettable, at best.

After introducing herself, my mother was told something like, "Oh, so you are Robert's mother. That boy annoys me to no end with his incessant gum chewing. Perhaps, though, I annoy him by calling him Mr. Burke; he just doesn't look like a Robert to me!"

After recounting that encounter, Mom laughed and said she asked my teacher, "What's a Robert supposed to look like?"

Mom said that she suspected the teacher must have had an old boyfriend named Robert and had some feelings of transference. I still remember having to write five hundred times on the board, "I will not chew gum in Ms. _____'s class." She promised my mom that she would attempt to call me by my name, if I would no longer chew gum. So, that deal was done. Still, I did get mostly A's in her class. There were some positive reports. Mom and I especially liked the praise from my retail selling and psychology teacher, Mr.

Nicholas. Yes, he was the son of Mrs. Nicholas, my favorite grade school teacher.

There were many brilliant students there. Some got perfect or near-perfect scores on standardized national exams such as the SAT. This was new to me. No longer first in the class, the competition was unlike anything I had ever experienced. Previously, I could get straight A's without studying. No longer. It took some average to below-average grades for me to understand the importance of self-study. Even that had its limits. Certainly I would need to learn how to study. The teachers aimed to challenge everyone in the class, so more was expected. This is why Kingston had a reputation for preparation of students for college. Those who could not meet the rigorous standards dropped out or went to technical school. Even gym class, shop, music, and art classes were intimidating for me. Such resources had been available for those who had always been in the Kingston school district, but never for me.

As an outsider, I had difficulty making strong friendships. There were a few students whose company I really enjoyed, but most of those dropped out or got into trouble with the law. Having no money for meal tickets, I brought my own lunch. In the cafeteria, I seemed out of place. So I hung out near the corner store, which had a reputation as a site for "hoodlums." The kids there smoked cigarettes, played pool, and also felt estranged. Many of them skipped school and bragged about how they faked illness to do so. One peer could purposefully vomit, and he would do so on the school walls if his request to leave for not feeling well was rejected. That maneuver worked every time. Some of these students were brilliant but did not fit in. In fact, one of my friends dropped out of school because of this. By stereotype, he was like the Fonz on television. Evidently he and I had similar IQ test scores, so we were both asked to participate in some research as to why such students would have starkly different success in school. More than one of these social "outcasts" went on to college with me. There were some other students who did not hang out there, with whom I developed friendships. All of those went on to college.

Emotionally traumatic is descriptive of my first two years. Eventually, I assimilated and overcame the outsider bias. One particularly painful memory made me so self-conscious that I believe it adversely impacted my public speaking and confidence for years. As I was giving a verbal report to the class concerning our favorite hangout, a student in the front row exclaimed, "Hey, it looks like he doesn't have any teeth!" My upper teeth had been extracted due to the dental problems alluded to earlier, and I had to wait three months for some gum recession before getting dentures. The teacher commented about the incivility of that remark, the class stopped laughing, and I finished my presentation with applause. However, the damage had been inflicted. I was humiliated and felt both tearful and angry enough to want to physically harm that student. He was one of the few people in my life for whom I felt hatred—the son of a preacher man, but I called him a son of a ... something else!

Although my overall high school experience was challenging, it exposed me to diverse personalities. It exposed me to socioeconomic bias in its rawest form. Some of my social experiences, however, were positive. I was a member of the Latin Club, the French Club, the Student Council, and the Ars Medica, a club for those aspiring to become physicians. My participation in intramural sports, basketball and volleyball, was limited as I often could not arrange transportation or had employment conflicts. Similarly, there were barriers that prevented my participation in any extra-curricular activities involving after-school hours. Occasionally I was able to attend a class dance and Friday night football.

How well was I prepared for college? After all, that was my purpose in choosing to go to Kingston. My self-esteem was certainly diminished. I was no longer the confident and self-assured person who started there. Although I got good grades, I did not excel and barely finished in the top twenty-fifth percentile of our graduation class of 256 students. My college board scores were low, with raw scores of 440 verbal and 563 math. That was sufficient for me to enter college. However, that admission was "on probation," contingent on earning a cumulative average of 2.0 as a freshman. Nevertheless, I had no doubt that I would succeed and become a physician. The quest was threatened, but still on.

Employment

Preparedness for success in life requires more than good grades. As Dad emphasized, a strong work ethic is necessary. "Once a job is first begun, never leave it 'til it's done; be a job great or small, do it right or don't do it at all." He lived by it. He expected no less from us. Perhaps it is the most enduring personal quality that he helped to instill in me and my siblings. "Perseverance son, perseverance …" That is all that it takes. Never doubting him, and always admiring him, I tried to live by that same ethic.

Not only did I work as described earlier to save money to go to high school, I continued to work during school. After school, I would rush home to deliver the evening edition of the newspaper produced by the *Wilkes-Barre Times Leader*. I do not recall exactly when my brothers and I stopped delivering newspapers. Certainly, we did this throughout elementary school and the first year of high school. Sometime thereafter, conflicts with better-paying jobs ended that role. During the school year, I worked evenings at a plant where we potted artificial flowers. That company was owned by the Kingston-based California Fruit and Flower Company, whose retail market employed me on weekends. Sometimes I worked in the evenings and on special occasions with my best friend at the Kingston Catering Company. One summer, I drove their food truck to construction sites. During the summers, I worked at least forty hours a week, sometimes at more than one job.

Some of my favorite work memories occurred while employed at the Pocono Downs Race Track as kitchen help. We sometimes got to talk with the horse or sulky jockeys, who would offer tips on betting. One day a coworker asked to borrow a dollar from me to play the "daily double," for which he had a tip. I knew that he would never repay me, so I told him no, but that I would buy half of that two-dollar ticket with the expectation of half the winnings. Incredibly, he later returned with ninety dollars for me. That was a lot of money, considering that I was getting a dollar per hour wage. Although we were both underage, he talked one of the runners into buying the ticket. She gave us the rewards, after taking a forty-dollar service fee.

By the time I got home, it was midnight or later. Going past my parents' room, I whispered, "Are you awake?"

"Yes," Mom said.

"Guess what?"

"What?"

"I won ninety dollars at the track tonight!"

"Sure, Bobby, quit joking and go to bed."

"Honest, look!" I said as I turned on their light to show the winnings and to tell the story.

"Why didn't you bet some for me!" Dad exclaimed.

"Next time I will, if you reimburse me."

"Sure thing. That's great, now go to sleep."

The next time that we got a tip and made a bet, we were not

so lucky. I had bought a separate ticket for Dad. When I told him about the loss, he said something to the effect that I should know better than to gamble, and I should have checked with him first. He did not pay. That, indeed, taught me a lesson about trust. As President Reagan once said, "Trust, but verify!" reciting an old Russian proverb.

On another occasion, I did not see the stop sign, covered by a tree branch, as I drove through the intersection after midnight. The police officer waiting in the dark for violators pulled me over and cited me for the traffic violation as well as driving illegally on a junior license after midnight. The fines were more than I would earn the entire week. In addition, I would have my license suspended for three months, and that would get me fired! Mom perceived the injustice of this, as I had to work late that night and could not have avoided coming home at that time. She also sensed it was the borough's fault for not keeping the stop sign visible. Fortunately, her former classmate and friend was our state representative, and he squashed the fine and had my license reinstated before it was revoked! Lessons learned: be responsible, argue for fairness, and make friends in high places.

My parents were not always calm about such things. One time on my way home from the job at the artificial flower company, an elderly gentleman started through an intersection prematurely and ran into the back quarter panel of my dad's car. Upon hearing this, Dad overreacted, yelling and screaming that he would be sued and lose everything that he had worked for, and telling me how irresponsible I was. He verbally punished me, took my driving privileges away, and started arguing with Mom, who asked him to give me the benefit of the doubt. Just as things were going from bad to worse, the phone rang. Dad threatened to tear it off the wall, but instead answered the call.

"Yes, sir. I am sorry that my son ... what ... okay, thanks."

Dad had just been informed by the gentleman's lawyer that his client was in the wrong, wanted to apologize, and would pay for all repairs. Relief was apparent in Dad's face and demeanor, as was some embarrassment for his behavior. After that, he trusted my judgment and stories a little more. He reinstated my driving privileges, to work only.

Those jobs taught me more than the lessons above. I learned how to deal with long work days, cold, tiredness, hunger, frustration, uncontrollable events, and varied personalities. They taught me the value of a dollar and gave me a sense of pride in accomplishment. They provided me the opportunities to learn new skills, gain confidence in myself, and really understand the meaning of perseverance. The same could be said for future jobs that I would take on during the college years, and for jobs that I would take to provide for my family. The rigors of graduate school, medical school, and residency would require perseverance. Remembering those work experiences and alternatives to the career quest would support my motivation during trying times.

Adolescence and Friends

"Partners in crime" is how Mom described us with a smile. "His shadow" was another apt description. Billy and I each had a lot of friends, but our bond was stronger. He respected my abilities and aspirations. I idolized him, along with Mickey Mantle, Elvis Presley, and comic book superheroes. As noted earlier, twins could not be closer. He often felt compelled to protect me. We shared a bed, clothing, toys, sports, friends, work, church, illnesses, and the same likes in music and movies. In school we shared classrooms. And we got into trouble together.

Did I say trouble? "Let my brother plan it," was what Billy told the others gathered in our favorite cave in the woods. So, who will go in, who will be lookouts, and what will we do with the loot? Our small group of preteen boys was planning to rob a grocery store on Courtdale Avenue. Actually, we had met a few times previously and daydreamed about getting all the candy, fruit, sodas, cigarettes, and maybe money we could bag and carry away quickly without getting caught. There were details to be worked out, and now it was my job to plan its success. We decided the time, date, and how we would divvy up the goods. We would go through the small basement window on the side of the building early in the morning, while it was still dark. My brother and I would scout it out. Everyone swore allegiance not to squeal.

Perhaps it was our fear of getting caught and punished. Maybe our alliance fell apart. Did the dry run highlight unexpected problems? Did our consciences get in the way? For some reason, we did not do it. Why had we planned it? Who knows—was it a sense of adventure? After all, the Hardy Boys engaged in scary escapades, although their adventures were more altruistic. Or were we just tired of not having those things we wanted? All of us lived in poverty. All of us knew it was wrong.

As teenagers, trouble centered more around getting into fights, reckless driving, smoking cigarettes, drinking beer, and too often following the lead of our friends. These were the years wherein acceptance by peers outweighed reason. For better or worse, a local hangout called Flanagan's Danceland USA seemed to be where we spent a lot of our idle time. There is where we learned to play billiards, pinball machines, and shuffleboard. It is where we danced to records played in the jukebox or to live bands. It is where we met other teens from Luzerne, Larksville, Pringle, and other nearby towns. Parents mostly hated that place, but probably every kid in town loved it. There were no other options in town. It was located on the main avenue, just below the school. The owner always engaged us as to how we were feeling or to offer unsolicited advice about behaviors he saw in others. He was our friend, as he was always willing to listen.

"You just missed it," Mr. Flanagan said when I walked over to get a cherry coke. "Billy knocked out that kid with one punch."

He was a hero that day, defending some girl against the unwanted advances of another teen from out of town. I knew Billy could box, but a one-punch knockout! My brother's stature had just risen. He was well-liked, but this was big. It was not unusual for Billy to come to others' defense. Even complete strangers would benefit from his sense of what was right. He would try to break up or else join a fight where the assaulted was being outnumbered.

Billy's popularity blossomed at Flanagan's. After a heartfelt and impromptu singing of the Hank Williams song about a lonesome whippoorwill, his peers would encourage a karaoke rendition repeat or ask him to sing with the live bands. As his circle of friends increased, our time together decreased. I became so proud but also envious of him. Still, Billy and I spent a lot of time socializing with some of the same friends, working together on the farms or at the golf course and other places, as well as playing recreational sports. We spent one summer away, working as stable hands at a camp in the Poconos. The downside was that he was easily influenced, and friends engaged him in risk-taking behaviors. Ever the protective brother, he discouraged my participation with the rowdy crowd. We often had talks about careers, and he would remind me of how I should stay on track. Often, just thinking about how an action may adversely impact my future stopped me from doing it. His goal was to join the navy and see the world. He, indeed, did that.

How or why we choose and keep specific friends is often unclear.

Likely there is something special for each one in a particular relationship. Sometimes specific shared experiences bring us together.
Those experiences also may strengthen the bonds. Choices may
also be limited, based on where you live. Just like the need to be
loved and to be recognized, friendship is a universal need for most
humans. Older than me by three weeks, my best friend and I were
the youngest in our class throughout grade school. He had no
brothers. I had plenty. His mom and dad fought a lot, as did mine,
but his eventually divorced. I remember one year when he literally
threw his drunken father out of the house, after his dad had pulled
down the Christmas tree and threatened his mother, with whom he
was always very close. Perhaps he and I were even closer than some
brothers, for the first two decades of our life. In fact, he was at our
house so much that Mom would have to do a recount when she was
checking on her brood. Once, just like the cowboys and Indians in
western movies, we cut our skin and rubbed the wounds together
to become blood brothers!

Adventurous, impulsive, wonderful, competitive, and dangerous would be accurate descriptors of our friendship. In early
childhood games, we always chose to be on the same side, and
we inspired each other to do exciting things. Together always, we
would ride bikes, ice skate, sleigh ride, play sports, fish, swim, play
billiards, and hang out. We had other friends, but those were special
in other ways. Baseball was a different story. We were both pitchers.
He had the added advantage of being left-handed. Not then, but
now I would admit that he was better. Fortunately, our little league
coach gave us equal playing time. In teen league, it was different.
A different coach wanted a winning team, so you earned the right
to play. He and I were both versatile players, with special strengths
as infielders, so we rarely sat out. He became the star pitcher; I was
substitute. After puberty, he went from being the smallest kid in

the class to being the most muscular and handsome. He also got taller than average. Everyone thought he lifted weights, but he was just endowed. Our competition intensified to batting as well. Again, he had the highest home-run record. But he also held record for the most strikeouts. My performance was more consistent, giving me a better batting average. Academically, though, there was no competition.

That handsome, athletic, adventurous friend put both our lives at risk often. He had his own car, so we went everywhere together and often just cruised around for fun. At the beach, he flirted with all the girls, kissing some sleeping sunbathers (on the belly no less!), and getting us in trouble with others' boyfriends who would be nearby. He enjoyed speed and reckless driving, often driving the middle of the road and passing dangerously. Fortunately, we only had one accident, as he could not stop fast enough at a red light and rear ended the car in front.

During late adolescence we both worked with a drilling corporation. For me it was summer work during college. For him it was employment after high school. It was rough work, test-core drilling for new highways and buildings. We would carpool, drive out of state to New York or Connecticut, and share some low-cost, cockroach-infested housing with some of the older construction workers. After long and hot, dusty working days, we would go to a local bar and drink beer, with a dash of salt to make up for losses through sweating during the day. The older workers reassured a few bartenders that we were of age. Incredibly, this carpool group would buy a few six-packs of beer to drink during our long drive back to our homes on Friday nights for the weekend. Drinking and driving became common for us.

Every time one of us boys would get hurt playing, our dad would say, "You never get hurt working," as if we should not have been playing. Of course, many people are injured and tragically some die on their jobs. His "all-work-no-play" bias was balanced by our mom's "live-for-today" bias. Perhaps that is how some of us got the work-hard, play-hard attitude. But I did get to prove him wrong.

In the summer of 1969, I was working on the drilling rigs in the mountains near Suffern, New York. The foreman told me to prime the pump he had trouble starting by pouring some gas into the hole from where he had removed the spark plug.

"Are you sure we won't blow ourselves to hell?" I asked.

"No, we do this all the time."

He wasn't supposed to turn the starter, but he did. Flames ignited from the spark and followed the gas to the five-gallon can I was holding. Dropping it, I then realized that not only the rig started to burn, but I was on fire. My impulse was to run. Then I remembered that you should drop and roll.

"You are out. You are out," the foreman yelled as I continued to throw dirt on my chest and arms.

By the time we descended that mountain via our own bumpy truck path, it would be almost an hour to get treated. The foreman had a small burn on his forearm, but I had second-degree burns of the abdomen, chest, forearms, and hands.

The next day, the nurse told me that my sister, brother, and mom wanted to see me. They had driven from Pennsylvania. I was in reverse isolation but certainly gave permission. *Wait a minute*, I thought, *did she say sister?* Only immediate family members were allowed to visit. Mom had covered for my girlfriend, and future wife, to visit. Her brother had driven them. They couldn't stay long, but that sure made my day and relieved their anxiety about my condition. There was some question as to whether I would need skin grafts of my fingers and abdomen, but I healed well.

Another surprise came the next day. Several of my coworkers

dropped by after work. Sitting in their dirty clothes at the edge of the bed, they handed me a can of beer hidden in a bag. "They said you were in isolation, but we're not worried about getting anything," is how they said it. Laughing, I explained the idea of reverse isolation, just as the nurse came in to kick them out. Painful burn debridement and skin care, an allergic reaction to the sulfur-based burn cream, and loneliness marred the rest of my stay. To this day, I get nostalgic when I hear Stevie Wonder's song, "One is the loneliest number …." My dad was empathetic, but his opinion about not getting hurt working never changed. He would just cite my experience as an exception to his belief. He did have a dry sense of humor and noted that it was ironic for me, a Protestant, to be treated in a Catholic hospital in a town named Suffern, by Jewish doctors!

Our friendship persisted into late adolescence and the college years. However, our lives diverged as each of us pursued different life tracks and marriage. Those thousands of special moments and memories will be with me forever, and I can't help to think that in ways he helped me to become me.

Although he was totally unaware, Elvis Presley also played an important part in my life. There were times during adolescence that my friend's persona reminded me of Elvis. He didn't sing, but perhaps it was his smile. A large part of adolescence is dealing with emotions. Elvis's music addressed every emotion that I experienced. Adolescence was a time of moodiness for me. It was a time of reflection. His music was my friend. Even one of his songs confirms, "Without a song a man ain't got a friend." No matter how I felt, one of his songs expressed that feeling better than anything. It was not necessarily the words, but more importantly his emotional rendering of those words and its connection to my spirit. When I was happy, I played his songs and danced. When I was sad, I would sit in the dark, playing song after song, and often the same song, until I felt at peace. Even today, my tiredness disappears, my spirit lifts, and my challenges are more easily met after listening to his inspirational music.

Anecdotally, my admiration for Elvis started in early grade school. I would do karaoke at the Wednesday-night dances held for children under eleven at our local Fire Station. These were supervised events that involved more than just dancing. We played some indoor games and participated in contests. My Elvis impersonation, though, was always a big hit at our talent show, especially my leg shaking and pelvic gyrations while singing "Hound Dog." Some of my brothers and I attended every Elvis movie, and periodically I still sit down and watch one, a half century later. My love for the "King" is known by everyone who knows me. In fact, one of my pediatric colleagues dubbed me the "blond Elvis."

Perhaps this quote from Kahlil Gibran better describes the niche that Elvis's music filled in my adolescence: "Music is the language of the spirit. It opens the secret of life bringing peace, abolishing strife."

"This is my brother; you can't out run him." That was how my brother Billy introduced us to a new kid in town. He easily outran me and immediately gained everyone's admiration, since I was one of the fastest runners among our peers. He was Billy's age and would become his best friend. That would prove to be tragic. By default, he also became my friend. However, he was reckless, he had no particular goals in life, he was fun-seeking, and he came from a split home. His dad was an alcoholic, and his mom never supervised or disciplined him as far as we could tell.

I had few encounters with his parents, but one memorable one with their dog. The dog was barking, and his parents reassured me that he would not bite me, as I approached to collect their payment for the newspaper. Remembering that "a barking dog never bites," as Dad would say, I ventured forth reassured. That German shepherd dog's bite was painful, deep, and bruising. It made me fearful of dogs for decades. When I challenged Dad about his proverb, he explained, "The dog has to stop barking to bite, stupid!"

Juvenile delinquent would be an apt description of his behavior. Teenage alcoholic would be another. He was not always like that. In many ways, he reminded me of my best friend. He was fun-loving, and at worse, he was impulsive and adventurous. However, the challenges of adolescence under the best of circumstances are difficult. They could be deadly in dysfunctional family situations. Similarly, untreated mental health issues adversely impact lives. In retrospect, I suspect that he had attention deficit hyperactivity disorder, as well as anger management issues. He would drive us around looking for adventure, drinking beer. Sometimes he got the beer from his dad's supply after his dad passed out, and other times he would enlist the aid of any drunk coming out of the local bar to go back in to buy some. Depending on who was tending bar, he would go in and purchase the beer himself. Some of his actions made me fearful, and as they worsened, I spent less and less time with him. Specifically, he would shoot hunting arrows at cows, dogs, and mailboxes for fun. He would get himself and my brother Billy into countless fights.

To say that he was a bad influence on my brother and others would be an understatement. Billy's adventurous spirit kept him engaged in that friendship, despite the concerns I and my parents and older brothers voiced. Soon, in mid-to-late adolescence, Billy would start to drink regularly and come home drunk, more often than my parents knew. Inexplicably, he was not disciplined much for this behavior. Perhaps my parents were so affected by the loss of their eighth son, David, at birth, that they started to mellow. Mom had a special bond with him, possibly in part because he looked like her father, had a lot of charisma, and reminded her of her brothers. For the same reasons, Dad detested Billy's behavior and disdain-fully called him a "Gallagher." These reactions only encouraged the behavior and strengthened his bond with our wild friend.

Seemingly, Billy did not understand the path he was taking. His girlfriend did. She was his girlfriend off and on for several years but started to drift away. At times, Billy would change his behavior to keep her friendship. Eventually she gave him an ultimatum to stop associating with his buddy, or to at least stop his drinking and risk-taking behavior. She wanted to get married in a few years. That was the last thing on Billy's mind. Their separation seemed to finalize after Billy joined the navy and stopped communicating regularly with her. However, they always remained friends.

Although Billy had many girlfriends, she was special. My mother and I knew that and often voiced how we hoped that she would set him on a better path. One time, he and his best friend got beat up outside a diner for defending her honor, by a couple of grown men who Billy had politely asked to stop cursing around her. I wanted to help, but Billy told me to stay inside the diner with his girlfriend as they were stepping out to fight. "Two on two is fair," he said. Besides, he and his buddy rarely lost a fight, so I wasn't worried. After their breakup, Billy would frequently listen to a sad Ritchie Valens song that was about a girl who left him. Billy and I also shared a love of another heartbreak song by Valens entitled "Tell Laura I Love Her." The late '50s and early '60s had many emo-tional ballads such as "Running Bear," "Patches," "Transfusion," "Ode to Billy Joe," and a dozen or more other ones that Billy would bring to my attention. Typically, while he was hurting on the inside, he tried not to say anything out loud. When Old Yeller died (1957 movie), nine-year-old Billy had tears coming down his face in the movie theatre, which he wiped away and denied when I teased him about it.

The adolescent years are typically divided into early, mid, and late. The cognitive, social, and emotional impact of pubertal changes is often immeasurable and inexplicable. But it is significant. Peers become more important than parents or family. Experimentation with risk-taking behaviors such as smoking, sex, and drug use is not uncommon. Finding one's self is paramount. By mid-adolescence, those hormonal influences have stabilized, and friendships have become more selective. Career goals and lifestyles become more personalized. By the late adolescent years, career, beliefs, personal relationships, and life goals take center stage. At this time, adolescents may revisit the parental values they rejected earlier, but their independence from parental authority is finalized.

For some, transitioning through these years is challenging, but for others it is truly life-changing and consequential. Those who come from functional families with positive parental involvement seem to do much better. It is my observation and belief that the most significant positive influences on the outcome for adolescents is twofold: 1) having long-term goals, and (2) having good decision-making skills. The paths we choose on our journey throughout life are fateful. True, there are uncontrollable experiences. Making good decisions, however, is a skill that does not just suddenly appear. Teaching or at least providing opportunities for children to act independently, responsibly, and with good decision-making are requisite parental and societal roles. Those opportunities must be available throughout the formative years especially. Close supervision of children's activities and involvement of loving and supportive adults is necessary. Decision-making that considers the impact of one's actions on achieving one's long-term goals is crucial. Personally, I often chose not to participate in some risky behaviors for that very reason. Billy often cautioned me that the behavior and action that I sought was not worth the risk to my career goals. Sometimes he wisely refused to let me join him and friends in those activities.

Risk-taking behavior was a significant part of my adolescence. Smoking, drinking, fighting, sexual exploration, associating with peers and adults who reinforced these behaviors, and some bad decision-making could easily have been tragic for me. Most of my friends and family members smoked and drank. Our parents' behavior, unfortunately, supported the concept that in order for one to have a good time and to totally relax, drinking and drunkenness were important. That happened at home parties, on picnics, and for most celebrations or get-togethers such as weddings or funerals. That celebratory style influenced me and extended relatives, and it has become ingrained in the families of my siblings. Unfortunately, there have been related tragedies. Our family history is replete with alcoholism, tobacco use, and unhealthy lifestyles. Science does support that alcoholism and drug-seeking has a genetic component, much like obesity does.[25] The lifestyle that I was living was not conducive to the one that was my quest. Some of those behaviors persisted throughout college and put that quest at risk. What changed, and why?

---

[25] www.niaaa.nih.gov, "Collaborative Studies on Genetics of Alcoholism (COGA) Study.

PART 2

The Quest

CHAPTER 5

Questions of Readiness

A Liberal Arts Education

"It is the mark of an educated mind to be able to entertain a thought without accepting it."

Attributed to Aristotle, born 2400 years ago, this quote continues to ring true.

Similarly, there is wisdom in the following description of what it means to be an educated person, formulated and adopted by the Wilkes College faculty as a guide to learning.[26] This can also be found in our class's student handbook at Wilkes, where my lifelong education began.

An Educated Man or Woman:

- *Seeks truth, for without truth there can be no understanding;*
- *Possesses vision, for we know that vision precedes all great attainments;*
- *Is aware of the diversity of ideas and beliefs that exists among all people;*
- *Has faith in the power of ideals to shape the lives of each of us;*

---

[26] *Wilkes Physicians Report*, "An Educated Man or Woman," Wilkes University, 1989.

- *Knows that mankind's progress requires intellectual vigor, moral courage and physical endurance;*
- *Cultivates inner resources and spiritual strength, for they enrich our daily living and sustain us in times of crisis;*
- *Has ethical standards by which to live;*
- *Respects the religious convictions of all people;*
- *Participates constructively in the social, economic, cultural and political life of the community;*
- *Communicates ideas in a manner that assures understanding, for understanding unites us all in our search for truth.*

I was truly impressed by this description and vowed to become such an educated man.

Wilkes College, dedicated to a liberal arts education, became a university in 1990. Why did I attend Wilkes College? The only family member before me to go to college was my oldest brother. He went to Mansfield State College, to major in music, as that college had a good reputation for music. He eventually changed career goals, so the original choice of that college was no longer relevant. There were also extra costs and adaptations to living away from home. My choice to attend Wilkes College in 1966 was simply practical. Staying at home and commuting daily would save a lot of money, as Wilkes was only four miles away. There would be grants and loans for which they would help me to apply. Wilkes had a local reputation for providing a solid liberal arts education. The other local choices were related to the Catholic Church, with which I was not affiliated. So, I applied nowhere else.

Why choose a liberal arts education? I sought exposure to a broad spectrum of studies in the sciences and humanities, to be sure my education would be conducive to career flexibility. I wanted my life and study of the sciences to be enriched by exposure to art, music, philosophy, political science, foreign languages, and the diversity of ideas. I wanted to learn analytical and critical thinking, as well as good communication skills. How well Wilkes College would prepare me for my quest to become a physician was not well researched. Instead, I relied on reports that some of our respected local physicians had attended Wilkes. I never sought their opinions.

Day commuters were not spared the freshman hazing.

"Hey frosh, lie on the sidewalk and sizzle like bacon."

"Here, carry my books."

"Frosh, do twenty-five pushups now."

Commands such as these could be made by any upper classman. We had to wear a funny cap and a cardboard sign that clearly indicated our status. Failure to comply would require your presentation and defense at a tribunal set up by the student council at the end of the first semester. It was considered a rite of passage but clearly now would be considered evoking a hostile environment, abusive, and illegal. Many students suffered humiliation, discrimination, and injury as a consequence of these actions. Thankfully, Wilkes University and most, if not all, colleges and universities now have anti-hazing policies. I forget the reason, but I refused to comply fully and had to present to that council. At the tribunal, the person bringing charges flipped his cigarette at me, causing ashes to get into my eye and burn the eyelid. That ended my participation. I walked out despite the tribunal's protest.

Several faculty members also created an abusive and hostile environment, interpreted as egocentricities, that would not be condoned today. Some of those behaviors were instructive and provided useful life lessons. Others were simply bullying. Faculty with tenure were given complete freedom of style for teaching. Out of respect to the memory of those otherwise wonderful mentors, I will only discuss some examples, not names.

"Hey, fatso, stop right there, get on your knees and beg the class for admission."

The girl he was speaking to cried with embarrassment and left. This professor believed that all fifty minutes of class should be dedicated to learning. Anyone who was not punctual was considered to be an intrusion on the learning environment, for which the students were paying. So, if you were not through the doorway by the time the bell rang, you had to show respect to the class by getting on your knees and begging for admission. To his credit, he expected excellence and precision. Cross-sectional drawings of a leaf as viewed under a microscope had to be centered within one millimeter of the center of the page, or you would receive a letter grade lower. Similarly, questions such as, "How many steps are there from the first to third floors of Stark Hall?" or "Which way does the man in the moon face?" would have as equal importance on an examination as biological questions. He believed that scientists need to be observant, and we should practice these skills inside and outside of the classroom. To this day, I count steps wherever I go.

Another professor would pace back and forth in front of the room with a long stick, as he discussed the Civil War (a.k.a., "the war of northern aggression" as he referred to it) or other historical events. That stick came crashing down onto your seat if he thought that you were inattentive. He also believed that only one student in the class should get an *A*.

A "hippie-like" French teacher, dressed in a leather miniskirt and jacket, would consider taking points off your final grade for her course if you came to class instead of participating in a student protest against the Vietnam War.

Despite waning the number of biology majors from over a hundred in the freshman year to less than two dozen in the senior year, some professors insisted on "down-curving" grades. They remarked that their exams were not tough enough if too many of those students got *A's* and *B's*. We reminded them about how we had been selected from the pack and now had similar educational experiences. That did not change everyone's opinion.

Most of these eccentricities did not bother me much. But I did learn the importance of observation, paying attention to details, being precise, developing a broad base of knowledge, tolerance for dissent and diversity, and analytical-critical thinking. At Wilkes, we learned how to learn. The latter was the most significant attribute that would carry me through multiple career changes. That same style of teaching that was so beneficial created problems for me with standardized, multiple-choice exams such as the MCAT (medical college admissions test). At Wilkes, we had to recall sufficient information to answer open-ended questions on exams and rarely had multiple-choice questions. For example, our final written examination in comparative anatomy would have one question at the top of each of perhaps ten pages, to be answered thoroughly. One such question might be, "Compare and contrast the ontogeny and phylogeny of the respiratory system in vertebrates." Such questions required a significant depth of knowledge and the ability to think deeply in a logical manner. By contrast, answering MCAT multiple choice questions accurately required test-taking skills such as how not to be distracted by choices and how to navigate quickly among unrelated questions with little opportunity for in-depth thought about a single topic.

Our critical thinking was stimulated by examinations such as those we had in organic chemistry. A typical exam would allow fifty minutes to read the article presented in a scientific journal and then answer ten questions about the author's conclusions based on your understanding of nucleophilic substitutions or some other concept. During my first semester of organic chemistry, taken in the spring, this was problematic. I was a slow reader and had difficulty concentrating in group situations. Thus, by the time I read the article, I only would complete four or five questions in the time allotted. Usually I received full credit for the answers provided, but since I only completed half the questions in the time allotted, I failed most of the lecture examinations.

By contrast, I had an *A* in the laboratory section, as I was able to apply my knowledge and accurately analyze data to figure out the unknown chemicals that we tested. Fortunately, I passed that four-credit course because of the laboratory grade and having done better on the final examination, which allowed more time. The excessive time I spent studying just to pass organic chemistry adversely impacted my performance on my other courses. By the end of the second year, my grade point average was only 2.61. This was certainly a barrier to my quest to become a physician.

Interestingly, something extraordinary happened to me in the third year. Learning seemed to come easier, and I developed a more analytical approach to studying. A friend taught me how to anticipate examination questions and to prepare and memorize outlines that would facilitate my test-taking speed. At home, I finally got a bedroom to myself and had a place to study and concentrate better. During my first two years, I had studied at the dining room table, among the noise of rowdy brothers and their friends, and sometimes arguing parents. Occasionally I could get away to Wilkes and study in the library.

The second semester of organic chemistry was during the fall of my third year. I decided to devote equal time to my courses, so as not to let one course adversely impact the others. Surprisingly, I now finished all lecture exams on time and earned all *As*, including the laboratory. In fact, because of extra credit questions, I scored above a 100 percent on the final exam. Despite that, our professor recorded a *B* for me for the semester. I brought the error to his attention, but he said it was done purposefully because "you are not an *A* student, and you failed last semester." I argued that I had an *A* in lab the preceding semester and did pass. The dean told me that he could not do anything about this unfair grade because the professor had tenure and they would have to respect his judgment.

Finally, I had learned how to learn. In addition, my testing performance improved. The course load of sixteen to eighteen credits per semester was similar for all four years. But my performance for the last two years of college was much better. Those semesters recorded grade point averages as 3.4, 3.6, 3.7, and 3.9 respectively. That boosted my cumulative average at Wilkes to 3.14 for all four years, and an impressive 3.68 for the last two years. Because it was the philosophy at Wilkes College that the first two years of college required significant adaptations toward learning compared to that in high school, they based graduation with honors solely on the last two years of performance. Thus, I graduated magna cum laude.

Key to the Door to the Future

In 1989, I wrote an article for the *Wilkes Physicians Report* on the "Education of a physician-scientist."[27] I would like to share some of the same sentiments as reported therein about my experiences at Wilkes. Some memories have been indelibly imprinted. In particular, the close personal relationship of faculty with students was nurturing. We were challenged to open our minds, to explore new worlds, and to strive for excellence. The faculty and other leaders were synergistic with seriousness of purpose. As future leaders of our society, we were reminded frequently that the pursuit of

[27] Robert E. Burke, "Education of a physician-scientist," *Wilkes Physicians Report*, Wilkes University 1989, 12–13.

excellence was tantamount to achieving our goals and meeting that responsibility. Frustration was often borne of that pursuit, but it was soothed by the insights to truth gained through steady, hard work and attention to the wisdom of our mentors. They were the templates from which we gained the attributes of an educated person.

There were many good times and a camaraderie that is remembered to this day. That included but was not limited to Biological Society projects and camping trips, homecoming displays and events, science fairs, ecology projects and seminars, eyeball-to-eyeball talks with Dean Ralston, intramural sports, dances, concerts, Nobel laureate guest lecturers, plays, social parties at the homes of faculty or colleagues, and the development of incredible friendships.

For me, Wilkes was a key to the door to the future. Wilkes helped me to find the financial resources, the internal strength, and the educational readiness to open that door and to proceed. Passing through that door was challenging for me and resulted in taking a tortuous path through multiple other doors. Although my quest was delayed, that path enriched my life beyond anything that I could have imagined. Since I met my soul mate at Wilkes, I can state that I also found a key to the door to happiness there.

Soul mate: n. a person ideally suited to another (The Oxford American Dictionary).

Little did I know that a broken leg would reveal my soul mate! Something in the conversation attracted me to this beautiful blond at our table, several months into the first year at Wilkes College. The commons was a place where most of the commuters met for lunch, or just to socialize. She was talking about some annoying boyfriend who was too serious and too old for her, but she was unsure of how to break off the relationship. Evidently she had tried, but he persisted in the chase.

"Hi, have I seen you here before?"

"Well, I've been meeting with this group since we started." Laughter and disbelief from our colleagues put me to shame, but I continued.

"We could pretend to be dating, and I'll tell him to buzz off. Besides, I have an old girlfriend who is still in high school and wants me to go to the senior prom, so I could tell her about my new relationship and decline."

It was that easy! Bonnie agreed. Then I said something about a date, so we could be more convincing, and she agreed again. That was the beginning of what would become a lifelong relationship— although at this point, neither of us realized it. In fact, it seemed unlikely. Her parents strongly disapproved of my cigarette smoking, and I disapproved of their puritanical, controlling natures. They allowed conditional dating, primarily to group events, and insisted that she be home by ten o'clock, even though the college dances did not end until much later. I obeyed, for a while. Eventually Bonnie and I asserted ourselves and they relented. Over time, I came to admire her parents for their strong values, their interests in gardening, antiques, and carpentry, and their work ethic. But that would be much later.

Off in the woods to relieve my bladder, I heard a couple of college friends enjoying each other's company at the far end of the ice pond. Deciding to scare them, I ran with my ice skates on, through some deep snow toward the pond. Unfortunately, the snow ended and I stepped into a frozen mud rut, heard a snap, and fell to the ground. Unable to get back up, I shouted out for help.

"Have another beer, Burke," was one response, followed by laughter.

"Seriously, I broke my leg!"

"Sure!" they said, laughing. After a few minutes, Bonnie came to check on me.

My diagnosis was right. I had fractured the distal tibia and disrupted some ankle ligaments on my left lower leg. Against my instincts, I agreed to be hospitalized overnight for pain relief. "Overnight" became two weeks. Our family doctor (not the one from earlier years) arrived the next morning, explained that my leg was too swollen, and that we would have to wait another twenty-four to forty-eight hours before a cast could be placed. Some overzealous nursing, following the doctor's order to apply heat, and failure of my doctor to return for over a week, prolonged my stay. Frustrated, Mom had to appeal to the hospital board in order to change doctors! Two weeks after the injury, I had a cast placed and was discharged.

"Sorry, you will get an *F* for the final exam that you did not take," said my genetics teacher. Previously he had warned us that there were only two exceptions for missing an exam: personal death or hospitalization. He noted that I had been dismissed from the hospital a half hour before the exam and should have been able to get there. My plea that I was unable to get there and had been at a study disadvantage for having missed two weeks of classes was acknowledged, and he let me test at a later date. Fortunately, my mom had continued my home fruit fly experiments during my hospitalization, following my instructions. Subsequently, I was able to make an accurate analysis of the "unknown" genetic mutation of the *Drosophila melanogaster* flies given to me earlier to breed and analyze.

"Please, let me help."

Bonnie offered to carry my books to classes. It was not easy to walk with crutches on icy paths and walkways, or to climb the steps to get to classes in the old coal-baron mansions of the college, where there were no elevators, so I did not hesitate to let her help. During those six weeks, we got to know each other much better. Such loyalty got my attention! Perhaps it never dawned on me to use a backpack to carry my own books, but then again, perhaps it did.

"Really? Is that what it means!"

So was my response to friends who were congratulating me upon return from the 1967 Christmas break. Prior to Christmas, I had asked Bonnie's best friend what she thought would be a great present for Bonnie. "Oh, I am sure that she would just love a Wilkes pin." That is how I "pinned Bonnie," and learned that it was supposed to be a symbolic "engaged to be engaged" thing before the final question of marriage is popped. Marriage was the furthest thing from my mind at that time. That was not my intent. Although Bonnie knew the meaning, she denied any collusion with her friend! Encouraged by Mom's opinion that "Bonnie is such a wonderful girl!" I willfully presented an engagement ring three years later. Bonnie made me the happiest man in the world, five years after that first meeting in the commons.

It is amazing how meaningful relationships make a difference in one's life. This is true at any age. Just as it is true for the dependent newborn who learns to trust those who cuddle, feed, bathe, and nurture her, so it is true for the centenarians who profess that social connectedness is a key to their longevity. Our relationship has made a difference in countless lives, more than we could ever have imagined.

College was, early on, no exception for me in terms of those risk-taking behaviors of adolescence that I described earlier. Bonnie's influence was key to my enlightenment regarding such things. In addition, the time shared with her reduced the time spent with risk-taking "buddies." Although it would be years before

I would successfully quit smoking, the habits of occasional excessive drinking and drunk driving were not broken until a particular near-tragic experience for us. Bonnie had saved the day, but it would be a few more days of introspection that would change me forever. At a friend's lake cottage, we were partying away the stresses of college, by drinking. Most of us were still under the legal age for alcohol consumption. Nevertheless, beer and hard liquor were abundant at the party. One peer challenged me to drinking beer and vodka, mixed. After several mugs, I was totally drunk. Stubborn and stupid, I refused to give Bonnie the keys and drove drunk the full nine miles around the lake. She had to prod me awake and steer from the passenger side to avoid head-on collisions. Fortunately, we made it to a diner in Luzerne, where we got coffee and breakfast and safe rides home.

"Where is my car?" I asked Mom.

"Last night you said it would not start and so you left it at the Sunset Diner."

"Oh, that's right." As my brother Carl drove me to the diner, I kept hoping that the car was there. It was. It also started on first try.

For several days, I physically felt the effects of the excessive alcohol intake. I also was frightened to think that I had a not-so-clear memory of what happened. There were images of the party, seeing headlights coming at me on the lake road, burning my tongue on hot coffee, vomiting at the diner, and people forcing me into a car. But there was not much else. Bonnie filled in the details for me several days later. Literally, she had saved our lives, and the lives of our not-yet-born children and grandchildren, as well as helped tens of thousands of people who would benefit from my actions as a physician in later years.

Old habits are hard to break. I did it again. Not the drunk-driving, but I drank excessively, on the occasion of my twenty-first birthday. At lunch, several friends took me to a bar near campus, and each bought me a shot of alcohol and toasted my milestone. After four or five shots, the bartender told them, "No more." Sitting on the stool in bacteriology lab after lunch, the professor's words began to sound strange to me. Several students were looking at me, shaking their heads, and laughing. My best college friend took me to the restroom, where I vomited relentlessly. He drove me home. The next day, Bonnie reminded me about the stupidity of my actions and that I missed the date that we had planned for that night. Upon reviewing my lab notes, there were several pages. I had started in English, changed to German, and eventually just wrote squiggly lines for a page or two.

There would be other instances of partying, playing darts with my friend at the local bar, and numerous other occasions of drinking in college. Sadly, there would be other parties and occasions throughout my young adulthood of excessive drinking. Fortunately, I never got out of control again. There would only be one or two other occasions where I would drink until I was sick, but I never drove drunk again, giving Bonnie the keys ahead of time.

Bonnie has been there for me and our loved ones ever since those early years of college. As later chapters will support, we have shared a wonderful life and are truly soul mates.

Soulful: adj. having or expressing or evoking deep feeling (Oxford American Dictionary).

Billy's death affected our family for decades. How it happened we think we know, but none of us was there. Why it happened is what every grieving person asks. What led to it? Could it have been prevented? What was its purpose? He was just twenty. Dad blamed Mom for her tolerance and encouragement of his wild side. Mom complained that Billy always knew Dad despised him for exhibiting her family's worst traits. My brothers blamed the driver, Billy's best friend. I questioned how God could take away my closest brother.

After high school, Billy joined the US Navy. Back then the draft enlisted every boy upon his eighteenth birthday for two years of service in the military. By joining, you could choose in which branch to serve. His idea was to see the world, serving his time, and then go to college. He served on the USS *Donner* LSD-20, Amphibian Squadron-Two, Sixth Fleet. Some ports of call included: France, Spain, Italy, Sicily, Ephesus, Izmir, Soros Bay, Greece, Turkey, Morocco, St. Thomas, and Puerto Rico—naming those recorded on his duffel bag. Many of his letters home discussed his friendships, chores, and joys. He also was sentimental and reported being homesick on occasion. During his last year of enlistment, he was especially looking forward to the Christmas holidays. Unfortunately, he broke his femur and was unable to get in on time. Although he told us that he had fallen down the ladder on board, a friend later told me that Billy and some sailors were attacked after leaving a bar while on shore leave, and his leg was broken by someone evidently doing a "flying side-kick" into his thigh. By June of 1968, he completed his service and enrolled in the Luzerne County Community College. He was excited about this new path in his life—a path he would never take.

"Bob, wake up. It's Billy. He was in a car accident, and they don't know if he will live." These were the awful words my oldest brother spoke to me around 2:00 a.m. on July 5, 1968. Mom and Dad were trying to keep their composure, telling us to hope and pray for the best. Just a half-mile from home, his friend had fallen asleep at the wheel and hit the large maple tree near our old home on Courtdale Avenue as they rounded the corner. He and Billy, who was asleep on the backseat, had been out drinking and celebrating

Independence Day. Although the driver incurred a minor laceration and contusion of his leg, Billy was unconscious and had been taken to the Nesbitt Hospital in Kingston. There were no seatbelts. Although he had no external signs of trauma, the impact caused a severe hemorrhage of his brain.

Without a doubt, those thirteen days that he survived were the longest and most horrible days of my life. Even now, forty-seven years later, I feel tearful as I write. I visited him every day, for as many hours as I could. Mom, Dad, and my brothers and I would go into his room, watching over him ever so vigilantly. We visited together, we visited with close friends and relatives, and we visited alone. None of us believed that he would not make it.

"He's a fighter, and he will win this one."

"He must be in pain."

"Look, he is trying to breathe on his own," we imagined.

"He knows we are here; he squeezed my hand while I was holding it," more than one of us said with contained excitement.

"He moved his arms and his legs," we exclaimed; likely it was de-cerebrate and decorticate posturing.

Always looking and hoping for signs of life, we interpreted every movement as communicative. Yes, he is in a coma. But he can hear us. He knows we are here. All of us could sense it as we looked painfully at his dependence on that ventilator for life. We also looked at every aspect of his face, remarked about how slender his fingers and toes were, and noted the broad shoulders and lanky arms. His toenails were long, and we worried he would be embarrassed by that, as he was always so well-groomed and particular about his appearance. His pallor, his cold extremities, and how he appeared to be wasting away bothered us.

For thirteen days, I would cry next to him, begging him to be full of life again. I would think of things that we had done together;

how it was before he left for the service; how I wrote to him weekly at first but then monthly and then intermittently. His smiles, his worried expressions, his voice, his mannerisms, and his closeness to me were all remembered. Life lessons he taught me, concerns we had talked about, and our hopes and plans for the future would occupy my thoughts. This was painful. It was confusing. It was so tragic. At times, I could not talk, but Bonnie's quiet embrace as her tears met mine meant so much. Together, we blocked out the world, at least for some moments of respite.

In retrospect, our grief was not unlike that described by Elisabeth Kubler-Ross in her book on *Death and Dying*.[28] Although her model was based on terminally ill patients that she interviewed, and not on those who experienced the loss of a loved one, the five common stages of denial, anger, bargaining, depression and acceptance have been extrapolated to include all grief reactions.

The acceptance of our loss, though, took decades. Each of us grieved in our own way, and along our own timelines. To each of us, it meant something different, although we understood each other's loss. Some of these stages occurred long before Billy died, while he was comatose. Some re-cycled after he died. The denial was evident in the hope that we placed on every non-purposeful movement. It was not long before anger took hold: anger at his friend, anger at God, anger even at Billy, and anger about our loss. Surely I was not alone in trying to bargain with God. Please, make him better and I will do anything. My brother Len was recalled from the front lines in Vietnam per my mom's request. Her friend, a state representative, came through again and got him home before she "lost another son." Len felt guilty that he had bargained with God to get him home and out of harm's way. It was hard convincing him

---

[28] Elisabeth Kubler-Ross, *On Death and Dying*. (New York: The Macmillan Company, 1969).

that Billy's injury had nothing to do with his hopes. All of us were depressed for an uncertain but long time. We told each other that Billy would have wanted us to go on with our lives. For decades every holiday, every birthday, every family celebration, and every event that I wanted to share with him brought pain. Although well-meaning folks exhibit empathy, the meaning of one's loss is never exactly the same as another's loss. Acceptance just takes time—a very long time.

After a week or so, the stress of watching Billy die was such that I, with guilt, was hoping that God would just pull him through this now or end it. How could *He* be so cruel as to let this tragedy unfold slowly to its inevitable end? Didn't *He* know that this was torturing Mom, Dad, me, my brothers, and all those relatives and friends who knew him? Would a just and loving God allow this young and compassionate person to die, causing so many to grieve? Why weren't my prayers, and our prayers, being answered? What kind of God did this? Then I remembered the life and death story of Christ, and somehow knew this was the same God. Indeed, *He* had let *His* only Son die, and millions to mourn for that, for millennia.

Of course, I was being selfish. It was my loss. It was my grief that produced such anger and doubt. However, my view of God, as I was taught, was that He was omnipresent, all powerful, and omniscient. Why then, would *He* not do something? It is too bad that the book *When Bad Things Happen to Good People,* by Harold Kushner[29] was not yet written. It may have helped. It may not have. But clearly, the answers I was getting from others were not acceptable: "Only God knows." "He is going to a better place." "God is making a bouquet and needs fresh flowers." "You need to just keep faith in God." "We know how you feel, but ..." "Accidents happen." Some words just

---

[29] Harold Kushner, *When Bad Things Happen To Good People.* (New York: Schocken Books, Inc., 1981).

made me angrier or question more. Do accidents happen, or are some preventable? Many "what if" questions came to mind. What if he never met his friend? What if they left the party earlier? What if they were not drinking? What if his previous behaviors were better disciplined? *What if, what if, what if!*

Perhaps this was the beginning of my belief that most accidents are really preventable injuries. This was the single most important loss I have ever experienced. For better or worse, those days and that loss changed me forever. Undoubtedly, that change fed my determination to pursue the quest. That change became the basis for my future career choice to be a general pediatrician, focused on well-being and preventive medicine. There could be no better purpose in my life, I thought, than to be able to prevent such a tragedy for others.

How did this tragedy impact my college performance? Fortunately, there was a month or two after Billy's death before I resumed classes at Wilkes, starting my third year there. That gave me some time to adjust to the realities of life. Previously, I mentioned that something extraordinary happened to me that academic year. Learning seemed to become easier. My performance improved. Why? I had always tried my best, so it likely was not effort related. I did learn better study techniques and test-taking strategies, but that could not explain it all. There was less chaos in my study environment at home, and I am sure that helped. However, my focus was very much improved. Perhaps I had unrecognized attention deficit disorder (ADHD) that resolved or improved with brain maturation. Certainly, I exhibited hyperactivity, inattentiveness, and impulsivity during the high school years. But ADHD was not a recognized condition back then, and certainly no one was treated with the medications that are now used successfully to treat it. I am sure the symptoms were present in a few of my brothers and in some relatives as well, and it is known that ADHD runs in families. There is also data that suggests more than a fourth of all children who require medications for this improve spontaneously in young adulthood. Our experiences literally change brain function and structure, so I suspect that my brother's death was no exception. It energized my dedication to the quest, but did it improve my focus? Who knows?

Despite being quite successful in college, apparently this came too late. Mentally, I was more than ready for medical school. Academically, it appeared that I was not. It was well known that a grade point average of 3.5 and competitive MCAT scores were required for admission. Certainly my 3.68 GPA of the last two years should have qualified me, but the first two years had lowered my four-year GPA to 3.14. The difficulties that I had with standardized tests, as alluded to earlier, resulted in my MCAT scores (V: 505, Q: 575, GI: 525, S: 425) being not so competitive. None of this deterred me, as I knew that anyone reviewing the reasons for my overall GPA and board scores would understand. Besides, there was no one more committed than I, so that would seal the deal.

All that was needed now was to get that interview. One after another, the letters came back. Hershey, Hahnemann, Jefferson, Medical College of PA, Temple, Pittsburgh, Penn, Johns Hopkins, University of Chicago, Emory, and Meharry each sent a standard letter of rejection, citing the large number of highly competitive applicants. A few had the sensitivity to say that I might be qualified, but competition was keen and there would be no room. That interview for which I hoped never came. The applicants were first screened by a secretary, based solely on GPA and MCAT scores. It may not have been as painful if the letters all came at once, but they did not. Nevertheless, I remained hopeful for months until that last letter of rejection was in hand. Only then did I consider an alternative.

Once again, my mom perceived an injustice here. Some students, who did not graduate with high honors as I did, successfully made it into medical school. So she wrote an anonymous letter to the editor of the *Wilkes-Barre Times Leader* newspaper complaining that the process is unfair. She also condemned Wilkes College administrators for not being as helpful as they should have been. Some letters of response suggested that a sponsor was needed, so she once again tried to get her state representative to help, but to no avail. Bless her, she was always doing battle for me. I believe those rejections were as painful for her as they were for me.

Not yet ready to give up the quest, I tried a different approach.

CHAPTER 6

The Quest in Peril

Perseverance is encoded in my DNA. Dad made sure of that. I thought if one door closes, then go through another door to get to where you want to go. I had a master key. It was called a liberal arts education, and surely I had learned how to learn. Which door to choose was not apparent to me. However, one of my professors suggested that I go to graduate school to beef up my credentials and then reapply to medical school. That sounded like a plan, so I did.

Master of Science: Botany

Would you believe it? I actually scored competitively high on the standard graduate school admissions test (GRE) and was accepted at the only place that I applied, The Pennsylvania State University. My good fortune got better when I received a letter from a member of the admissions committee. "I am a physiologist and happen to sit on the admissions committee. I am impressed with your application and would like to offer you a graduate research assistantship ...." The offer would cover tuition, books, dormitory living, and then some. How could I refuse? My plan was to do medically related research if I did not get into medical school, so a master's degree in physiology would certainly prepare me. The assistantship and research work experience would enhance my credentials as well.

"Excuse me, where is Dr. _____'s office?" I asked the secretary of the physiology department in the Life Sciences building at Penn State when that magical first day of graduate school fall term arrived in 1970.

"Dr. who? There is no one here by that name."

"Why, there must be. Here is a copy of the correspondence that he sent regarding a research assistantship for me in physiology. Is this not the physiology department?"

Upon checking with someone else and the directory, the secretary made a call.

"It appears that he has an office in the old Botany building, and I can direct you there."

Botany? I thought that was strange. So, I went to his office. After our greetings, I asked him about the research and its location, wanting to confirm that it was medical or animal physiology.

"Oh, I'm sorry for the confusion. I guess that I neglected to mention that it is *plant* physiology. You see, I happen to be a plant biochemist. We are looking at the metabolism of hormones in the *Parthenocissus tricuspidata* crown-gall tumor tissue cultures."

Wow! I didn't even know that plants had physiology. I proceeded to tell him that his research sounded interesting, but I was not interested in plants. My intent, I naively stated, was to reapply to medical school in a year or two and perhaps do medical research in the future. He looked a little concerned but then tried to reassure me that the nature of the tissue studied did not matter as much as the understanding of biochemical and physiological processes.

"You will be prepared to do any type of research, including medical research, after your graduate studies. In fact, this next year I will be doing a sabbatical at a federal research institute in Switzerland."

He continued to explain that his colleague, another plant physiologist, had agreed to be my mentor in his absence. "You can focus entirely on your graduate courses in biochemistry, biophysics, and plant physiology. Then you will be able to focus 100 percent on the research when I return. Meanwhile, you will actually be doing a teaching assistantship for him. He will also introduce you to our lab team and give some insight into our research."

Confused would be an understatement of how I felt. As soon as I left his office, I went back to the Animal Physiology Department to see if I could, naively and hopefully, exchange my research assistantship for one in an area that I preferred. The department chair explained that it does not work that way, but if I wanted to apply for one next year, my chances would be good. That was not what I wanted to hear. Angry, I thought about dropping the research assistantship, but I had no other way to pay my expenses, so I felt trapped. I reasoned that *plant physiology* studies would enlighten me about an aspect of the plant world of which I knew nothing. Besides, I would do as he suggested and focus entirely on getting all or most of my graduate courses out of the way. Disheartened, I accepted the assistantship.

During that first year, I really enjoyed graduate school. Wilkes College had prepared me well, especially in the areas of analytical and critical thinking. I felt much further ahead of those in my classes who had come through their undergraduate years at Penn State or elsewhere. My courses included plant physiology, plant physiology seminar, general biochemistry, molecular biophysics, plant growth substances, and summer research. In those nine months before the summer term, I had taken nineteen credits and maintained a GPA of 4.0. The teaching assistantship required teaching beginning laboratory courses to undergraduate students, and that went very well. Socially, I developed several close friendships.

That was the year during which Bonnie and I got married. Before getting into the summer term research, we moved into graduate housing on campus. When reminiscing, we still laugh about how everything we owned and needed fit into the bed of a half-ton pickup truck that we had borrowed from her dad's employer. The entire efficiency apartment was less than four hundred square feet! The hallway upon entering had a closet, stove, cabinets, and refrigerator on the right. It extended to the bathroom, which had a sink, toilet, and tub. One could easily sit on the toilet, brush one's teeth over the sink, and soak one's feet in the tub, all at once. Of course, I never tried that, but would laughingly demonstrate that for visitors. To the left of the hall was the living room, separated by a counter, and adjacent to the one bedroom, which was closer to the bathroom. It was cozy and convenient. One of our favorite pastimes was to rearrange our wall-to-wall furniture every couple of weeks. The campus location was really appreciated when I had to go to the laboratory in the middle of the night to change solutions or to do other actions my experiments required. Some things just could not be planned around my sleep schedule.

After my mentor's return, my research got underway full-time. My goal was to complete my work for the master's degree by the end of summer term 1972. So I worked many evenings, most weekends, and several holidays in the laboratory or the library. There was no Google or easy way to research the literature on a particular topic. Hours of painstaking, boring card catalog searches, followed by retrieving the articles, were necessary. What could be done nowadays in a few hours literally took weeks. Like Dad, I was and still am a workaholic. During the same year, I took more plant physiology, biochemistry, and biophysics courses, as well as courses in botany and biosynthetic macromolecules.

The quest to become a physician was still front and center for me, although I now had a clearer backup plan than at any other time in the past. Hoping to be accepted and to start medical school in 1972, I applied once again for admission to the medical schools in Pennsylvania. Touting my perfect GPA and likely master's degree completion that year, I thought things would be different. I do not recall taking the MCAT again, as I believed I was now competitive. Once again, I received rejection after rejection. This time, I did get past secretarial screening and was invited for interviews at Jefferson and at The Medical College of Pennsylvania. Both interviews went very well, but the outcomes were the same. Both agreed that I was very qualified and would do well. However, competition was keen, and there was no room for me. One dean of admissions, who was truly empathic and transparent, told me that if I were a minority applicant that my application would have been readily accepted, but affirmative action literally took my place. Both recommended that I complete my graduate work, and if still interested, specifically prepare for the MCAT, as better scores would be key to my gaining admission. Once again, my quest was in peril.

The amount of research I did that year resulted in an overwhelming amount of data. I decided that it was time to write my thesis. My thesis adviser suggested that I skip the master's degree and continue this work for a doctoral (PhD) degree instead. Being wary, I told him that I would like to write the thesis and receive the master's degree before testing as a doctoral candidate. He agreed. I suggested that I might change research fields and do something more medically relevant. He reminded me that there would be only a few more course requisites, and I could accomplish enough in two years, using the current model and research goals, to get the PhD in plant physiology. Changing to an entire new field for the PhD might take much longer.

By September, I wrote and defended my master's thesis, entitled "Nature of Indoleacetic Acid Oxidase Preparations from *Parthenocissus tricuspidata* Crown-Gall Tissue Cultures." The major objective of the research was to characterize the metabolism and mechanism of action of indoleacetic acid oxidase (IAA), in regulating the plant hormone known as an auxin. Chromatography and spectral analysis were employed to identify the degradation products of IAA, and those products were assayed for biological activity as auxins. This was truly exciting for me, since no one else in the world had done or reported similar research. My research studies, data collection, and analysis were unique. As was the custom, I submitted it for review and oral defense to a select research committee consisting of botanists, biochemists, and plant physiologists. The thesis was accepted, and my efforts earned me a master of science in botany, awarded September 16, 1972. This research supported a larger study that was published years later.[30]

A Broken Trust

Per my advisor's recommendation, I enrolled in the fall term. In order to pursue research toward a doctoral degree, a doctoral candidacy oral exam must be passed. My goal for the doctoral research was to study the IAA-oxidase metabolism in normal callus cultures for comparison with that identified by my initial studies on the crown-gall tumor tissue cultures. Perhaps that would provide some

[30] Hamilton, R.H., Myers, H.E., Burke, R.E., Feung, C.S., and Mumma, R.O. 1976, "Metabolism of indole-3 acidic acid II. Oxindole pathway in *Parthenocissus tricuspidata* crown-gall tissue cultures." *Plant Physiology* 58: 77–81.

insight into the metabolic basis for the auxin hormone-independent growth of crown-gall tumors in this ivy plant.

"Your intentions are what? To pursue *medical* research?" asked one botanist.

All committee members looked at my advisor with incredulity. Suddenly, something sinister seemed surfacing.

"This is news to me," was his reply.

Now I must have looked incredulous. How could he say this after all of the discussions that we had over the preceding two years concerning my research goals! Later it was explained to me, by one of my favorite professors, that researchers are admired for their work as well as, and often even more so, for the quality of researchers they train in their field. Even if my research advisor truly did not care about my post-doctoral goals, he had to save face, even with a bold-faced lie.

That was one heckuva way to start my examination. Perhaps it was over analysis, but I truly believe that they purposefully tried to fail me. Two examples follow. First, after discussing the research that I planned to pursue, I was asked to write the chemical structures and reactions for all of the enzymes and substrates and anticipated metabolic products that would be involved. That was easy for me at that time and seemed to be an appropriate request. However, the biochemist, after a glance to the others, then looked at me and asked me to show him where in these reactions free radicals were formed and to diagram a likely sequence of molecular movements. It seemed like a "gotcha" demand. But I was at the top of my game, having had those biophysics and biochemistry courses, and did so perfectly.

The second effort came from the botanist. Since there was no formal degree in plant physiology, I had a choice of either a master of biology or of botany. He knew that I chose botany to reflect the area of my research and seventeen graduate credits in plant physiology. He also knew that I had only taken one botany course per se. Having anticipated his question, I memorized the complete nomenclature for the plant kingdom. Unfortunately, there were two or three sets of nomenclature, but it was considered practical to only use one. Nevertheless, he recognized, with surprise, that the preferred nomenclature that I had described was correct. He then asked for the other two nomenclatures, which I could not do. None of my research depended upon that knowledge, and he knew that many botanists would also not be able to answer that correctly.

After the candidacy examination for pursuing the doctoral degree, my professor met with me and congratulated me on passing. "There is," he proceeded to explain, "a condition. The committee requests that you be required to do research for four years before writing and defending your thesis."

I reminded him of our prior discussions. He apologized for his response to the committee's surprise about my goals, as he thought and meant to have said, "He had put that goal behind him." In terms of his expectations of me, he said that he would require four years as the committee recommended, even though we both knew the status of my research and studies was such that two years would be an easily reached goal.

It was not a hard decision. There was a broken trust. There was clearly an injustice here, and my mother's sense of fairness had also been encoded in my DNA. My advisor said that he understood my decision but wished that I would stay on with him. I just could not, so I withdrew from further graduate study at that very moment. There was no backup plan, but I was confident I could develop one.

Becoming a Carpenter

Fortunately, there was an unexpected opening for an instructor in a biology course for non-majors. That position was for one term, but I applied and got it. Having had some positive experiences as a teaching assistant, I looked forward to this and hoped something similar would follow. There was nothing available for the spring term. By this time, I had become an expectant father. I applied for many jobs in town but was denied because the owners or managers suspected that I was too educated to stay on. I was even refused employment as a janitor. After those rejections, I was frantic. We now had to use food stamps, and I had no other income.

So when I responded to an ad for a full-time carpenter, I exaggerated my experience. Although I had worked as a carpenter's helper during college, I had never worked alone or with folks like the ones with whom I joined. They were on incentive and literally could build a house within three to four weeks from start to finish. By example, instead of two working together to sheet rock or panel a room, each carpenter was assigned a room. On my first day, I had completely paneled one wall and a closet by noon and was feeling quite proud. However, at lunch the foreman wanted to know why I was so slow, as the others had completed their rooms except for the ceilings. Within a few weeks, it was obvious that I could not keep up with those highly skilled and experienced carpenters, but I was working better and harder than ever before and becoming quite skilled. The owner had hired me at minimum wage, with a promise to adjust my salary depending on how I "panned out."

"Sir, I am requesting an increase in my salary. I can't make ends meet on minimum wage and believe I deserve an increase. A quarter an hour more would help a lot."

I was shocked. He refused, saying he had thought about firing me because the other carpenters complained that I was slowing them down. However, he would keep me on as unskilled labor to clear lots and do landscaping as well as to unload materials from railroad cars and any other support work needed. In two weeks, he would give me the wage requested if all went well. That perseverance and work ethic advice that Dad always gave would now be put to the test. The other labor crew worker had to tell me to slow down, as I was putting his job at risk by raising expectations. He had taught me to use a chain saw, and I was clearing a full lot in one day, cutting and stacking a couple of cords of wood as well. For his sake, I heeded his request. He also had a good work ethic, and he was right about the owner's exploitative personality. Two weeks later, I was called into the office. The owner let me know that he was totally impressed with me and gave me a better raise than I had requested or expected!

Eventually, a position for a carpenter opened with the company for which my father-in-law worked. He knew how my skills had grown, most likely thought about his pregnant daughter as well, and offered me the job. Excitedly, we moved back to "the Valley." We rented a second-floor apartment initially in the town of Forty Fort. Our first child was born there, but we moved again within a year to Kingston, where we rented a larger but dilapidated apartment. I talked the owner into letting me remodel it, as long as he bought the materials. He agreed. My father-in-law thought I should have billed him for the work, but we were just glad to get a better living arrangement out of it.

Becoming a Father

Labor Day became labor day for us in 1973. Less than two months after our move from the State College area, Bonnie went into the labor of childbirth. Prior to that, we had established prenatal care with a local obstetrician. Our friends recommended him, as he let the father in the room and allowed him to cut the umbilical cord. That was quite a novel idea at that time. Usually the father just waited nervously in the waiting area outside of the delivery room. Dr. Hazlett offered me even more participation. He handed me a manual on the emergency delivery of a baby, stating that he expected to let me deliver the baby with his assistance. Wow! All that I had hoped for was to be able to observe and then cut the cord. We also went to Lamaze classes together, so I knew what to expect and how to coach Bonnie through this. Little did I know how both stressful and joyful this would become.

For seventeen hours, I rubbed Bonnie's back, while she experienced the progressively harder and more frequent contractions of childbirth. We were in a special birthing room, for labor only, at the Kingston Nesbitt hospital. The nurse visited frequently, monitoring the fetal heart sounds, which we could hear. Despite how tired we were, something suddenly sounded different. I asked the nurse why the sounds were different and slower.

"Oh, don't worry," she tried to reassure us as she quickly left the room.

Within moments, Dr. Hazlett came quickly through the door, listened to the fetal sounds, and asked the nurse to call anesthesia stat. Quickly they wheeled Bonnie out of the room on a gurney. Standing there dumbfounded, I knew something was wrong but had received no explanation.

My worrisome thoughts were interrupted by the doctor, who quickly came back through the door and said, "Come on, you have a baby to deliver!"

As we headed to the operating room, he stopped to scrub and to explain that there were fetal heart decelerations, so we would need to facilitate a quick delivery with forceps.

"Are you sure I should help?" I asked nervously.

After all, I was just a carpenter who read a manual on emergency delivery of the newborn, which said nothing about forceps or fetal decelerations. My interest hardly qualified me to do anything, especially if there was a suspected problem.

"Of course you should! I will get things started for you and let you finish the delivery."

Bonnie was already breathing oxygen and pushing. We could see the baby's head crowning.

"Sunny side up! Give me the hockey sticks," he told the nurse.

He then told me what he was about to do. He expertly applied the delivery forceps to each side of the baby's head and began to steadily pull as Bonnie pushed. He showed me how to continue holding the forceps and pull while he further prepared for the baby's imminent arrival. My thoughts about how dangerous this was, and that I hoped it did not crush her head or twist her neck, were soon dismissed as the head popped out. As he assisted, I caught the baby. While holding her prone in my hands and asking what I should do, he looked at the nurse, who had been taking photographs of the entire delivery, and said, "I think he is doing just fine. Oh, that is just poop," as some dark rectal discharge fell onto the floor. I also got to cut the clamped cord.

Incredibly beautiful and wondrous, but no words can fully capture the experience. Helping to deliver Christa, our first baby and daughter, was an experience that gave me a lifetime of joy. Even now, I can feel the presence of her weight on my hands. In future years, whenever I would hold a newborn, that same feeling enabled me to guess the weight within an ounce or so. That always amazed the nurses at the delivery who heard me hazard a guess about the weight in response to the mother's query. Still, I can envision Christa, that tiny little body covered with vernix and blood, turning her head in my direction while suspended in my hands, and crying. That special event would be unique for me, as I would not be allowed to participate in our other children's deliveries. However, I did get to witness the joy and wonder of each of their births. The joys of becoming a father for the first, second, third, and fourth times are among the greatest gifts I have ever been given!

Becoming a Doctoral Candidate, Again

Life as a carpenter was enjoyable. Like most, I would venture into "side jobs," independent of my employer. My brother Kevin, fresh from technical school where he studied to become a carpenter, joined me. For me, there is joy in building something new or re-modeling something old. At the end of a day, one can look back and see what was accomplished. The challenge of planning, gathering the materials, and completing the task is satisfying. It is also hard work, and it is done in hot, humid, cold, windy, dusty, hazardous, and other challenging conditions. Such work also often requires the acquisition of painting, plumbing, masonry, and electrical skills as well. Being able to do these things for oneself as well is a time and money saver. Often it is the only way to get it done the way you want it and when you want it. There is much opportunity to be creative, changing plans as the project moves along enticed by new ideas. These are lifelong skills. I still utilize them. Over the past several decades, I have embraced the hobbies of remodeling our homes, landscaping, painting, and creating and building decks, a gazebo, arbors, children's play-scapes, furniture, and toys.

In the summer of 1974, I received a call from my friend with whom I associated while working on my master's degree. He recalled my desire to do medically oriented research, and the laboratory in which he was working toward his doctoral degree suddenly had an opening for another graduate student. This professor and his graduate students were working with cell cultures, doing NIH-supported breast cancer research. My friend had told him about my prior graduate studies and suitability to his needs. His advisor offered me a research assistantship, so I could work full-time on the doctoral degree and not have to borrow much money. He also thought that I would possibly be able to earn my PhD within two years, if I worked as hard as I had done previously. Having already passed a candidacy examination, another would not be required.

The timing was perfect. The possibilities for career development awakened an excitement in me that had been dormant the past two years. This offer came unexpectedly, as I had taken no actions and had made no specific plans for further study. Perhaps I was so focused on providing for our family needs, and still reeling from the deceit experienced during my prior studies, that I had put my career goals on hold. Now it was time to move forward and do something special with my life. Despite the start of the fall term in a couple of months, I had time to accept the position, reapply to graduate school, find a place to live near the university, and move. The quest to become a physician had been in peril, but this new quest was exciting. Personally, my interest in breast cancer research was also stimulated by the fact that my mother had bilateral radical mastectomies for a pre-cancerous condition. The psychological impact of that on her lasted for decades. Fortunately, that would never happen now, because breast cancer research has provided better diagnostic and therapeutic measures.

Breast Cancer Research

Although I had worked with tissue culture systems during my earlier studies, cell culture research was new to me. Some of the cell lines we worked with were derived from breast milk, breast tissue from reduction mammoplasties, and tissue from cancerous breast tumors. Normal cells have a defined life span in culture, spontaneously lysing or otherwise dying after so many cell divisions. By contrast, malignant cells such as those from breast cancer tumors can grow *in vitro* cultures indefinitely, provided they are given the appropriate nutritional solutions and transferred to new flasks when they get overcrowded. These cell lines can be tested with chemicals such as estrogen, thyroid hormone, anti-estrogens, and many potentially therapeutic chemicals to determine the effects on cell growth, differentiation, or viability. In some of my post-doctoral research, I also looked at the effects of radiation on these cell lines. Similarly, the normal cells can be treated with chemicals suspected of causing cancer as well as treating it. In brief, my research interests were in studying hormonal action at a cellular level, in particular, to study their effects on cell proliferation and differentiation in culture.

Human breast–derived cell cultures are uniquely suited to providing a means to evaluate the role of hormones on differentiation of human mammary gland epithelial cells. Most breast cancers arise from the mammary ductal epithelium. Normally, this epithelium specializes in the unique synthesis of casein, a milk product. Estrogens, progesterone, corticosteroids, growth hormone, and prolactin are all known to play some role in both mammogenesis and lactogenesis. Studying the effects of these chemicals at the cellular level in the intact organism is complicated by the multiple interactions of body systems with the mammary gland. However, casein synthesis in cell culture could provide a useful marker in assessing the role of hormones and other chemicals in the differentiation of the mammary epithelial cell. At the time of my research, there were no reports documenting the production of casein in human cell cultures. Therefore, my goal was to develop a protocol to measure casein products in human breast–derived cell cultures and to test the effects of hormones on that production.

As anticipated, I enjoyed research and committed to devoting as much time as possible to earning the doctoral degree. Most of the course credits needed for the doctoral degree had previously been completed, but I took several additional courses relevant to my research. This included studies in dairy science radio-physiology and in mammalian cell cultures. Hard work and perseverance once again got me through some difficult times over the next two years. Part of that difficulty related to how unexpectedly independent most of my research became after the first year. My thesis advisor went on sabbatical to England, so much of my completion of the research and writing the doctoral thesis required independent initiative and assertiveness. I passed the required comprehensive examination on October 24, 1975, and the doctoral thesis defense on May 19, 1976. The thesis was entitled: *Studies on casein synthesis in human breast-derived cell cultures.* Some of this research was published later.[31] Completing requirements for submission of the thesis to the graduate school and seeking post-doctoral research opportunities were part of my challenge. The doctor of philosophy in biology was conferred in August of 1976, at which time I had already moved to San Antonio, Texas, for my NIH-sponsored

---

[31] Burke, Robert E. "Prolactin Can Stimulate General Protein Synthesis in Human Breast Cancer Cells (MCF-7) in Long-Term Culture," 1978 *Life Sciences* (23): 9 pp. 901–06; Gaffney, E.V., Polanowski, F.P., Blackburn, S.E., Lambiase, J.T., and Burke, R.E. 1976 "Cultures of normal human mammary cells," *Cell Differentiation* 5: 69–81.

post-doctoral breast cancer research in the laboratory of William L. McGuire, MD, at the University of Texas at San Antonio Health Sciences Center. I had several other offers for postdoctoral research in Michigan, Virginia, and North Carolina but decided to go to Texas because of the different cultural experience we would get. Dr. McGuire was as well-known as the leaders of the other research laboratories where I had interviewed.

CHAPTER 7

A Cell Doctor

Post-Doctoral Research

"Why are you putting those rocks in the car?" I asked Christa.

"They may not have any in Texas," she said with a worried look.

We had rented a U-Haul trailer, and my father-in-law gave us his Chevy station wagon, for which he said we could pay some time in the future. The trailer was completely filled with our stuff, and our kids were hard to find among the lamps and other items stored inside the station wagon. In fact, there was only about four inches of clearance between the hitch and the road. We were Texas bound.

By this time, *we* included me, Bonnie, Christa, and our first son, Bob, who had been born during my last year of doctoral research. His birth I could view through a window, but I was not otherwise allowed in the room at the State College Community Hospital. The obstetrician brought him to the window to show me that our new-born was a boy, and because I was so excited, I didn't take a picture but lowered my camera to look. Still, the miracle of his birth was special, and I wondered how our life would change with this new addition to the family.

En route to San Antonio, we stopped one night at a motel in

the Tennessee mountains to sleep. The next day we got off early yet had what seemed to be an unending drive to just outside of San Antonio, where we stayed at a Holiday Inn, in a town called San Marcos. During the long drive, I was getting sleepy as we were passing through Arkansas. At that time there was only a two-lane highway from Memphis to Little Rock, and one could drive the entire length and see only a few other vehicles. Suddenly in the dark on that lonely road midway between Memphis and Little Rock, we came across a car that was on fire alongside the road. As I slowed down to see if anyone needed help, we noticed that the entire side of the car was bullet-ridden. There did not appear to be anyone around. As my adrenaline surged, I became wide awake, and we sped out of there, talking about the scene for the next several hundred miles.

Before moving to San Antonio, I had talked with a laboratory assistant named Mini. She offered to find an apartment for us based on what we could afford. The only place affordable was government housing on Dean Pannill road in San Antonio, which would be close to the medical center and research laboratory, so we took it. That was a decision we later regretted.

"Bonnie, look what's happening," I said as I looked out of our cockroach-infested apartment at the kids near the outside staircase to the second floor. Our daughter was on her tike bike, and several other children were pulling at her hair, pulling the bike, and trying to get her off it. She was crying. I immediately chased the kids and brought her into the apartment. "The next time those kids pick on you, hit them back," I said, much to Bonnie's disapproval.

One day, not long afterward, as I pulled into the parking lot at our apartment after work, our daughter came running to greet me. But she stopped to do something that she would never have done previously, as she had always been a polite child who would strive to please others. She had passed a girl sitting on the sidewalk. Christa then ran back to her and pushed the girl onto the grass.

"That's my sidewalk!" she exclaimed in a threatening tone.

That three-year-old, sweet little girl of ours had now become the ringleader of the group that had picked on her previously! That incident and the hostile environment there triggered our search for better housing. Some cars in the parking areas adjacent to the apartments had rags instead of caps covering the gas tanks, and the guy in the apartment above us frequently fought with his wife and threatened her with a gun. Because of my career and potential for better earnings (my fellowship was for only $10,000 per year), we were able to get into a new $25,000 house on Ambling Drive by including the required down payment in the mortgage. Although we only lived in the apartment complex for six weeks, it took six months and a lot of parental guidance before Christa trusted other kids again. Lesson learned for me: environment and personal experiences are critically important in molding the behavior and personality of young children.

My quest to become a physician remained in peril, as a consequence of my graduate studies. I became disinterested in the pursuit, as I lost hope in ever achieving it. Although I was rightfully called "doctor," a title conferred by earning the PhD degree, that title was not my *raison d'etre*. It had been much more than a title of respect for which I had yearned. My postdoctoral research in breast cancer was very exciting and meaningful. Thus, I was reconciling myself to that role in life.

There were several other researchers in our laboratory who had also earned their PhDs. They had been involved in some of the early studies that documented the clinical importance of classifying breast cancer tissue as estrogen or progesterone-receptor positive or negative, as there would be different implications for therapy based on the classification. In addition to my research, my role was to supervise the day-to-day technical activities of the laboratory to ensure quality in maintenance of the cell lines. I was the problem solver for any problems related to contamination or culture failures. This was an intense working environment, as Dr. McGuire and the others were nationally and internationally known for their work. That put us under closer scrutiny as well as greater expectations for productivity and leadership in our area of breast cancer research. Meeting research grant demands added stress. This was transitional research at its best, as that would take basic scientific laboratory studies and link them to clinically relevant needs. We "PhD-types" worked out the scientific approaches, following the highly knowledgeable medical internist's clinical queries and goal-oriented research. Dr. McGuire also worked part-time as a practicing clinician who taught residents and medical students. He would arrive at the laboratory before his clinical duties started early in the morning and stay late into the evening. We held "data review" sessions every Friday morning and plotted our research strategies.

My expertise was developing and simultaneously being recognized. Other clinicians or researchers coming to our laboratory to study our approaches to clinically relevant research and to learn our cell culture techniques would be trained and oriented by me. New departmental hires were also put under my wing until their research took hold and grants allowed them to fund their own operations. In fact, two of these researchers went on to become prominent leaders in clinically relevant breast cancer research, one developing soft agar stem cell assays for testing new pharmaceutical agents and the other pursuing the use of anti-estrogens such as tamoxifen in therapy. Ironically, the latter young doctor who I had helped to get his start in cell culture studies did not remember me decades later when I asked for a letter of recommendation from him. There were other physicians in different specialty areas within our area of the building with whom I also became associated. In order to help financially, Bonnie would baby sit some of their children in our home. This would become significant in a way that we never imagined.

Those years with Dr. McGuire were very productive. Most of my work was published in the reputable journal *Cancer Research*. This included studies on estrogen action following irradiation of human breast cancer cells,[32] the use of lactate dehydrogenase as a marker in studies of estrogen-responsive human breast cancer cells,[33] and the detection of nuclear thyroid hormone receptors in a human breast cancer cell line.[34] Pursuing my doctoral thesis goal of measuring casein synthesis in breast cancer cell lines, we were able to document the detection of both casein and alpha-lactalbumin, both human breast milk products, by immunocytochemistry of breast cancer cells.[35] I also found time to publish some of the research done during my graduate studies on the ability of prolactin to stimulate general protein synthesis in human breast cancer cells in long-term culture.[36]

Often it takes years for basic research to become applied and

---

[32] Burke, R.E., Mira, J.G., Datta, R., Zava, D.T., and McGuire, W.L. 1978 "Estrogen action following irradiation of human breast cancer cells" *Cancer Research* 38: 2813–2817.

[33] Burke, R.E., Harris, S.C., and McGuire, W.L., 1978, "Lactate dehydrogenase in estrogen-responsive human breast cancer cells," *Cancer Research* 38: 2773–776.

[34] Burke, R.E. and McGuire, W.L., 1978, "Nuclear thyroid hormone receptors in a human breast cancer cell line," *Cancer Research* 38: 3769–73.

[35] Herbert, D., Burke, R.E. and McGuire, W.L., 1978, "Casein and alpha-lactalbumin detection in breast cancer cells by immunocytochemistry," *Cancer Research* 38: 2221–23.

[36] Burke, Robert E. "Prolactin Can Stimulate General Protein Synthesis in Human Breast Cancer Cells (MCF-7) in Long-Term Culture," 1978 *Life Sciences* (23): 9 pp. 901–06;

clinically relevant to the diagnosis and/or treatment of medical conditions. Goal-oriented research, as required by most grants from NIH and other sources, facilitates this transition. Some research never gets published or is discontinued, as grant-directed goals move in different directions in order to study or solve more pressing problems. Good researchers become nationally and internationally known for their work, their laboratories expand with personnel and projects, and the leaders (principal investigators) spend much of their time spreading the results of their work and ideas among the scientific and medical community.

Although competition is keen, scientists share knowledge readily. One professor put it this way: if I give you a dollar and you give me a dollar, then we each have a dollar; however, if I give you an idea and you give me an idea, then we each have two ideas. Unfortunately, getting money to continue such studies becomes a full-time endeavor. This is called "grants-man-ship" by some, and not every good researcher is good at it. Most money for research comes from the government or philanthropic organizations and individuals. In industry, research and "intellectual property" are often much more guarded.

The area of my research was intellectually challenging and personally satisfying. I could look at the long-term and accept the delayed gratification that would come for a lifetime of work in research. The results of one experiment often inspires several others, and creativity could blossom unexpectedly or as a result of perseverance with steady, goal-directed research. Asking a question and pursuit of the answer requires experimental designs that account for variables and unbiased analysis and interpretation of data. The revelation of a truth comes in the application of that knowledge to a successful practical end, or in the ability of such results to be repeatable by different groups in different laboratories consistently over time. So a hypothesis is set, then tested and retested, and eventually becomes a theory, which then requires further studies and confirmations that result in it becoming a scientific law or truth. Many "truths" become modified as more scientific inquiry and research provide new data.

Basic laboratory research and transitional research differ from "clinical research." In the latter, data may be gathered retrospectively from medical records and interpreted as to relevance to a particular inquiry. Many biases can be introduced into this type of study. The best clinical research, however, comes from what are called prospective, controlled, randomized, double-blind studies that eliminate many biases and give greater validity to the results. The value of this research over basic and transitional research is that it often can be applied faster to clinical needs. Thus, there may be more immediate gratification for the researchers. All three types of research are important and require different levels of expertise and have varied, meaningful applications. Often research results or techniques in one area overlap and benefit other closely or even unrelated areas.

Although the non-physician researcher can participate in any of these types of research, the physician-scientist is more likely to understand the relevance of clinical data in its application to treating patients. This would be due to the art of medicine, which could only develop or be applied in the actual practice of medicine. The lay public is often confused by the changing nature of medical recommendations, based on new research data and interpretation. This problem is confounded by sensationalism in the media trying to capture a greater market share of readers or viewers. Often the significance or applicability of the new findings are exaggerated to create interest or due to other known or unknown bias.

There is both an art and a science to the practice of medicine.

Most recommendations are evidenced-based (EBM) and change only as new evidence comes to light. However, new questions that lead to EBM often arise from experience and reason related to anecdotal cases. The third quality of importance for the clinical practice of medicine relates to how meaningful it is for the individual being treated. How information is personalized is part of the art of medicine. The rapport established with the provider (physician or other healthcare professional) is an important component of trust that enhances compliance with recommendations and better outcomes. Understanding the interactions of EBM, experience and reason, and individual needs is crucial to providing excellence in patient care. In future years, this is a theme that I would repeatedly emphasize as a mentor for students and physicians.

Perseverance

Becoming a physician-scientist was not my original quest. However, the paths I took in becoming a scientist have been heretofore described. My quest to become a physician met many barriers and was almost abandoned as I came to appreciate the value that my life as a scientist could contribute to the field of medicine and scientific knowledge. Call it serendipity or call it fate, it does not matter to me. But what happened next did matter. It was a life-changing event, precipitated by a random discussion between my wife and Dr. O'Connor, whose child she was babysitting. She mentioned the struggles I faced in pursuing the quest to become a physician, especially the problematic MCAT. He knew me and told Bonnie that he thought that I would make an excellent physician as well as physician-scientist. That goal was attainable, he said, as the nature of the MCAT had changed. The exam now was primarily focused on both qualitative and quantitative analytical skills, rather than a general fund of knowledge. Since those skills were required in my current career and used daily, he reasoned that I would earn highly competitive scores.

Although I was content, my wife knew there would be an underlying regret that I was not a physician, since that had been my quest since early childhood. She told me of her discussion and the new knowledge that she had gained regarding the MCAT. This was truly interesting information, and my mind began to race with all the possibilities. First and foremost, I have always believed that my *raison d'etre* was to become a physician. Perhaps that quest could be achieved, if I were willing to retake the MCAT. It was a long shot, considering my past performance. Being a physician-scientist would enable me to treat patients and perhaps gain insight to clinically relevant and needed research that I could also pursue. Maybe this was why my life followed so many paths. Was this my fate? Was this what I would do?

As usual, Bonnie encouraged me to follow my dreams. The lyrics of that 1961 Elvis song "Follow That Dream" came to mind:

> *When a dream is calling you, ...*
> *Well, you gotta follow that dream wherever that dream may lead ...*

So I did. The excitement in my soul was palpable, but I tried to contain it. There was a real fear that, once again, I would be rejected. But there was also a new confidence and an old voice in my head. "Perseverance, son. That is all it takes."

The third time was a charm! Not only did I do well on the MCAT, I scored in the top 3 percent nationally. Game on. We enjoyed living in Texas, and saw no reason to move. In fact, we thought we would like to stay in San Antonio. We already had a house, and we were familiar with the medical school. Nevertheless, I thought it was prudent to apply to all of the medical schools in Texas.

Most medical schools still had the same criteria of competitive MCAT scores and a total GPA above 3.5. Now I had both, having done so well in graduate school. But the final decision rests with the admissions committee following an interview with the candidate. I was not sure if the fact that I had earned a PhD and was so involved in research would be held against me. Also, at age twenty-nine, I would be older than many of the applicants. To my relief, at a meeting with Dr. Carlos Pestana, associate dean for student affairs and professor of surgery at the Medical School at San Antonio, I learned that these would be positive factors. This was the only medical school with a formula, or at least sharing the formula, that would be used for selecting the 1978 entering class. It was reassuring that rejections would not be issued in a capricious manner.

The dean shared that formula with all in attendance:

$$8x \text{ GPA (up to 3.5)}2 + (\text{cumulative MCAT x } 1.5) + R\,2 + D\,2 + Q\,2 + I\,2$$

This formula took into account grade inflation over the years, as well as gave extra points for outstanding MCAT performance, for a maximum of ninety-eight points. The last four categories related to non-cognitive assessments: R = pre-medical advisor's letter; D = academic distinctions such as advanced degrees, research, publications, and other achievements not covered in the MCAT; and Q = non-academic achievements such as employment and volunteer work. These three variables would contribute a maximum of 121 points. The fourth factor, I = individual's personality, maturity, motivation, and likelihood to fulfill society's needs for medical care, were all subjectively judged by the interview. This would be worth 100 points. He told us that the majority of applicants score relatively few points in the subjective areas, as a way of boosting an outstanding candidate to compensate for a less-distinguished academic record. Dr. Pestana also reminded us that there would be many exceedingly well-qualified applicants who would not get in due to the limited number of spaces. The maximum possible score would be 454 points, but scores above 300 almost would assure admission, based on past years (the preceding year cutoff point was a score of 260).

A quick calculation with my known GPA and MCAT scores gave me at least 200 points. Certainly I thought that I would earn at least half, and likely more than two-thirds of the subjective points. Thus, my expected score (even with an average or below average interview) would be over 300! That made my day. Time to celebrate, almost. Those who were well above 300 would receive immediate notification of acceptance, and then there would be a second round. By some time in February, all accepted applicants and those on an alternative list would be known.

Once again, disappointment came as I had not received a notification with the first group of accepted applicants. Agonizing over this, I kept recalculating my score and wondered why I was not in that group. Oh well, certainly I would be in the next group. That letter never came! Once again, the quest was threatened. Fortunately, I had become more assertive over the years. The registrar told me that if I had not received a letter, then I was not accepted. I asked what the cutoff score had been. He looked it up, and I recalculated my score based on the formula, to show him that I should have been accepted unless I got a zero for my interview. "Please," I begged, "look into my case. See what happened, and let me know." He said it was an unusual request but my argument made sense. After what seemed like an eternity, he reappeared from the back office.

"I have some good news; you will be accepted."

I was shocked! Was this true? After all these years, was my quest going to be successful? How could he be sure that I was accepted, when less than an hour ago he was certain that I had not been? He explained that there was an error of input for my scores, but double-checking and correcting that placed me among the top-scoring applicants. Fortunately, he said, this was discovered before the deadline date, which would have made it too late to correct. Suppose I had not known about the scoring formula? What if I had not been persistent and assertive? Before leaving, I shook his hand, but I really felt like hugging and kissing him!

The joy, exuberance, and news of my acceptance to the medical school at San Antonio moved through our circle of family and friends like wildfire, almost as fast as Facebook would allow today. No one could believe it, especially me. Thank goodness for the fair, transparent, and objective scoring formula that San Antonio used as a tool for the admissions process. Thanks to Dr. Pestana for sharing that formula. Other schools in the state were more capricious, and I could recall questions during some interviews that reflected bias relating to my family, motivation for changing careers, and flexible long-term goals that would possibly include research as well as direct patient care. I still had an interview scheduled at Baylor, but I cancelled, knowing that San Antonio was where I wanted to stay.

"He used to be a *cell doctor*, but now he will be a *people doctor*." That is how Christa explained it to her friend when she told her that I was going to become a doctor.

Informing Dr. McGuire about my career change was a little daunting. One never knew how he would react to change that he did not implement. He reported surprise but congratulated me. Then he asked me how I would meet the obligations of my NIH-supported research agreement. Evidently there was a stipulation that failure to do two years of full-time research beyond the two years that they financially supported me would require payback. The formula for payback was equivalent to about four times the amount of money they gave me! Borrowing money for medical school was going to put me into significant debt, but this additional $80,000 would be extremely burdensome.

Dr. McGuire's advice was to find out what NIH defined as full-time research. It was twenty hours per week. That was doable. Dr. McGuire hired me as a consultant, and for the first two non-clinical years of medical school I also worked twenty hours a week in his lab, advising on cell culture development, maintenance, and problem-solving. During that time, I continued to do research. My research aimed to develop a normal breast cell line—one that would allow long-term comparative experiments with breast cancer cell lines. That was challenging, as normal cells have a defined *in vitro* life span. But the research possibilities made it worth the effort. However, only short-term experiments could be done with the cells that I separated from human milk or surgical specimens from breast reduction mammoplasties. They would lyse and die unpredictably in culture, so it was difficult to separately analyze the effects of treatment versus those effects due to normal ageing processes.

CHAPTER 8

Dad Misses It

Personal Challenges

Admission to medical school was the major final and consequential step toward succeeding in my quest to become a doctor. But entrance to medical school does not guarantee that the medical degree will be earned. Because medical school entrance is so competitive, very few students fail to graduate. Some, however, never make it for various reasons that may include bad choices or uncontrollable events or both. Sometimes it is a bad fit for that person, and for some persons, cognitive difficulties or previously unrecognized pathological behavior erupts.

For me, there were specific unique challenges. Medical school classes consumed about six to eight hours daily, Monday through Friday. The amount of material to learn, the reading assignments, and other out-of-classroom responsibilities entailed an equivalent amount of dedicated time. Specifically, my NIH payback required twenty hours of actual presence in the laboratory weekly, so that occupied my full weekend and occasional other commitments. That left about four or five hours for sleep. In addition, I tried to be involved in all of our family affairs, and certainly with our children on a daily basis. At the start of medical school, my wife was pregnant with our third child, Galen (yes, named after the famous Greek physician, surgeon, and philosopher). Usually, I spent the first couple of hours with the kids as soon as I got home and waited until they went to bed to resume my studies. Often, I would then run a few miles to the local school, run a dozen laps around the track, then run back home refreshed and ready to study. Actually, I was only good for an hour or two of studying before falling asleep at my desk.

Financially, I still had debts from my undergraduate and graduate studies. Borrowing throughout medical school to pay for tuition, supplies, and fees, as well as to support a family of our size, added significantly to our debt. The residency years would add even more debt, as residents' salaries were not enough to live on ($13,000 per year, with an approximately $1,000/year increase over the three years). Bonnie worked at Sears and later at the University of Texas continuing medical education office in order to help. However, the cost of child care, and the overall family stress, did not make this practical. We could not elicit grandparent or family help, as all of our relatives lived more than eighteen hundred miles away from us. Bonnie also would provide some limited child care in our house. One year, she recruited me to play Santa on weekends at Sears during the Christmas holidays. That was an experience that still makes me appreciate all commercial Santas. I developed a mild hip synovitis as a result of the heavy adults sitting on my leg. Jokingly, I talked about sending a letter to the editor of a medical journal describing a new occupational risk: "Santa synovitis."

Our house was small, at less than one thousand square feet. Since we rarely used the one-car garage for the car, we decided to remodel it, converting it to an additional living space. Once again, my skills as a carpenter came into use, and we remodeled the garage for the cost of materials only. This I did in my "spare time." In order to prevent the need for a wall heater-air conditioning unit, I decided to extend ductwork from our house into the ceiling space above the garage. This required buying flexible ductwork that could be cut into the fixed duct structure, and directed to a couple of ceiling vents. Of course, there were not enough daylight hours, so much of this remodeling was done in the evening.

"Bob, Bob, are you okay?" Bonnie's worried voice alerted me. She had not heard any noises, and it was now 11:00 pm. I could hear Bonnie's voice, but it seemed like a dream. Where was she, and where was I? In a few moments, I realized that I had fallen asleep in the attic while installing the ductwork. "Like father, like son." I was and still am a workaholic.

Unlike my father, I found ways to spend quality time with my wife and children while pursuing my career goals. Although Dad engaged us in his projects, he rarely involved himself in our interests. In fact, our needs were often viewed as a disruption of his work. Consciously, I decided to not create such a void in my relationships with our children. I would make up for the scarcity of hours by giving undivided attention to them while enjoying family activities such as going to the park, camping, visiting the zoo, playing in the yard, and other low-cost highly involved activities. I engaged them in gardening and other activities. We brought in enough dirt to create a small garden in the backyard, and I extended the concrete patio off the back door and built a roof structure over it, while closing off one end in the cold season to create a plastic enclosed greenhouse. They "helped" in the construction of a raised playhouse to substitute as a treehouse. They spent hours on a swing set we bought and installed in the yard, as well as time on a teeter-totter I made.

Fortunately, at that time, the medical school at San Antonio had a pass-fail-honors grading system. Although the venture into that type of system has proved to not be as effective as a grade point system, it was perfect for my needs. The idea was that a pass-fail-honors system would take the emphasis off grades and place it rightfully on learning. Of course, this assumes that all the students are highly motivated to be the best doctor possible and would give 100 percent effort. That assumption did not account for the fact that some students do just what is needed to get by. Apparently, there is also difficulty in the comparative evaluation of the vast majority of students who pass but do not achieve honors. Having applied my prior studies to another career before medical school, I was perhaps better able than younger students straight from college to understand what information was needed as a fund of knowledge for rapid decision making. Thus, I could discern what had to be memorized and what was more suitable as reference material. I also understood the importance of being able to apply knowledge to patient diagnosis and treatment. The advantage for me was that I would not have to memorize dozens of reference tables and charts, just to get by on an exam. I could set priorities. My thoughts were always centered on what I really needed to do know to provide excellence in patient care, rather than how would I study and compete for an *A* instead of a *B*+.

From a practical standpoint, the pass-fail-honors system allowed me to meet my other obligations to family and research. In other words, it was a boon to time management. It also helped me to keep my priorities right. For example, the night before a renal pathophysiology term examination, my daughter was to perform in her first Christmas play at church. By the time we went there and returned, I would have to stay up all night to study, or else get sleep and hope to do well on the exam. As her dad, it was a no-brainer; I would attend her performance and worry about review for the

examination later. I still remember the excitement of her participation, the proud look of accomplishment for her, and our feelings
of joy as parents. I remember very little about the exam, for which
I did not cram, except that almost everyone, including me, failed
it. We were rescued by a grade curve. In addition, I still remember
stopping to help a child who incurred a compound fracture of
his lower extremity in a motor vehicle-pedestrian accident that
occurred in front of us en route to the play. That child was someone I met again the next day, while rounding on our hospitalized
patients.

Medical Education

Medical school is four years in duration. It would be such an incredible loss to miss those years of your children's development,
and to miss the joys and responsibilities of parenting. Those early
childhood years are especially critical to developing the capacities
to learn, and for social-emotional-cognitive development. Taking
time to read to my children almost nightly helped to lay a foundation for their future learning and a lifetime love of books and learning. I am sure that many parents face these same issues of balanc-
ing careers with parenting. This is now almost taken for granted,
whereas back then, the traditional one parent stays at home while
the other is employed or pursues a career was more prevalent.

As a parent and pediatrician, I am impressed by the ingenuity
and time management skills of my children and others who advance their careers while spending quality time with their families. What previously was seen as a detriment to families has now
become almost a necessity and is considered an enhancement of
one's life.

The first two years of our medical school concentrated mostly on laying a foundation of knowledge about the human body and behavior. There was very little to no clinical experience. We learned about creating a differential diagnosis list and making accurate diagnosis by deductive reasoning. Treatment was not as important a focus for us. We learned that most diagnoses were made based on history-taking and physical examination skills and that laboratory and imaging studies were secondary and confirmatory only. So that is what we focused on: learning the pathophysiology and etiology of diseases, and how to take accurate and complete histories and to engage in excellence of observation during physical examinations. All else was reserved for the "clinical years," where focus would be on diagnosis and treatment. The third and fourth years would be so time-consuming with real patient diagnosis, treatment, and care, that further in-depth learning would be self-motivated, based on the problems encountered with our patients.

Out of necessity, our history and physical examination skills were learned on each other, during those preclinical years. That's right, we learned *on* as well as from each other. This made for interesting relationships among the students, as we learned a lot of personal information about each other, which we learned to keep private. There were some "proxies" hired by the school, to enable us to learn to do pelvic examinations and to take appropriate histories. Sometimes, though, we did embarrassing things to each other in order to desensitize ourselves appropriately and to gain experience that would not be at a cost to patient care. It also gave us an appreciation for how patients would feel about those invasive examinations. For example, members of our gender-mixed work groups would agree to exchange breast examinations for prostate examinations, by lottery, or as we called it the "un-luck of the draw"! We also practiced taking blood pressures, doing complete physical examinations, and starting intravenous lines on each other. Details of anatomy were learned in class, and on human cadavers that we dissected. Those people who donated their bodies to such studies were highly respected and appreciated. That experience helped to desensitize us to the surgical aspects of our profession, as well as to learn specific skills.

Animal labs also provided meaningful experiences. It seemed cruel but necessary to learn on animals, as there were no computer graphics or models to learn from back then. It was my understanding that those dogs were scheduled for euthanasia before being donated. One day's experience in the dog lab helped me to later save a child's life in the pediatric intensive care unit (PICU) as a resident physician. Specifically, I learned how to create, diagnose, and treat a pericardial effusion in an anesthetized dog, and how to do percutaneous injections of medicines into a beating heart.

The patient referred to was a child who suddenly got worse in the PICU. I was called to see him, checked his heart and lungs, read the monitor and EKG, and then diagnosed a pericardial effusion. We did not have ultrasound-guided procedures, so I had to rely on the skill that I had learned on a dog to aspirate the fluid from around the beating heart by placing a needle through the skin and into that small space. On another occasion, I had to inject epinephrine into the heart of a child who was not responding to our advanced life support measures. That patient's life was also saved, in part due to that procedure.

The Clinical Years

Everyone, it seemed, looked forward to the clinical years. After all, that is why we went to medical school. The first two years had felt more like college than medical school, with the exceptions of physical diagnoses and the cadaver and animal labs. By the time the third year came around, we were ready. At least we thought we were. Suddenly it dawned on us that we knew very little about the treatment of disease, although we thought we could make accurate diagnoses. The best way to learn, we were told, was to read extensively each day about the differential diagnosis, etiology, pathophysiology, and treatment strategies for a patient we were following. Usually, we would pick the case that seemed most interesting to us, or the one assigned by our resident or staff physician mentors. This was a strategy to learning that I continued during and after the residency years. I would view each patient encounter as an individual with something new to teach me. So, although I had seen hundreds of cases of diarrhea, there would always be some "take home" message for me in the diagnosis, treatment, or particular meaning of this disease to the patient and/or the patient's caretakers. This attitude made both lifelong learning and patient care interesting for me and never routine.

Armed with a short white coat, stethoscope, tongue depressors, ophthalmoscope and otoscope kit, head lamp, tourniquet, reflex hammer, and tuning forks, I ventured forth with my black bag on my first day. Not to be unprepared for anything, I also carried reference books on emergency procedures, medicines, differential diagnoses, and specific manuals for that month's particular clinical rotation. (Lucky students today just need access to a smartphone or computer!) This was the typical medical student gear. Being a student was going to be an important part of the medical team taking care of patients. In San Antonio, we rotated through experiences at the teaching hospitals and clinics, which included the Bexar County Hospital (later called Medical Center Hospital), the Veterans Hospital, Santa Rosa Children's Hospital, and the Brady Green indigent clinics. Most of our medical school mentors were faculty at the University of Texas Health Sciences Center at San

Antonio (UTHSCSA). However, some were clinical instructors who were physicians in private or small group practices and who may have had affiliations with other hospitals as well.

"Do you know why they call you medical students slugs?" queried our intern. "It's because you are so slow," he continued.

The reference analogy was clearly to the shell-less mollusk. That only added to the trepidation that I had for having read *The House of God*.[37] The point was accurately made. As students, we would take an hour or more to get the history and do the physical examination that an intern or resident could do in fifteen minutes. Getting lab and imaging results, finding charts, drawing blood, writing orders, or doing any of the scut (short for scuttle, an oxymoron for "slug" work; primarily used to denote the less-desirable deeds) jobs we were assigned or expected to do would all occur at what would seem an eternity to those in the hierarchy above us. That hierarchy was student to intern to resident to fellow to attending. Oftentimes one could place nurses and other experienced personnel well above us, and sometimes above the inexperienced interns. There are many reasons for that, but inexperience and fear of missing something or making a mistake or doing less-than-perfect work all contributed to the slowness.

Our (my) goals were simple. Do no harm. Please the intern. Please the nurse, who could be the best resource. Please the upper level resident. Please the attending. And somewhere in there, please the patient. Patience, perseverance, and productivity would be paramount. Learn something new. Be a "gunner" and outperform your peers. That is how one will be evaluated, by immediate comparisons. If you rotate through with exceptionally talented students, then you look unprepared. If you rotate with less-talented students,

---

[37] Samuel Shem, *The House of God*. (New York: Berkley, 1978).

then you look exceptional. Be sure to know everything about your patient and the information needed to manage that patient. Also, read broadly about the patient's problem, and be prepared to present a two- to three-minute in-depth discussion about common as well as uncommon conditions on rounds. (By the way, there was no Google, no PubMed, no WebMD, etc.; the library was closed or not helpful; computers were not yet in routine use; laptops or other personal devices were not yet invented; medical records were handwritten and mostly unintelligible; there were no instant readings of x-rays; and you had to find and read them yourself.) It doesn't matter if you don't sleep when on call; what matters is your performance and how you make life easier for everyone else. Be prepared for work rounds, resident rounds, and attending rounds. Then be prepared to act normal when you get home.

Expectations of medical students seemed widely variable, depending on whether one was on surgery, medicine, or psychiatry. Similarly, there were variations as to expectations in the clinic and hospital and variations depending upon whom your residents and attending physicians were. The amount of autonomy might or might not depend upon your proven responsible behavior. It would only be predictable once you identified the leaders of your particular team. How thorough or brief your presentations were also depended on the noted variables.

Typically, surgeons wanted quick, concise, actionable information, and short written notes that updated the patient's status. They believed you should be able to see one procedure, do one, and teach one. Internists wanted you to wax elegantly about the differential diagnosis, the options for care, the immediate plans, and actions should the patient's status change. You would be expected to teach everyone on the team something they didn't already know or remember. You would be "pimped" in depth about topics that may or may not have related to your patient, as a means of determining your basic fund of knowledge. The psychiatrists wanted to talk, and most plans were to observe or refer. Rarely was medical therapy recommended, in contrast to today's healthcare, as mostly there were no good or effective medicines. Most of their patient care related to group or psychotherapy or cognitive behavioral management strategies. Any other medical or surgical problems, regardless of simplicity, were expected to be referred to those specialists.

After being assigned specific patients, we would be expected to turn in write-ups (within twenty-four hours or less) that summarized the history, physical examination findings, the results of laboratory and imaging studies, procedures performed, differential diagnosis with deductive reasoning arguments for choosing the most likely diagnosis, and plans for management both short- and long-term.

One of my attending physicians required us to be able to summarize all the pertinent information in one sentence, claiming this would demonstrate one's insight to the patient's status. It would also enable one to present necessary information verbally and concisely to colleagues to whom a patient is referred. For every body organ or system, we had to include an endless description of all negative as well as positive findings. For example, the eye description alone would require a listing of the normal and abnormal findings of the external eye, sclera, tear ducts, eyelids, conjunctiva, eye muscle movements, pupil, iris, retina, and optic disc; it would also include presence or absence of symptoms such as diplopia, scotomata, blurred vision, pain, visual disturbance, history of foreign body or trauma, itchiness, and so forth. Multiply this descriptive approach by all the organs on physical examination and how burdensome a report it becomes is obvious. That really made me appreciate the concise and precise surgeon's approach, for example, the "eye exam was *normal, except for* minimal redness of the bulbar conjunctiva; there was no history of foreign body or injury." The assumption was that one's description of "normal" followed an in-depth evaluation of those things as noted in the preceding longer version of the eye report. What could be presented in one page, and summarized in one sentence, often would become a four-plus-page report. At this stage of our education, the attending usually preferred to see thorough and exhaustive reports, rather than precise and concise presentations that would be expected as residents. Brevity of reports should not substitute for thorough evaluations. They were only to facilitate rapid communications.

Students quickly learn to adapt to the eccentricities of each attending physician or mentor. Doctor A may be obsessed with cutting tape for bandages perfectly without irregularities of the ends. Doctor B requires a rectal examination of every patient in GI clinic who presents with chronic abdominal pain. Dr. C requires a list of ten possible causes of every prominent symptom. Dr. D requires dilation of the eyes for thorough evaluation of the retina. Dr. E rarely prescribes antibiotics, for which Dr. F almost always prescribes antibiotics. Dr. G always recommends cough suppressants, whereas Dr. H lectures one against prescribing any cough suppressants. Dr. I prescribes modified diet and anti-diarrheal medications, whereas others never do, electing to let diarrhea run its course and simply replace losses with nutritional liquids. Dr. J wants brief presentations with only pertinent positives and negatives, whereas other attending physicians require in-depth presentations. Dr. K resists most referrals. Dr. L refers almost everyone. Dr. M always wants supportive lab and imaging studies. Dr. N rarely orders lab or imaging studies. Dr. O rarely visits the bedside, whereas others conduct all patient rounds and discussions at the bedside and involve the patient. The lists of variable approaches to patient care and physician eccentricities can be endless.

Fortunately, nowadays there is a concerted effort to standardize approaches to patient care, meeting what are considered evidence-based criteria, and diminishing variability in diagnosing, testing, and treating patients. Meeting those standards must be documented, risking financial consequences, accusations of impropriety, and public disclosure of "quality" issues for not. Patient satisfaction and meeting standards of care affect physician compensation as well as employment or career development. The clinical performance evaluations of medical students are also now more standardized and reflect on how many of these expectations are met.

Although EBM (evidenced-based medicine) is considered the gold standard for patient care, there continues to be an art of medicine that is important. Someone once told me that the nature of our profession is such that it centers around two people: one looking for help, and one offering help. The art is to personalize that care. That is difficult to teach but easier to demonstrate. Thus, good mentors can facilitate what may or may not be intuitive to the student or primarily "left brain" person. Over the years, EBM changes as new information is realized. Thus it is important, as part of that art, to consider experience and reason in all therapeutic options. Often anecdotal experiences fit patterns that stimulate further research that then leads to new information and new EBM. Personalizing patient care means involving patients in decisions about their care. The physician is obligated to know and to keep up with changes and to present EBM in an easy-to-understand manner. The physician also must consider the value of anecdotal experiences and reason in meeting the patient's expectations. Thus, I believe that the science and art of the practice of medicine are inseparable.

It behooves us to resist "cookbook" standardization of care, just to facilitate the access and affordability of that care. For example, advanced practice professionals (physician assistants and nurse practitioners) serve many valuable roles in underserved areas and specialty care. They are also more affordable than physicians. Thus, there is a national endeavor to promote their use throughout the system. That is fine, but those roles need to be clearly differentiated from that which requires the expertise and in-depth training of physicians. Physician-led healthcare is a must, to ensure the highest quality care. The accountants and politicians, important in making that care affordable and accessible, must not be at the pinnacle of care. Although it is understandable that "no manpower" and "no money" means "no mission," the needs of the patient must be the foremost consideration in delivering that care. Surely our country has the resources to educate and provide the manpower needed to deliver the highest quality of personalized care to *everyone*, not just to those who could afford it. We just need the political will to do so.

As medical students, we learn as apprentices of specific mentors but also by experience, reading, attending seminars and grand rounds or other continuing medical education lectures, and reviewing care presented at morbidity and mortality conferences, and from other members of the healthcare team. We learn from the patient and families. We learn by frequent introspection, review of our actions, and holding ourselves accountable to the highest professional and humanistic standards. There are extrinsic motivations to learn, such as grading, liability, lifestyle, and licensing. However, the best students are intrinsically motivated and curious. They understand the importance of professional responsibilities and personalized care. They understand the importance of changing practice parameters, as new research is confirmed and as it changes existing evidence-based medicine. Excellence as a physician is their *raison d'etre.*

Often, students learn from each other, as well as from other members of the healthcare team. Sometimes that is a good thing, whereas it can also be detrimental. One particular experience stands out in my memory. First, let me point out that I am very indebted to the many nurses who guided me as a student, welcomed me in my new and challenging role, and helped me to understand care from the patient's point of view. Indeed, nursing is "the caring profession" and is exemplified by the willingness to go above and beyond job descriptions to comfort, to be compassionate, and to be caring in very personal and effective ways. In fact, one of my pediatric attending physicians in the intensive care unit emphasized that we should listen to the nurses caring for the patient and include them in our data gathering and plans for the patient. After all, they spend an entire shift and multiple days with our patients, whereas the physician's time with the patient is extremely limited to minutes each day. That made sense, and that was a commitment I made for my entire career. More often than not, a nurse's input made a huge difference in the care I provided to my patients. However, when that input seems to contrast with your own intuitive belief or analysis, then caution is advised.

Sadly, there is one experience that stands out in my memory. In the process of evaluating and treating a pediatric patient who was admitted for seizures and possible meningitis, it was my role as a student to do a thorough examination and the procedures necessary to gather critical data and provide treatment. This often included blood drawing, placing intravenous lines, and doing a so-called septic workup, which also involved percutaneous bladder aspiration of urine to rule out urinary tract infection, and a lumbar puncture to obtain cerebrospinal fluid for analysis. Most often parents are asked to wait outside of the room until these procedures are done. As a parent, I thought it was very reasonable to allow parents in the room whenever they so choose. As a medical student, this added to my performance anxiety, but I thought it was the right thing to do.

"Don't you ever do that again!" the nurse scolded me.

"But the parents asked, and I thought—"

"That's probably why you couldn't get the intravenous line placed."

She continued to say that the problem is that parents will think less of you as a physician if they see that you are unable to obtain a specimen or start a line when needed. Then she proceeded to show me how easy it is, and some tricks of the trade. This nurse was an LVN but was very skilled with procedures and was often called to help resident physicians and students having difficulty. Her assistance was appreciated, as often these infants or children are so sick that the effectiveness of care depends upon rapid, efficient testing and treatment.

However, her advice just seemed wrong to me. Perhaps it was my paternal instincts or just my maturity as an "older" student, but I believed it was every parent's right to stay with their child during the entire course of care, even during procedures, as they would better appreciate the challenges of care and would be there for the child as well. I still believe that. In the PICU at Bexar County Hospital, that skillful nurse always seemed to be the first person at a respiratory or cardiac arrest and would initiate life-saving procedures. In retrospect, that nurse, Genene Anne Jones, may have had duplicitous reasons for wanting parents absent. Eventually she was convicted of killing fifteen-month old Chelsea McClellan with succinylcholine and attempted murder of Rolando Jones with heparin, but likely had a role in the deaths of somewhere between one and forty-six infants and children in her care.[38]

Emotions are front and center for the student. One feels empathy and compassion for the patient and family. Resentment for time away from one's own family may not be consciously recognized, but it may present as difficulties with team members or others. Similarly, the stresses of meeting everyone's expectations, especially your own, carry over to the home environment. Paradoxical feelings of confidence and incompetence, exuberance and depression, satisfaction and disappointment, altruism and selfishness, and anxiety and calm are ever present like the twists and turns of a roller coaster ride. Experience, education, efficiency, and effectiveness in one's role as a student eventually ease the emotional journey but never erase it from the career. The emotions are what make us human, and acceptance of that makes the journey enjoyable.

Decision to Become a Pediatrician

Some memories of my medical experiences beg to be told. For each one told, there are dozens if not hundreds more, some remembered holistically and others in part, but still felt.

One kind elderly gentleman was admitted to our team's medical service for chronic cough. He gave me two gifts that I will always remember. The first was a Susan B. Anthony silver dollar, which he said would be worth something more someday, and it was given in appreciation of the care and compassion that he experienced. The other gift was a conversion of my skin test for tuberculosis (PPD) from negative at the entrance of medical school to positive by the end! He was the only patient for whom I cared who was

---

[38] Peter Elkind, *The Death Shift: The True Story of Nurse Genene Jones and the Texas Baby Murders.* (New York: Viking Adult, 1989).

unexpectedly found to have active tuberculosis. Unfortunately, my failure to take appropriate precautions against airborne pathogens also gave me a lesson not to forget. After nine months of isoniazid therapy, the tuberculosis bug was evidently eradicated, as all of my chest x-rays since then have been negative for disease.

Fortunately, professionals as well as hospitals and clinics are nowadays more cognizant of the need and are required to always take precautions not only against airborne pathogens but also against those transmitted by human body fluids. Thus, extensive education about how diseases spread, the universal use of gloves, masks, appropriate gowns and gear, environmental service procedures for decontamination of surfaces, hand washing and antimicrobial gels, along with restrictions of food and drink from patient care areas, and other precautions are now expected and routine.

Never before had I realized how extraordinarily burdened some people are with disease. The very first surgery for which I attended as a medical student made me count my blessings. This poorly controlled diabetic who recently had a below-the-knee amputation for gangrene needed a cholecystectomy for recurrent painful gallstones and acute ascending cholangitis. The appendix would also be removed, as a precautionary measure, as that is a useless organ and could put this fragile patient at risk for peritonitis in the future. Unexpectedly, as the surgeon entered the abdominal cavity and performed a routine manual exploration prior to the planned surgery, some adhesions from a prior surgery were disrupted, causing extensive bleeding from the spleen. This patient also needed an emergent splenectomy to save his life. Post-operatively, he expressed his gratitude for the care he had received. His emotional acceptance of his condition was an example of the grace that I would witness numerous patients exhibit over the years.

"Doctor, don't let her fool you. She needs help," warned the tearful mother.

Her beautiful, quiet, and calm teenage daughter was well-groomed and wore prominent red lipstick and rouge. Convincingly, she reported that her parents overreact to everything and that she was brought in for evaluation simply because she had thrown a mild temper tantrum at home. She had thrown more than that, as her parents reported that she also threw a chair out her closed bedroom window and threatened them with a butcher knife. They recounted many other incidents of psychotic behavior. Paradoxically, this girl appeared normal, using the mnemonic device AMSIT, whereby psychiatrists assess the appearance, mood, sensorium, intelligence, and thought processes of patients. My attending counseled that she should be admitted to the hospital for further behavioral observation. The goal was to determine if she was indeed psychotic or just a teenager with anger management difficulties. She did not use tobacco, alcohol, or illicit drugs. A drug screen supported that statement.

Indeed, she was psychotic. On my nights on call in the hospital, she would seek my attention, endlessly, until I firmly insisted that she be allowed one discussion session with me. Any other non-emergent issues should wait for group or individual sessions the next day. To ensure my privacy, I had closed the call room door in order to document on patient charts, read, or have discussions with other team members. Eerily, I could hear footsteps in the hall, and the shadow under the door revealed that a person turned to stand outside my door. After five or ten minutes, she would say, "I know you are in there." I would answer, "Go back to your room." For hours, she would repeat this behavior frequently, standing there for ten minutes, but saying nothing. She also acted out in the hospital, angrily threatening support staff at times. On occasion, she was found in bed with other adolescent patients. Her affect and behaviors during those several weeks of observation confirmed the parents' earlier reports. The psychiatrists recommended transfer to a facility for longer-term psychiatric care.

Those clinical years were replete with strange, sad, and wonderful patient experiences. With each rotation, I envisioned myself as having a career in that specialty. Before beginning medical school, I thought that I would become a general practitioner (now called family physician), pediatrician, or psychiatrist. The excitement, for better or worse, of each rotation gave me insight to my own true feelings and enticed me toward other career opportunities.

Rotating through surgery, I envisioned myself as a general surgeon always fixing things, as an orthopedist ("the carpenter doctors") using saws, hammers, and drills, or even as a brain surgeon who perhaps one day would be able to save people who had been injured like my brother. My attraction to psychiatry was stronger, as human behavior is intriguing for me and understanding and treating mental health issues is a unique challenge and joy. Dad's advice in jest to become a psychiatrist to figure out "what makes this family tick" was an earnest interest for me. However, I soon learned that I was unable to get patients' problems out of my mind, even when I was at home or on vacation. The emotional toll on me and my family would be too great to pursue that as a career. As a general practitioner or family physician, I could set bone fractures, analyze and help family dynamics and mental health issues, deliver babies, do minor surgeries, and have continuity of care with my patients throughout all aspects of their life from cradle to the grave. That was really attractive. Surprisingly, I found that sometimes I resented time that I spent with some patients because of their resistance to help to change their behaviors to ensure better health.

Knowing what needs to be done and not getting it done was more than frustrating; it was exacerbating.

By contrast, as a pediatrician, I could take care of medical and surgical problems for newborns, infants, children, and adolescents. I could assist at high-risk deliveries to ensure full attention to the health and survival of the newborn, and I could help new parents to begin their long journey with a confident step forward. Moreover, my impact would be greater, since there would be an opportunity to correct unhealthy behaviors by appealing to the parents or other caretakers as well as the patient. There could be no greater opportunity for preventive healthcare measures. Encouraging immunizations and parental involvement with positive, warm, and nurturing interactions with their child, and teaching parents how to provide opportunities for their child's development, would be primary objectives. The early detection of disease could allow early treatment and considerable reduction in childhood morbidity and mortality. Certainly, if I could teach patients and parents about risk-taking behaviors and provide insight for healthier lifestyles, then maybe I could help to prevent injuries and tragedies such as happened with my brother. The opportunity to devote a lifetime to the optimal growth and development of those in the first two decades of life was irresistible. Any impact that I would have could last a lifetime, or even transfer through generations. Thus, I concluded that the best profession in the world for me was to be someone's pediatrician!

More Heartbreak

To become a pediatrician, one has to complete three years of specialty training beyond graduation from medical school and successful specific testing for certification by the American Board of Pediatrics. There are lifetime requirements of periodic testing and other activities for maintenance of that certification. During that training, known as a pediatric residency, just like in medical school, there is ample opportunity to decide what area of pediatrics interests you the most. Subspecialty training, such as becoming a pediatric cardiologist, would require an additional three years of specific cardiovascular education, relevant skills development and experiences, as well as certification in that subspecialty.

By the end of my third year of medical school, I was committed to becoming a pediatrician, so many of my elective rotations were directed to extra experience with child psychiatry, physiatry, orthopedics, and as much exposure to the care of children as possible to help prepare me for specialty training in a pediatric residency. My preference would be to get accepted into the pediatric residency program at the UTHSCSA, since I was familiar with the program and facilities and we would not have to move. That preference was almost changed by a trip home to Pennsylvania during the Christmas break in 1980.

"Oh, Bobby, I want you to check out your dad. He has had a bad cough and some chest pain," Mom said.

"Dad, how long has this been going on?"

"Oh, just a few weeks."

Mom interrupted, "It's been going on for months."

"No it hasn't, Betty. It all started after I had been breaking up some concrete with a sledgehammer, last month."

As a very concerned son, and thorough medical student, I must have asked a few dozen more questions relevant to the cough and chest pain. Then I proceeded with a physical examination. Two or three times, I tapped the diaphragm of my stethoscope to be sure it was working appropriately. It was. The absence of breath sounds on half of Dad's lung fields alarmed me. So I talked with him and mom about the possibilities, giving a differential diagnosis, and insisting that he get in to see his doctor immediately.

They hospitalized him and drained more than a liter of bloody, thick pleural fluid. Chest x-rays had confirmed complete absence of air in half of his lung and diminished aeration in the other half. No wonder that he coughed and had chest pain! The news was bad. Most likely cancer or tuberculosis would be diagnosed. The final tests confirmed that he had mesothelioma. Evidently his exposure to asbestos filled air when they insulated the pipes in the boiler room at work thirty some years ago was the cause. Workers were not protected with masks or respirators. Dad reported that at the time, the air was so thick with the asbestos that he could hardly see the other workers. That is not atypical, as mesothelioma arises three to four decades after inhalation of asbestos into the lungs. I do not know if any of his coworkers lived long enough to develop mesothelioma.

Prognosis is poor for mesothelioma, even now. The doctors told Dad that he could have a pleural decortication, fluid drainage, and medications to ease his symptoms, but his life expectancy would be six months or less. Sad and determined, I talked with oncologists I knew from working in Dr. McGuire's research lab. They confirmed the prognosis. Yes, they could try some experimental treatments, if they could get institutional review board approval, but at best it would buy him another six months. It could hasten his demise. Excited about the possibility of buying time until better options developed, I presented the option to Dad. He refused. I was angry. How could he not take advantage of this slim chance for treatment? At least it would give him, although infinitesimal, some chance of survival. He argued that no one lives forever, and he would rather just quietly die at home. He wanted no part of treatments that would make the last six or more months of his life full of pain, vomiting, and other side effects. There was no way he would want to spend those precious months in a hospital environment. There was no way he would burden his children with the financial debt that would be incurred.

Eventually, I realized that Dad had made the right choice. Dad always was "ahead of his time" in his thinking, as he not-so-modestly often proclaimed. We knew almost nothing about the research on death and dying. Hospice care emphasizes the psychological preparation of the patient and loved ones for death, and the provision of comfort and quality of life in the final days or months of a terminal illness. Hospice care and the dignity of dying at home, among your closest loved ones, did not flourish in the United States until 1982, when Medicare agreed to cover some of the cost of services provided for that. Although there were no such services provided for Dad and his family, dying at home made a personal event personal. However, it was heartbreaking. This strong and perfectly healthy man who had never been sick "one day in his life" got a terminal illness at a relatively young age, sixty-six. He had always looked at least a decade younger than his years, but in the course of the next six months, he would look a couple of decades older. Mom felt guilty for having wished a slow, painful death on him in the heat of those horrible arguments they had. Dad felt guilty for not spending more time with her and his children. "We get old too soon, and smart too late," so goes a Pennsylvania Dutch adage.

Because of my desire to be near Dad and Mom during the last months of his life, and to support Mom emotionally after his death, I applied to a couple of residency programs near them in Pennsylvania and Connecticut. Trips to those interviews also gave me opportunities to visit with both Mom and Dad. Dad was thrilled beyond belief that he helped to raise a son who would soon become a doctor. Perseverance was what he taught, and he knew that would be key to the success of my quest. He hoped to live long enough to witness it. However, he missed it. Dad lived almost eleven months after his diagnosis but died seven months before the quest was realized and celebrated. How I wish he could have been there! He also had hoped that we would move back closer to family. However, that did not happen. I decided to accept the offer of a position in the pediatric residency at San Antonio and not to uproot our family. Mom had encouraged me to make my decision independently of our heartbreak, explaining that there was enough family close by for her. She was right. It was the right decision. But would I continue to make the right decisions?

PART 3

Beyond the Quest

CHAPTER 9

No Time to Sleep

After years of arduous study and accomplishments, overcoming barriers and distractions, I was proclaimed a doctor of medicine. The quest was realized! Now what? The Texas State Board of Medical Examiners would need to authorize and license me to practice medicine in the state of Texas. To practice in any other state would require separate licensing. I would have to pass the Texas Jurisprudence Exam to demonstrate knowledge of the laws of Texas and restrictions on my practice. In addition, a fee would be paid for licensing. Proof of continuing medical education would be required, and annual or biannual fees would need to be paid in subsequent years. Separate licenses to prescribe controlled substances, such as narcotics or certain stimulants, would be required from the state as well as federal governments. The quality of practice would forever be scrutinized by employers, colleagues, insurers, the medical board, other governmental agencies, and special interest groups.

Legally, I would be able to practice medicine once licensed. However, most doctors upon graduation have had very limited practical patient care experience. Thus, almost everyone has to go on to complete three years of supervised training in the area of one's career choice. Traditionally, that is called internship (the first year) and residency (the second and third years). Now those years are lumped together as a "residency" and referenced as specific postgraduate levels (i.e., PG1). After a three-year residency, another examination is required for board certification in that specialty. Subspecialists have additional testing and certification. Maintenance of certification requires ongoing compliance with board regulations and periodic future testing.

Where to begin? How to begin? Where to practice? What benefits are anticipated? What lifestyle is desired? Those are questions that would have been anticipated earlier, but now they are revisited. Residency provides new experiences, expertise, and introspection. Thus, career opportunities are researched and employment options reconsidered. Does the lure of an autonomous practice drive one's decision, or is a guaranteed income and group practice more appealing? What setting is desired, academic or not? How do family considerations and debt affect one's decisions?

The practice chosen may seem perfect or less fulfilling than anticipated. Over time, one's perspective may change. There may be financial debt, emotional damage, strained relationships, boredom, waning confidence, less autonomy than expected, required continuation of the quest for new knowledge in order to keep those special healing powers, subservience to patients' demands as well as employer, government, insurer, and professional association regulations that affect one's happiness. Happiness, though, comes from within and how we respond to what we experience.

Much lies beyond the quest to become a physician. Reality confronts idealism. As physician, your life continues even more integrated with people than ever before. What is different is that now thousands of lives will enter your life. You will enter their lives as well. It will become your privilege and responsibility to touch bodies in many ways, some of which are quite invasive. You will be privy to private information that others will not. Your actions may change lives forever in good and bad ways. You may save lives. You may take lives unintentionally. You may be a physician, skilled in the art and science of medicine or surgery or both, but you will remain a person with the same needs as those you serve. Preparing for how your life evolves thereafter is every bit as important as the quest. What will be your additional roles in the family, in the community, in the schools, in the profession, and in this life?

Following are some tales and memoirs of my experiences and career changes. Hopefully they will provide insight for those students and physicians pondering the above questions or struggling with career decisions.

Residency

Startled awake by the sound of honking horns, I realized that the traffic light was green. Where was I? What was I doing? En route home after having been on call at the hospital, I had fallen asleep at a traffic light on Bandera Highway. How long, I did not know. However, it sent a chill through me to realize that I had fallen asleep behind the wheel.

Pediatric residency was challenging physically, emotionally, intellectually, and socially. Unlike today, there were no restrictions on our work hours. Residency programs offer specialty training and supervised experiences to those who have become physicians, before releasing those physicians to the independent practice of medicine and surgery in the "real world." Close supervision of these rookie doctors saves lives and prevents much morbidity. This necessary and important post-graduate learning experience helps one to become confident as well as competent and compassionate. The realization that one's actions or inactions may be the difference between life or death, can be a daunting acknowledgment of the caveat to "do no harm."

Nevertheless, much harm can occur as a result of that training. The long hours without sleep impair one's judgment, decision-making, and the skill with which procedures are performed. Nighttime call is often not well-supervised, as interns or higher-level residents may be unwilling to disturb the attending physician, for various reasons. The attending may give strict instructions not to be disturbed except for something that truly cannot wait until the next morning, or for the death of a patient. The resident physician may feel too confident. Or the resident may not want to show any signs of dependence. The quantity of patient care affects the quality as well. Patients who suddenly worsen may require the bulk of the resident's time, leaving some care of the other patients to the less-experienced physicians, medical students, or nurses. Attention to detail wanes. Specimens may not make it to the lab, or the critical results may not be reviewed timely to prevent further morbidity. There were too many times that I witnessed these consequences of sleep deprivation. There were more occasions than one wherein I personally put patients at risk because of my fatigue or out of necessity for lack of resources in personnel, supplies, and communications.

"Dr. Burke, the pharmacy is calling and wants to know if you meant milligrams or micrograms," the nurse reported to me in the wee hours of the morning when I had been up all night caring for patients in the neonatal intensive care unit (NICU) and attending high-risk deliveries. The question was in reference to one of the ingredients in a NICU patient's hyper-alimentation order. Hyper-alimentation is specifically formulated nutrition that is given by intravenous route to keep patients alive until they are able to take food or formula orally. Upon reviewing my orders, I realized that I had indeed written for a thousand fold more salts than intended. Fortunately, the pharmacist, who also initially missed the error, realized something was wrong when he could not get the salts into solution! Catastrophe was avoided. Lessons learned: double or triple check all orders; listen and act earnestly when orders are questioned.

One of the benefits of training at the UTHSCSA hospitals and clinics was the experience gained from caring for a high volume of pediatric patients. In addition, one is exposed to a variety of illnesses, injuries, or diseases that may later be experienced only once in a lifetime. This exposure to an incredible gamut of pathology, the entire menu, allows one to create a meaningful differential for presenting symptoms, and to not miss what may be a rare or unusual condition presenting in the future. The long hours also allowed one to follow the presentation of an illness from beginning to end, providing a continuity of care and understanding of the progression of disease and the effects of treatments that may otherwise only be gained by reading or hearsay. Since I am a better visual learner, the hands-on experiences were critical to making me a better physician. One neurosurgical resident half-seriously complained to me because he was only on call every other night, thereby missing half the potentially valuable experiences!

Sometimes there were insufficient numbers of persons to care for the hospitalized patients due to a high census or sudden admission of numerous patients, thus requiring a dedication to providing timely and thorough care for one's patients. This meant that the physician (me) often had to perform duties that would be considered better leveraged to nurses or lab technicians or others. For example, it was not unusual for me to check vital signs, do frequent and serial examinations of the patient's status, obtain and take specimens to the laboratory, take the patient to imaging, follow-up on lab or imaging results, start intravenous lines, talk with worried or upset family members, change diapers, clean up soiled bed linens, and other tasks to ensure patient comfort and safe, timely treatment.

On call is an expression used to designate who is responsible for patient care during specific hours. The assumption is that the care begins after regular day hours and continues until the next regular day shift. It also refers to whom is responsible over the weekend or on holidays or as backup for other physicians. That call may require one's physical presence or consultation by phone (texting had not been invented yet, but pagers had). The reality is such that during my residency years, on-call hours were just longer days without sleep or with occasional sleep.

Typically, I would begin my usual day at 5:30 a.m. to visit all of my hospitalized patients and to gather the results of studies that had been performed and to check that the treatments ordered had actually been done. The plans for discharge or for continued hospital care would be formulated. Next would be a meeting or rounds with the other residents on the team for discussions regarding each patient. Some educational discussions about disease processes, differential diagnoses, and optimal treatments would occur in preparation for later rounds with our attending senior staff physician. During those rounds, the attending would critique our care, assist with treatment plans, and ask us questions that were intended to increase our fund of knowledge. Often the hierarchy of questioning would be to start with the least-experienced persons, the medical students, and proceed up the level of residents from first to third year to demonstrate deficiencies in our understanding, educate us, and create a sense of responsibility or expectation unique to our level or status in training. Usually a medical student, one intern, and one upper-level resident were designated "on call" until the next morning when the entire team returned. The rounding for that day would require our involvement the same as though we had not been there all night. We were responsible to care for our patients, write notes, and do whatever was necessary before leaving around 5:00 p.m. Thus, on-call was actually thirty-six hours.

What were the other expectations for call during my residency? The on-call assignment was every three days. That meant thirty-six hours on, twelve hours off, twelve hours on, twelve hours off, then thirty-six hours on again. The good news is this was only for three years. The bad news is that there were times when "manpower" was lessened due to unexpected losses from the team by illness, injury, maternity leave, unexpected family moves, and occasionally by a resident being dismissed from the program. While on call for the hospital, we covered the needs for the entire team's patients (often a dozen or two), the pediatric intensive care unit (PICU), new admissions, and urgent needs for a pediatrician in the emergency room. Sometimes we even needed to assist at deliveries or in the nursery if that area was overwhelmed with patient care needs. Changes in patient status sometimes required a "code blue" attendance, where intense life-saving treatments were needed. Nowadays most residency programs have separate on-call teams for the PICU, NICU, ED, and patients not in need of intensive care ("the floor," "the ward").

Outpatient clinic on-call took place at the Brady Green Clinic, downtown. Usually one intern, one upper-level resident, and sometimes a medical student would be assigned to stay after 5:00 p.m. to take care of patients who came for urgent care until 8:00 a.m. the next morning when the rest of the team returned. We would have a morning report with the attending physician and other team members about the patients seen who required hospitalization or close follow-up or referral to subspecialty services. The on-call assignment was also every three days. It was not unusual to see fifty or more patients, many coming in after 11:00 p.m., when they knew we would give out samples of medications needed since there were no pharmacies open after that hour. Patients requiring admission to the hospital were transported by ambulance. Occasionally, one of us would have to ride with the patient, assisting in life-saving measures or closely monitoring the patient's status. This is where we learned expediency of care, due to the high volume of patients needing care. One was afraid that the next patient may be critical, so making quick evaluations, diagnoses, and treatments was essential.

Some of the sickest of patients came through those clinics. During those years, there was no vaccine against HIB (hemophilus influenza type B bacterium) or pneumococcal infections, so at least weekly we would admit someone with sepsis, meningitis, osteomyelitis, or pneumonia. Often these patients were critical upon presentation. The whooping cough vaccine, DTP (diphtheria-tetanus-pertussis), was not as good as today's vaccine and was not widely administered, so it was not unusual to encounter patients with whooping cough. Neonatal tetanus, rabies, child abuse, seizures, dehydration, respiratory distress, asthma, gastroenteritis, new diabetics in ketoacidosis, and numerous other pathologies presented, of course, without labels. Quick, accurate diagnosis and action were required to save lives. There was no shortage of cases to thoroughly train us.

"Please, could you help me with this Spanish-speaking-only family?" I asked of my upper-level resident, who was born and raised in Mexico. Unfortunately, I had studied Latin, French, and German, but never Spanish.

"Listen, man, if you are going to work with these patients, then you better learn the language," he said with his usual accent and strong demeanor as he walked away refusing to help.

His message was clear. The clinic demands were such that two physicians could not be delegated to taking a history and communicating with the patient and family. Eventually, I learned enough Spanish to take an uncomplicated history and communicate with patients who primarily spoke Spanish. Also, there was often a nice nurse or medical student or family member or friend who helped with communication. There was no translation by phone service or professional interpreter available. Now it is considered inappropriate to use family members or friends for translation, due to privacy and other issues.

The same resident alluded to above was actually a good role model. He worked endlessly for his patients, advocated for their needs, and was a great diagnostician and procedurally skillful. He was sometimes a maverick, unconventional. Once we were overwhelmed with at least forty or fifty patients waiting on the two of us, and having had such sick patients that we admitted several. He also rode with one patient to the hospital that evening, performing respiratory assistance en route.

"Come here, man, I'll show you how to get this under control," he said as we walked out into the waiting room. It was now just after midnight.

"Everyone who has been sick for more than a week or two, raise your hand," he said to the crowd. A dozen or more hands went into the air.

"All of you can go home and come back tomorrow, since we

aren't getting to you tonight anyway!" It worked. Our workload was now close to manageable.

Most of our outpatient subspecialty clinics were also held in this building. We would rotate through neurology, genetics, pulmonology, allergy, and adolescent clinics. We also had our own cadre of patients we could follow for one to three years in our "continuity care clinic" there, a relatively new concept at that time. That was a very rewarding experience, as it made care a lot more personal and effective for the patients and gave us insight to child development, during a time of tremendous and rapid brain growth. Most of "our" patients were recruited from the nursery or urgent care experience, having identified patients without doctors. This was our only real experience at preventive health measures.

There were other experiences at the Santa Rosa Children's hospital that were unique. This is where we could learn from physicians in private practice, who would refer patients who were interesting or complicated cases, in need of the teaching services expertise. Sometimes we were just a convenience for their indigent patients who showed up late on a Friday in their offices. Often though, these were quite sick and challenging patients. My rotations through cardiology, oncology-hematology, and PICU there were some of my favorites. Those attending physicians were some of the most dedicated, knowledgeable, caring, compassionate, and competent role models one could ever hope to emulate. In particular, Dr. Howard Britton in Heme-Onc and Dr. Colette Kohler in cardiology had a most positive influence on me, especially their ability to relate and communicate with patients and their families, their dedication to excellence, and their ability to demonstrate a balance of the art and science of medicine.

Our program provided many other valuable experiences related to coordinating care for patients with multiple subspecialty needs, interactions with clinical instructors as our attending physicians from the private sector, and the expertise of those who combined research with patient care and education. The morbidity and mortality conferences that taught us how to assess and learn from bad or unfortunate outcomes were valuable in teaching us to strive for better, always. Patients as well as multiple specialists involved in their care were present at grand rounds, a unique and especially effective way to teach us how diseases originate and are evaluated, diagnosed, and treated. The importance of collaborative care and consultation was highlighted by these conferences.

Changes in Healthcare

Today's residents are challenged in similar, yet different ways. There are now rules that limit the number of hours a resident can work when on call, and there are limits to the total number of hours a week. Concerns and lawsuits over the possible link between sleep-deprived residents and the death of an eighteen-year-old named Libby Zion[39] led to these reforms. It is thought that her death was due to serotonin syndrome, a consequence of adverse drug reactions between an antidepressant she was taking and an opiate-like analgesic administered by a resident in the hospital for her pain.[40] This case, these reforms, and the efficacy of reforms are still studied and debated. Often, we joke that today's residents are too coddled. But they should be better rested and not have impaired decision-making and actions due to sleep deprivation.

Some (more senior?) physicians are concerned that residents'

[39] Barron H. Lerner, "A Case That Shook Medicine," *The Washington Post* (Nov 28), 2006.
[40] Jane E. Brody, "A Mix of Medicines That Can be Lethal," *The New York Times* (Feb 27) 2007.

commitment to patient care and understanding of the progression of illness and therapy is lessened somehow due to time away from their patients. Certainly, accountability is different when more than one resident is responsible for a particular patient. The HIPAA (Health Insurance Portability and Accountability), JCAHO (Joint Commission on Accreditation of Healthcare Organizations), meaningful use, insurer, and other governmental and educational rules have introduced a whole new focus on quality of care, teamwork, financial aspects of healthcare, productivity, communications, and patient satisfaction. The electronic medical record and electronic prescriptions have enhanced documentation, readability, process improvement, and easier overview of patient care and needs. Moreover, the new focus on community or population health and preventive medicine encourages a dependence upon other members of the healthcare team in unique and different ways. Embracing non-physician advanced practice professionals (APPs) in meeting access and follow-up care needs has grown, and likely will continue to do so. Greater involvement by the attending physicians in every aspect of the resident's care of patients is now required and beneficial.

Of course, one of the most challenging aspects of care now is the patient and provider's easy access to information. "A little bit of knowledge is a dangerous thing." That axiom seems ever so more meaningful in an era when anyone can become an instant expert, simply by Google search, which was not available before 1997. My opinion is that *if you don't know what you don't know, then you may harm what you don't want to harm!* This applies to physicians as well as to non-physician providers, patients and parents, or others involved in the care of the patient.

"I knew we were in trouble when my child's pediatrician had to Google the answer to my question," stated my daughter-in-law

with concerned laughter. Physicians now have fingertip immediate access to the latest information on almost any topic. Patients
have similar access. This challenges physicians to be aware of what
may or may not be out there in terms of beliefs that substitute for
knowledge.

Information is useful when used in the appropriate context but
may be dangerous when not. How information is interpreted often
depends upon the additional knowledge held by the "interpreter."
Also, some information can be misleading if not associated with
additional information. For instance, reading about the potential
side effects of a particular medicine may sway the patient to be
non-compliant with a physician's recommendation, with adverse
outcomes. In turn, a new recommendation may need to be made.
More in-depth education of the patient about both the risks and
benefits, as well as alternatives, for a particular approach to treatment becomes necessary. There is also access to information that
may be misleading or outright inaccurate or deceitful. Such is often
the case about immunizations, and so getting appropriate herd
immunity to contain diseases is often more difficult. Before, physicians were simply trusted to be more knowledgeable and to be
acting in the best interests of the patient. Their professionalism
required dedication to a life of continuous self-education and to
do no harm. Although there are always exceptions, I believe that
professionalism still exists and is actually better at monitoring
those in the profession.

Simply put, physicians now are more challenged than ever before to fully involve patients in their own care. That is rightfully so.
Only the patient knows exactly how he or she feels. Most often there
is more than one way to provide appropriate treatment, and the
patient's wishes or choices should be respected. Where it conflicts

with the physician's preference, greater in-depth discussions are needed.

During my medical training, we were taught about the importance of continuing medical education. Much of the information we were learning would likely be out of date in one or two decades, we were told. Well, it happened faster than that. The rate of growth of research-based evidence in medicine has been geometric and is changing ever faster. What doesn't change much is the analytical approach to problem solving, based on a fund of knowledge and deductive reasoning through differential diagnoses. However, our understanding of disease and disease process, as well as its treatment, is what changes. There are also data that support better ways of teaching and learning. That is all good, striving to always become better.

Some examples of EBM (evidence-based medicine) that have changed follow. Gastrointestinal ulcers were primarily thought to be due to the type A-personality and stress. In fact, we now know that *H. Pylori* bacterial infections are the main cause. Asthma was treated with steroids as a last resort, as we did not want to make the patient "steroid-dependent." Now steroids are the first line of therapy, as asthma is now known to be primarily an inflammatory process. Post-surgery, it used to be thought best to "rest the bowel" and then advance the diet slowly over a couple of weeks. Similarly, acute gastroenteritis was managed by dietary restrictions, whereas now we know it is best to feed the pediatric patient whatever is preferred by the patient and to replace losses with a balanced electrolyte or nutritional solution. Depression and multiple other mental health problems that were previously managed by cognitive behavioral therapy (CBT) alone or with shock therapy, now are primarily managed with medications and/or a combination of medications and CBT. Eczema was managed by the avoidance of baths, but now it is known that hydrating the skin by staying in the bath longer is helpful. The list can go on and on. Some cancers are curable. The management of neonatal hyper-bilirubinemia as well as the high-risk newborn, pain management, antibiotic use, ear infections, bronchiolitis, hypertension, basic life support interventions, common cardiac conditions, urinary tract treatments and prevention, and a host of other diseases and injuries has changed over the past few decades since I was a resident physician.

There have been astounding advances in the surgical treatment of many conditions over the years. In fact, some are now managed without surgery. So, the cardiologist employs balloon valvotomy, the passage of a catheter through an artery to the heart, to treat mitral valve stenosis and a variety of other structural heart conditions that used to require open-heart surgery. Sound waves are used to shatter and treat some kidney stones without surgery. Many intra-abdominal conditions, such as appendicitis, gall stones, and other surgeries, are treated with laparoscopic approaches involving small one-inch incisions, rather than large abdominal wall incisions that require greater rehabilitation. Many orthopedic conditions are treated by arthroscopy and some with just observation and a tincture of time. Back and brain surgical approaches have been revolutionized. Biotechnical and other industrial advances have made the unthinkable possible. Imaging techniques and equipment and radiological interventions have enhanced diagnostic and therapeutic management of many surgical and medical conditions.

What has not changed is the need for experienced mentors to teach how to use technology and research, and new knowledge in meeting healthcare needs. What has not changed is the need to teach students and new physicians how to continue to adapt to new information throughout their careers, to learn how to learn. What has not changed is the need to employ both the art and the science of medicine. What has not changed is the fact that healthcare is still about two people: one seeking help, and one offering help. What has not changed is the fact that this is a profession, not just a job. Being a physician requires empathy, compassion, competence, and a commitment to excellence in meeting the needs of patients. What has not changed is the need to provide universal access to therapeutic as well as preventive care.

CHAPTER 10

Something Is Missing

Careers, Choices, and Changes

To paraphrase Elizabeth Barrett Browning's Sonnet 43, "How do I *serve* thee? Let me count the ways. I *serve* thee to the depth and breadth and height My soul can reach ..."[41]

Truly, for some—nay, for most—being a physician is a labor of love. Hence the analogy to the sonnet. There are many easier ways to be held in high esteem, to become financially well-off, to achieve satisfaction in life, and to help others, than to embark upon a quest to become a physician. Still, thousands of people take up the quest. The primary motivation for each, I believe, comes from within. My quest and its tortuous path has been presented. My love of this profession has only grown stronger with time and experience. However, how I envisioned that role and what it became differed.

There are many types of physicians, and there are many possible roles for each type. Why I chose to become a pediatrician was discussed briefly earlier. During the residency years, once again, I had the opportunity to decide my life's course. What type of

---

[41] Elizabeth Barrett Browning, "How do I Love Thee?" (Sonnet 43) *Sonnets from the Portuguese,* 1850.

2Robert E. Burke, MD, PhD

pediatrician would I become? Would general pediatrics be my favored role? Certainly therein is the best opportunity to provide anticipatory guidance for patients and families, to keep them safe and healthy, and to help provide for the optimal development of newborns, infants, children, and adolescents. Therein would be the greatest opportunity to be "someone's primary care physician."

But the lure of serving in other ways was great. To be a subspecialist in the care of newborns or adolescents would require additional studies as a fellow in the area of interest. Mostly, it would be another three years of commitment to life as a physician-in-training to become a cardiologist, pulmonologist, gastroenterologist, otolaryngologist, ophthalmologist, endocrinologist, urologist, dermatologist, hematologist, neurologist, rheumatologist, allergist, podiatrist, psychiatrist, physiatrist, orthopedist, sports medicine specialist, or critical care specialist in the intensive care unit or in the emergency department.

Becoming a hospitalist was not a career option at that time, as primary care physicians took care of their patients when hospitalized, coordinating care with the subspecialists as needed. Becoming an oncologist had particular intellectual appeal to me and was encouraged by those I met, because of my cancer research background and studies in cell biology. The possibility of becoming a general pediatric surgeon or a specialist such as a neurosurgeon crossed my mind. In fact, every rotation of service during my residency brought a greater understanding and interest in that particular field. At different times, I thought seriously about becoming a neonatologist, a critical care pediatrician, an oncologist, and a cardiologist. Finally, I narrowed my decision to general pediatrics and cardiology. I chose the former for the reasons given above. Besides, my wife said that it was now time to get a job! After all, I had two or three different careers, and was now the proud parent of four children, our last having been born during the residency years. The enormous debt accrued during all this training also was considered. However, that was not as much a consideration, as I knew that subspecialists, especially cardiologists, would be paid much more than a general pediatrician, making loan repayments easier and likely faster in the long run.

As a general pediatrician, how would I serve? The appeal of moving to a small town, "hanging my shingle," and becoming an independent physician who would meet a community's needs was great. It was humbling and intriguing to consider delivering pediatric care to families that I would come to know quite well, and who would come to know me, much like my admiration for our family doctor. In 1985, when I completed my residency, the majority of physicians in the country were employed, although private practice was much more alive than now. In order to start a private practice, I would have had to go into debt another $100,000 or more at that time. There would be some options for loan payback and facilitation of setting up a practice in an underserved, rural area. But practically, it would take decades to get out of debt. In addition, the financial costs and time devoted to running a practice, meeting salaries, buying and storing vaccines, buying liability insurance, and covering other overhead would distract from my goal of being a pediatrician. Autonomy of practice would be greater, but at a financial and personal satisfaction cost that was perceived by me as not worth it. So, being employed with specific benefits and guaranteed income based on productivity had a much more practical appeal to me.

During my last year of residency, I took elective rotations with a couple of small group practices in and around San Antonio, both to get some practical experience as to what a group practice would feel like and to begin networking. The main advantage associated with practicing in an area where I had done my medical training was familiarity with resources and people. A disadvantage is that those areas where residents train are usually near or in big cities and offer more cultural opportunities for families and therefore have become saturated; thus, competition for a thriving practice is greater. Indeed, most of the practice opportunities for me seemed to offer less than what would be considered average income and benefits for general pediatricians across the country. There was an exception, with a well-respected group in San Antonio, where the offer was average the first year but would potentially increase dramatically to full partner within three years.

In order to join that group, I would need to learn to do circumcisions. They had a great liaison with the hospital's obstetricians, did all the circumcisions there, and had the opportunity to bring in newborns to their practice. At that time, our department of pediatrics would not teach circumcisions, since our national association claimed there were no medical benefits. Thus, I learned from my family medicine colleagues who were trained in the procedure. Excited about joining this group and finally getting out into the "real world," my plans changed at the last minute, so to speak.

Dr. Cipriani was an upper-level resident with whom I had worked in San Antonio. She contacted me, to recruit me to Scott & White, a multispecialty group practice modeled after the Mayo Clinic. In Temple, Texas, this group was the site for clinical education of medical students from Texas A&M, and had a residency training program in pediatrics, as well as most other specialties. The opportunities to teach and for career advancement, as well as the possibility of doing clinical research, greatly appealed to me. The salary would be competitive with similar clinics and greater than the group that I had planned to join in San Antonio. The employee benefits were equivalent to an additional 20 to 25 percent of compensation. Scott & White enjoyed a reputation for high-quality and personalized care, beyond the borders of Texas.

Having landed the perfect job that would enable me to care for infants, children, and adolescents, while mentoring medical students and resident physicians, seemed to exceed my expectations and moved me beyond the quest to become a physician. Now I would be that physician and more. Now the rewards of personal satisfaction, a flexible, secure career, a healthier lifestyle, financial relief, and more time for family would be mine.

The next four years were as good as, if not better than expected. As I built my own panel of patients who identified me as their primary care provider, I was able to continue my own education while teaching. Patients were treated by me in the clinic, and I also could share in their care when admitted to the hospital. Newborns were easily cared for within the same complex of buildings. The "icing on the cake" was that when I left for the day, I could turn off my pager. There were after-hour responsibilities in the evening and weekend clinics, shared with a half-dozen or so colleagues and the residents. However, I would only be called if I was the attending of the month for the inpatient pediatric team and if it was about something that could not wait until the next day during regular hours. There was only one time in four years that I had to go into the hospital while the attending on call. Ironically, it was because one of our patients needed a lumbar puncture and intravenous line, and the upper-level resident, who eventually became an excellent critical care specialist, was unable to obtain those after a few attempts. Although I had not done either procedure in four years, my extensive experience at San Antonio had long-lasting effects, and both procedures were successful with a single attempt!

In addition to patient care, I enjoyed being on several committees and implementing new programs. Because it was now a

standard expectation of the pediatric residency programs nationwide, I developed, implemented, and directed the continuity care
clinic for our residents. This also gave indigent patients an opportunity for easy clinic access with the residents for preventive care
and to help keep them out of the emergency department by having
a specific doctor as their primary. It was also my privilege to participate in implementing and helping with the children's miracle
network fund-raising program at Scott & White.

Perhaps my greatest sense of accomplishments, beyond direct
patient care and teaching, were the implementation of a parent-pa-
tient educational program and the production of a manual called
Caring for Kids.[42] That manual, written by me on my own time,
provided information about our group practice and the roles of students and residents in patient care. More importantly, it provided
anticipatory guidance for parents as what to expect in terms of developmental milestones and preventive care for their infant, child,
and adolescent. It also provided written advice for dealing with
colds, gastroenteritis, skin conditions, minor injuries, and many
other common conditions. Scott & White copyrighted this and gra-
ciously provided it free to all new parents and to new patients to our
practice. We extended its use to the family medicine satellite clinics
as well. This would be used for another decade, at which time access
to such information was more readily available in electronic and in
other ways. The patient-parent educational center that I developed
was initially funded by the Children's Miracle Network proceeds.
This would later be expanded by our department and funded by the
Scott & White Foundation.

Some other benefits of working in this type of setting related
to the ease with which I could provide access to subspecialty care

---

[42] Robert E. Burke, *Caring For Kids*. (Scott & White, Temple, Texas 1987).

for my patients and other members of their families. At that time, there were several hundred physicians employed at Scott & White, and the potential to provide comprehensive care from cradle to the grave was there. Because I knew the doctors, the system, and the available resources, it was easy to get the additional care and services that my patients or their families needed. Our subspecialists were in the same building, I knew all of them, and I could just walk across the hall to get "curbside" advice and to introduce my patient to the physician to whom I was referring.

Although our Department of Pediatrics was growing and had most subspecialties represented, we were not able to create or sustain a children's hospital at that time. However, the concept of a hospital within a hospital, wherein an entire floor was renovated and dedicated to children's services, was conceived and implemented. Newborns were still cared for in the same area as labor and delivery, and the concept of rooming in with the mother was advanced.

During this time, there was much more time for family than I had enjoyed in the preceding seven years of medical training. We went camping, participated in community soccer, traveled some, visited distant relatives more often, and generally spent more time together. One of our adventures involved learning the martial arts as a family. Although our youngest child was not old enough to participate, she often spent time watching us do our forms and exercises at the dojo.

Kids raise their parents. That is true. The relationships are bidirectional. Parents learn to meet the needs and expectations of their children, and their kids learn to meet parental expectations. That is how we became involved in Tang Soo Do. One Sunday at dinner, I was telling our children that it would be important for them to do something that they liked, that would enhance their lives beyond their school experiences. Some suggestions were given, and each child gave thought to this. Our oldest child, Christa, took the lead on this. She had seen the movie *The Karate Kid* and told me that she would like to learn karate. The conversation continued something like this.

"Great. We will find a program and sign you up."

"But I want to do it with you, Daddy."

"Me? No, I'm too busy, and besides, I'm too old. This is what interests you, your adventure." Trying to get off the hook, I suggested that she get a friend to join with her.

Well, that was not what she wanted to hear.

A few weeks later, Christa persisted in her desire to learn karate. Finally, I gave in. I had some experience, extremely limited, with an introductory course to Isshin-Ryu, an Okinawan form of karate, while a graduate student at Penn State, so this could be fun. Besides, it would mean so much to her, and it could be quality time together. After meeting with Mr. Lawler, the sensei and founder of Martial Arts International Association of Tang Soo Do, he welcomed us with an offer of a family membership that would be a great value at not that much more cost. The boys were ecstatic and joined with us. Over the next few years, we attended classes for a couple of hours, several times a week. All of us earned the *cho dan,* first-degree black belt. The boys then turned to other interests, but Christa and I worked to earn the second *(Yi) dan.* The commitment to goals, the exercise, the mastery of the forms and creating self-defense moves from each step of each form, and the can-do, respectful attitude of the martial arts, and especially Mr. Lawler, provided invaluable attributes for our children and a lifetime of memories for us.

Fateful opportunities are not always easily recognized or embraced. One fateful call came during the Christmas holidays of 1988. There was a recruiter on the line, asking me what it would take to recruit me to join Geisinger, a similarly structured health-care system as Scott & White. There was a need for a general pedia-trician in the central region of Pennsylvania. This was in a rural and indigent town called Philipsburg, located in the Moshannon Valley. Geisinger was currently providing *locum tenens* pediatricians, but the town had not had a dedicated pediatrician since the only one there left two years ago. There was a small group practice associated with Geisinger there, the Moshannon Valley Group, consisting of several family practitioners, a couple of internists, an orthopedist, an ophthalmologist, a couple of surgeons, a neurologist, and a der-matologist who rotated from State College. They were located across the street from an old, state-run hospital.

"No, thanks. I am perfectly happy here."

"Certainly, I understand that. But our need is great, and espe-cially this community's need is great. We will do what it takes to get you here."

"How did you choose to call me?" I inquired.

"We searched similar groups to ours, nationwide, to find a pediatrician who had roots in Pennsylvania and might consider moving back to be near family."

The entire opportunity intrigued me. Although I was not searching for a job and was happy with my current one, there was something missing. Circumstances and decisions that I had made led me away from an earlier dream of being a small-town physician. Here was an opportunity to realize that dream, yet be financially secure as an employee and not needing to spend valuable hours that could be directed to patient care managing a private practice. The quality of the organization that I would be joining paralleled that of where I was. As long as I can remember, Geisinger was known in Pennsylvania as the place to go to if you had challenging med-ical problems. It had grown from its original small rural hospital to the expansive system that it is, located in many sites and cities throughout Pennsylvania. There would be the same opportunities as I had here for career development, yet it would meet what seemed to be an unattainable, lost goal for me. Besides, it would be nice to be closer to relatives.

After a further detailed discussion and suggesting conditions for my move and practice, the recruiter wasted no time to set up an interview. The week after Christmas, I found myself in Philipsburg, Pennsylvania, wondering why I would want to leave Scott & White to join the small group in the Moshannon Valley. The hospital was run down, but that did not bother me, since my expectation was that most of my patients would be managed in the outpatient setting, which was nice. Based on my experience in Temple, Texas, I naively thought that a dozen or two would be the maximum number of patients I would need to admit yearly. The group of physicians and nurses that I would be joining seemed nice, but of course, this was an interview. The more I thought about it, the more I realized that the life change to being on call whenever in town may adversely impact our family life. Other than fulfilling a dream, the reality of a move became more apparent.

"Bonnie, we are *not* moving here," I said in the phone call that evening after a day full of interviews and interactions. She said she understood and that it was at least worth having looked into it. Unfortunately, I could not get her personal impression of the place, as she was unable to accompany me due to having to take care of our four children.

"Bonnie, we *are* moving here," I said, to her surprise, during my call after the second day. Her response was something akin to, "What the heck are you smoking?!" Just yesterday, I had argued against moving, and now I was telling her how it was the right decision. So, what had changed? How sure can you be? This would be my "missionary" work. There was indeed a true need for a pediatrician—for me. Having met with the nurses and personnel in the hospital, strangers in the grocery store, and people in the gas station and having more in-depth discussions with the physicians with whom I would be working, it became apparent that these were nice people and they were desperate for a pediatrician. I was truly needed, and I would be greatly appreciated. Small town life for the kids could be a plus, as it had been for me, and the family physicians promised backup for me when I needed to leave town. Geisinger had a children's hospital in Danville, which could be accessed by ground or air transport for emergencies, and by a ninety-minute drive for less-urgent needs. We would be just over the hill from Penn State University and a college town. We would be only a two- to three-hour drive from relatives, and the kids would get the experience of growing up knowing their remaining grandparents, cousins, aunts, and uncles.

The next day, I met with leadership, reviewed the offer, negotiated some, and committed to the move. They were ecstatic, and as a show of appreciation, they offered me a slightly higher salary than that for which I had negotiated.

Not everyone was happy. Our teenagers would be moving during their high school years. Our youngest daughter, now old enough, would not be able to join Mr. Lawler's karate classes. The beautiful house that we lived in, and that I had remodeled, would be left, and there would be difficulty selling it as the market was bad. Our friends and neighbors were just getting used to these "Yankees," and Mr. Lawler was saddened. Our department chair was surprised by this impulsive career change but understood that there would not have been much to change my reasons for the move. It was more personal than practical. Many of my patients and their families also expressed their sense of loss.

Deep breath, here we go. My enthusiasm was tempered by some trepidation, knowing that I would be the most expert physician in town caring for kids and not having immediate on-site support for some patient needs and emergencies. It was four years since I had managed most emergencies, such as diabetic ketoacidosis, seizures, overdoses, lacerations, and high-risk newborns. Would my skills of providing advanced life support, repairing lacerations, or placing inter-venous lines, umbilical catheters, and chest tubes still be there? It was my belief that they would, and that it would be nice to resume using those skills when needed. But I was taking no chances, so I enrolled in a PALS (pediatric advanced life support) course and a new course called NALS (neonatal advanced life support) at a continuing medical education meeting in Toronto Children's Hospital before the move. There, I learned an emergent procedure, called intra-osseous line placement, that was newly in vogue. Little did I know that I would use that knowledge and skill months later to benefit a future cancer patient of mine. How would I handle being on call 24/7? How would my family handle it?

CHAPTER 11

Doing It All

Small-Town Pediatrician

Becoming a small-town doctor is what I always envisioned as my career. When the opportunity arose, I jumped at it, although with some trepidation, as noted. Exactly what that entailed I could not have imagined. It would be more than a full-time job. It would be a commitment to my friends and neighbors and their families. It would be a commitment to my children's friends. It would be a commitment to my family. It would be a commitment to the other professionals in town. It would be a commitment to the schools. It would be a commitment to sharing my knowledge with other health care providers. It would be a commitment to unrestricted access to my services. It would be a commitment to the organization helping to make this happen. It would be a commitment to excellence in patient care. It would be a commitment to the surrounding communities and their hospitals. All of this commitment would be in unimaginable ways.

Hospital Care of Patients

Although I thought the hospital would play a minor role in my provision of pediatric care, it became front and center. The absence of a consistency in patient care, through the use of multiple *locum tenens* pediatricians over two years, led to out-of-control disease management. Asthmatics were not well-educated about treatment and prevention strategies, and many were confused about their medications. Many were not on controller medications. Those who were, were confused about how to use them. There were myths abounding, in terms of the management of acute gastroenteritis and the prevention and treatment of dehydration. Many children had no preventive care visits (well-child checkups) and lacked in immunizations. Their parents needed more knowledge about expectations for their child's development. Appropriate approaches to good nutrition, dental care, and sports participation were not common. Adolescents lacked access to accurate information regarding puberty and high-risk behaviors. Consequently, I spent part of almost every day attending to patients in the emergency room and to those whom I admitted. Instead of a dozen or so admissions as anticipated, that first year, I had to admit well over 350 patients! That did not include newborn care, or one of my patients who was hospitalized a couple of dozen times that year.

Our local hospital was not well suited for the management of the pediatric patient, although there were some experienced and excellent nurses. If intravenous lines could not be placed, and if blood specimens could not be obtained, then I was needed to fill those roles as well. The emergency room was not staffed by those with specific training and in fact was often staffed by physicians who had dropped out of residency programs or were not board certified. Thus, I spent a lot of time assisting there, as well as checking on patients, multiple times per day, to be sure they were receiving the appropriate care and monitoring. Hospital privileges in pediatrics had to be reviewed and approved by me. I participated on several of the hospital committees, read the pediatric EKGs and reviewed all pediatric visits to the emergency room for appropriateness of care and to manage patient risk, and I was called at least once nightly to attend to patients in the emergency room or at a high-risk birth. Once I was both the assistant surgeon at a C-section birth, as well as the one to attend to the baby once delivered. My help with patients involved in motor vehicle accidents and life-threatening injuries was also needed.

One day, shortly after my arrival in 1989, I was reviewing the medical records of pediatric patients who had been seen in the emergency department (ED). To my horror, a newborn had been seen for a high fever, documented in the ED as well as at home. It is still the standard of care to hospitalize such patients and do a complete sepsis workup that would include blood studies and cultures, urine culture, possible imaging, and spinal fluid analysis and culture. The reason for such an aggressive approach is that newborns (under six weeks) may have a serious infection such as meningitis, sepsis, pneumonia, or urinary tract infection, yet the only initial manifestation could be fever and maybe fussiness. By the time those infections are clinically obvious, it may be too late to save that baby's life. Thus, tests should have been done, and the newborn should have been admitted for antibiotic therapy and observation for other support as needed.

"You are telling me that you want to admit our baby to the hospital and do all these tests? He looks okay, and the ED physician brought the fever down with Tylenol. You are new to town, so how can I trust you? Why did the ED physician not do these things?"

Those may not have been the exact words, but they are the

essence of that conversation with the appropriately worried mother. Fortunately, the parents decided to take my advice. Our evaluation revealed that the baby did indeed have meningitis. He did well with treatment and had none of the potential sequelae of meningitis, short- or long-term.

There were many other encounters with the ED that made me determined to always see the patient when notified, as the patient assessments and reports of findings were often inaccurate.

One occasion involved inappropriate attempts by the ED physician to intubate a child with bronchiolitis who was breathing fast but otherwise doing well. As often occurred, I had been called emergently from our clinic across the street.

On another occasion, I was called to assist with a patient who was having seizures. The nurse anesthetist had been called prior to me but could not get the patient intubated and had loosened her teeth and traumatized the gums. A quick assessment of that patient revealed that she would benefit from airway protection and assistance, so I agreed to intubate her and did so successfully, although I had not intubated an older child like her in the preceding six years or more. A quick history revealed that she was an asthmatic. My suspicions were confirmed by blood test, that her seizure was due to theophylline toxicity. It was later learned that the patient, known to me only as my daughter's friend, was on high-dose therapy to begin with, and when her asthma worsened due to illness, the parent had given her extra doses.

Perhaps the most convincing encounter that made me distrust future ED physician assessments of patients there was a response to a call that I received shortly after midnight. The ED physician suspected that my patient, who was on Tegretol therapy for behavioral management as prescribed by another physician, had Stevens-Johnson Syndrome and would need to be transferred to a burn center. Although he described the typical rash perfectly, and the patient had abnormally high liver function tests, the description that he was not on intravenous fluids and otherwise was fine did not make sense. Why would such a stable patient need transfer to a burn center? Despite his reassurance that I was not needed, that he only called to learn where the nearest burn center was, I insisted on going in to see the patient. Upon arrival, the ED had only subdued lighting, and the physician had gone back to bed.

"Dr. Burke, is that you?" asked my patient, who heard me talking with the nurse. "Please, get me out of here. I'm okay."

"Let me see your rash."

"Rash? I don't have a rash."

Upon examination, he indeed did not have a rash, and he looked perfectly well. Evidently he had fever and presented to the ED for that reason. The fever was now gone, and any flushed appearance that it may have caused was also gone. It was not unusual to get spurious lab results in that hospital, so I could not rely on the report of elevated liver functions, but Tegretol could cause that. As I looked around the physician's work station for the patient's chart, I found a book called the Merck Manual, opened to a page on Stevens-Johnson Syndrome. The ED physician had been reading the rash description from the book to me. No wonder that it sounded typical! I discharged the patient and later had a long discussion with the physician. This episode, as many others, was presented by me to our quality assurance committee. Unfortunately, such unqualified physicians continued to work there. When the hospital closed, I found that the ED physicians in Clearfield, Tyrone, and State College were much more reliable in their assessments of the pediatric patient, although there were times when one of the Philipsburg ED physicians moonlighted at Tyrone or Clearfield.

One evening, I received a call from one of these ED physicians, who I knew as usually unreliable. He called because my patient's mom refused to allow a lumbar puncture and CT scan to be done for her son, who had a brief new onset seizure with a fever. This toddler stopped seizing just before arrival by ambulance to the Clearfield ED. The physician called, asking me to get the mother's permission for the tests. He stated that the patient appeared fine but was hallucinating. So I talked by phone with the mom.

"Dr. Burke, he is not hallucinating. He just asked the doctor to get Donald Duck out of his ear, like you always do!"

The mom and I had a good laugh, I believed her assessment of her child, and I made the diagnosis of simple febrile seizure based on the history and re-discussed this with the ED doctor, who then discharged the patient to see me in follow-up as needed.

Previously, I mentioned that a procedure I learned at a PALS course in Toronto would later be useful. This anecdote reflects the state of the Philipsburg Hospital at that time.

"Dr. Burke, I have been paging you. Your patient has been seizing for over a half an hour, and we are unable to get an intravenous line, and the surgeon we called to do a cut-down for access has not arrived," lamented the ED nurse.

I had been out of town and answered the phone as I entered the house just after 11:00 p.m. The ED had not tried to contact the family physician who was covering for me. Minutes later upon my arrival in the ED, my patient was still seizing. One quick try at an IV placement was unsuccessful, so I tried to administer rectal Valium, but that also was not successful. When I asked for an in-tra-osseous needle, no one knew what I was talking about, as they were not yet in general use. Thus, I asked for a bone marrow needle, but they said they would have to find one and then autoclave it. In desperation, I opted to use a spinal needle, but it bent as soon as I tried to twist it into the bone in her lower leg. Finally, I inserted the

largest hypodermic needle available into the bone marrow successfully. The intra-osseous infusion of medication stopped her seizure.

Unfortunately, the weather was not conducive to transfer of the
patient to the PICU at Danville, Geisinger's Children's Hospital, so I
admitted her to our hospital's adult ICU overnight. As we encountered the ICU nurse just off the elevator, I gave precautions about
care of the intra-osseous line.

"The IV is in her bone? What is this, voodoo medicine!" she
asked incredulously.

"Don't knock it, it works," said the ED nurse.

The patient was admitted to the ICU, which was a large room
with several beds separated by curtains and illuminated by an incandescent light bulb over each bed. Overnight the patient did well,
despite losing her line. I referred her back to her oncologist the next
day. This was a patient who had presented to me within the first few
months of my arrival in town for fever and who I diagnosed with
leukemia (ALL). Further analysis by the oncologist revealed that
her seizure was a complication of her induction chemotherapy with
L-asparaginase, which caused a sagittal sinus thrombosis.

Interestingly, this case was referred to the quality assurance
committee for further evaluation, not because the surgeon never
arrived to assist but because I had employed a technique that they
thought was unconventional and outside the bounds of acceptable
practice parameters. The internist who chaired the committee had
to research it and was then satisfied that there was merit and data to
support this approach, and that I had been trained to do it. I made
sure that the hospital ordered the appropriate needles for possible
future needs. This also led to an opportunity for me to provide an
in-service on the management of seizures, and it reemphasized the
need for better communication of who was available for call at all
times.

Without going into it in depth, suffice it to say that state and local politics factored largely into the quality-of-care issues, resources, supplies, and personnel staffing at the Philipsburg hospital. Although I personally support collective bargaining, clearly the demands and political power of the hospital unions factored both in the demise of the hospital and its ineffectual reopening and subsequent final closure. There was always a constant battle to provide quality care, despite the expertise of many of the physicians and nurses. This was not unique to Philipsburg.

For example, I personally had to lead the charge to make both the Philipsburg and Tyrone hospitals smoke-free. The effectiveness of my efforts was limited by the unions and only partly successful as I finally was able to present this as a safety issue. The risks of fire and explosions and risks to employees factored into some restrictions. At Tyrone, the nurses' smoking lounge was right across from the room in which one of my severe asthmatics was placed. Ironically, that patient had previously almost died and had been admitted to intensive care at Philipsburg twice before I could convince the parents to stop smoking in the house or anywhere around her. After getting through to the parents, they were astounded to find that smoking was still permitted in the hospital and occurred around their child. Their concerns were also reported. Eventually, smoking was moved away from patient care areas, a partial success.

The resources available to rural communities and underserved areas are incredibly limited for the members of those communities as well as for the healthcare providers. Philipsburg was fortunate to have liaisons with Geisinger. In fact, more than 75 percent of the hospital medical staff were Geisinger-employed physicians. There was also a neonatal care unit independent of Geisinger in a town called DuBois that occasionally provided support when weather did not allow for helicopter transport. The DuBois team could arrive by ground within thirty to forty-five minutes, depending upon the weather. Ground transport from Geisinger at Danville was approximately two hours.

Although most of my years there were challenging and emotionally rewarding, it seems that the first year or two of experiences were beyond anything that I could have envisioned. There were times when I had to take care of premature infants at birth or assist in obstetrical, surgical, or emergent patient needs. The number of patients admitted to the hospital due to asthma and dehydration was incredible. But the effectiveness of my management strategies and parental educational efforts brought this under control and reduced hospital admissions to normal expectations within two years. Eventually educational efforts and needed referrals helped to prevent the delivery of high-risk babies there, tempered by the weather or other unpredictable circumstances. Still, there were many times when I attended high-risk births at Clearfield, Tyrone, and State College. Because of the distances to these hospitals, effective communication, education, and time management were necessities for quality care of the newborn.

Sometimes, things just happened. There was the rare or uncommon use of ultrasound during pregnancies back then, and the standards for management of meconium at birth, respiratory distress of the newborn, and jaundice were somewhat controversial and not as standard and evidenced-based as today. Thus, it was not unusual to deal with unexpected although sometimes preventable problems at birth. One anecdote is particularly instructive.

One of our family physicians, well-known locally for her obstetrical skills, was called to assist an elderly local general practitioner who unexpectedly encountered thick meconium while assisting a birth. Subsequently, I was called stat from our clinic to assist. Upon arrival, the anesthetist reported that he had intubated and suctioned thick, green meconium from the baby's airway twice, the newborn appeared lifeless, but he was now needed emergently downstairs in the ED. Upon handing the baby over, the endotracheal tube dislodged.

I continued resuscitation measures, re-intubating the newborn and providing chest compressions. The heart rate was not responding, and by ten minutes after birth it seemed that our efforts were futile. The blood gas revealed severe acidosis and hypoxemia. I thought that the meconium could have caused a pneumothorax, so prepared to test for that. At just that moment, a chest x-ray was presented to me, and I could see clearly that both lungs had collapsed. After providing relief with bilateral needle aspirations, the newborn began to respond to our resuscitation measures. While placing a chest tube, I also instructed one of our surgeons who had come by to help on placing the other, since he had never done one on a newborn, although he had done many on adults.

By the time the DuBois transport team arrived, this baby had umbilical catheters in place, was receiving fluids, had bilateral chest tubes in place, and was now pink and looking around the room. My elation was added to when the neonatologist introduced himself to me and thanked me, stating that prior to my coming to town, distressed newborns had to await their arrival for such care. My joy was even greater when I encountered the baby in my office in two days for follow-up from the NICU. Ultrasounds confirmed that there were no cranial bleeds, and there were no findings of neurological sequelae. Truly, I thought, miracles do happen!

One unexpected delivery at Philipsburg, of a thirty-three-week premature infant, also unexpectedly led to some notoriety for me. This premature infant evidently had more mature lungs than expected for her age. Her age was confirmed by history and by my assessment of her physical development, according to Dubowitz criteria. Called emergently, upon arrival, I assessed her status and proceeded to ensure that appropriate measures would be taken for her well-being. Usually breathing, feeding, and maintenance of body temperature are challenged by immaturity that puts these prematurely born infants at risk. They are also more susceptible to infection than term babies. Standard practice even at a major referral center would be to place the infant in NICU, to provide monitoring and supportive care as needed. The rule of thumb then was that it would likely be another five weeks or more before a thirty-three-week premature infant would be feeding well and could be safely sent home. I explained all this to the single teenage mother and cautioned that although her baby was not distressed, it would be twenty-four hours or more before we could reliably know how she would do with her breathing.

Believing that patients and/or their caretakers should be involved in all decisions about their care, I took risks with this newborn that perhaps were not wise. The mom's only social support was local, and transfer out of town was strongly resisted. After discussions with her and the maternal grandfather, I agreed to try to manage the infant locally. However, I emphasized, any change in respiratory status, or inability to progress with feedings in a couple of days, would necessitate transfer to a neonatal intensive care unit. Possibly, it would need to be emergent. Needless to say, I was anxious about keeping her there, but I was also confident because of my extensive training and experience that I would know when transfer would become mandatory. I would need to monitor her closely. During the next forty-eight to seventy-two hours, I made very frequent visits, including many during the middle of the night.

Fortunately, this premature infant never developed significant respiratory distress, just some tachypnea. I was able to begin feedings as that resolved. Excellent nursing care maintained her temperature well and kept me appropriately informed. The baby did well and was discharged home to parental care in three to four weeks, having gained weight well.

Somehow this story got out to a newspaper in my hometown area, the Wyoming Valley, and Mom proudly sent me a copy of the article with a title above my picture that proclaimed, "Courtdale Man Saves Baby!" The nurses and mother also expressed their gratefulness by giving me a white sweatshirt with the baby's pink and blue footprints on it. I still have that shirt, and it still fits!

Clinic Care of Patients

"Don't worry, Dr. Burke, we have rescheduled all of this evening's (sixteen-plus) patients for tomorrow," would be the response after my second or third call from the hospital that I was delayed by emergencies requiring my help. Sure enough, all of those patients showed up the next day, along with a few dozen others.

Fortunately, I had two wonderful, dedicated, well-respected pe-diatric-trained and experienced nurses who had their RN degrees and who had been a part of that community all or practically all of their lives. Sometimes I would answer a call to our clinic, made by a patient's parent requesting to speak to the nurse. When queried as to why the parent just didn't ask me, the nurse would report that the patient did not want to bother me with their questions. They knew they would get excellent advice from the nurse. More than once, my nurses would prepare me for a visit by an angry parent or discuss a patient's concerns in advance of their visit. Interestingly, the same parent who would tell the nurse, "If Dr. Burke doesn't give me an antibiotic for my child this time, I will pull out every one of his blond moustache hairs!" would be very pleasant and nice to me at the visit and would not bring up that concern. Fortunately, being forewarned helped me to be prepared to address the unspoken concerns.

In addition to the two nurses, I had one front desk person who was marvelous at multitasking, was always pleasant, and served as my appointment person, receptionist, and transcriptionist. Her communications with me and the nurses were timely and effective and allowed us to provide more access for patients than we could put on the books. Depending upon how on time or behind I was, they would advise the patients as to when to arrive to be seen. Literally, I never turned away a patient for same-day care unless there was a conflict with me having to be elsewhere.

One busy winter day, I had just returned from morning hospital rounds in State College Community Hospital, where I also attended newborns and high-risk deliveries. Upon arrival, my receptionist asked if I had my roller skates on. It was 8:00 a.m. and already I was double-booked. My nurses and she agreed that they could stay as long as it took to see all the patients calling in that day. My wife brought supper for us. By 10:00 or 11:00 p.m., we had seen and treated over a hundred patients! There were only eighty-plus registered, but parents who asked me to just take a quick peek into a sibling's ears or to listen to a sibling's chest were not denied. The number of siblings seen in that way put us over the one hundred mark. During that day, I ran almost two hours behind and would often find a parent asleep in the room with a child or two in her arms. It was a rare parent who complained, as they knew we were doing our best to meet the demand.

News of that day spread quickly, and I received an admonishment from leadership at the main site, a hundred miles away, that I was not allowed to run the clinic past 7:00 p.m. in the future. Thanks to those nurses willing to stay late, patients got better care than I could possibly have provided at the hospital emergency room, where they surely would have presented to see me.

There are hundreds of anecdotes that I could tell about my experiences as a pediatrician in Philipsburg. But clearly, those would fill a book, and most are best kept as my personal memories. However, some are told as a way of relating what it was like to be the only pediatrician in town for eight of those nine years that I spent there. The challenges patients have in getting needed healthcare services, and the challenges professionals face in delivering that care, thereby become somewhat more apparent.

Eventually, the state elected to close the Philipsburg hospital because of the costs associated with taking care of a relatively low number of patients. The unions had created over two hundred positions in a hospital that ran a daily census often under a dozen or two. Although the community and local legislators tried to keep the hospital open, the attempts failed. Consequently, I had to admit patients to the Clearfield, Tyrone, and/or State College hospitals, which were about twenty to twenty-five miles in different directions from our clinic and my home. To provide my patients with the appropriate care, Geisinger supported my requests and negotiated on their behalf for services in the other hospitals, whose private practice physicians feared the presence of this behemoth organization as potential competition and lobbied against it. Interestingly, the Philipsburg hospital would reopen under private management, but there would be several years without a local hospital, and eventually the hospital would close again.

In the absence of a local hospital, care of patients presenting to the clinic could be compromised. Patients with a problem that normally would require an overnight observation often were treated as outpatients with close follow-up by phone and subsequent clinic visit. We were fortunate to have laboratory and x-ray resources

within our clinic, so that mitigated some of the risk and saved patients the need to travel for those tests. Unlike today, when imaging
is available for review by computer and can be read quickly by an
expert, effective management of the patient required that I could
read x-rays in terms of fractures, pneumonia, foreign bodies, cardiovascular, and abdominal abnormalities.

The resources for managing seizures, specific injuries, and some
other emergencies are not as readily available in a rural clinic as in
a hospital. Patient care in our clinic was enhanced by the expertise
of our nurses and supplemented by the occasional assistance of
my non-pediatric colleagues. The need for me to attend high-risk
births and to assist with acutely sick, distressed, or injured kids at
a hospital more than twenty miles away often led to unsafe driving
practices that put me at risk as well. One particular near tragic
accident on a snowy, ice-covered road that I traveled en route to
Clearfield in the middle of the night brought me to my senses about
speeding and passing under dangerous conditions.

Care back then was also riskier than now, because there were
no cell towers or ways to communicate except by pager and access
to a landline phone. Thus, calls for which I was paged en route back
to my clinic from the hospital, or vice versa, had to await my ability
to find a phone booth or arrival at my destination. Because many
of my patients were my neighbors, knew where I lived, or had my
phone number, the expectation to provide advice over the phone
or to see the patient at my house would put the patient at risk for
care and me for liability.

Fortunately, I lived only two miles from the clinic and
Philipsburg hospital, so I would always ask to see the patient there,
rather than try to make a diagnosis by phone. Sometimes, like the
ED physician described earlier, parents would read symptoms of
chickenpox or some other illness from a home medical book, and

my presumptive diagnosis would change when the patient was assessed directly in person. After the closure of the Philipsburg hospital, I would refer the patient to other emergency departments or assess whether the patient's symptoms would allow evaluation the next morning once the clinic was open. It was not uncommon for me to see the patient in the Tyrone or Clearfield emergency departments, since there were no pediatricians there who could cover for me, whereas the staffing of pediatricians at State College Community Hospital was appropriate and provided effective triage. My presence there was only needed for the uncommon presentation and need for admission of my patients.

During my last two years of service in the Philipsburg-Tyrone-Clearfield-State College area, I was joined by a pediatric partner. That eased the clinic burden but did not help much after hours because he lived in State College and took call with the Geisinger pediatricians who worked there. He and the members of that group were reluctant to cross over the mountain to see patients in the Philipsburg ED when that reopened because of continued quality issues there. So, for the entire nine years, I was on call twenty-four hours a day and seven days a week while in town. In fact, I did not use as many vacation or continuing medical education days as allowed, because leaving often put my patients at risk. In fact, one of my daughter's friends died in the Philipsburg ED from her asthma when I was absent. My presence may or may not have made a difference, but it always did in the past.

Although I made a difference in the lives of thousands of patients, each impacted my life as well. I was privileged to be a part of their lives. Beyond the emotional touch, I enjoyed the intellectual and professional challenges, somewhat unique to the setting. There was much pathology in that area, for unknown reasons. Almost every pediatric condition imaginable came through my doors. In the first couple of years, I diagnosed several cases of leukemia. There were diabetics, asthmatics, abused children, injured children, newborns with congenital heart conditions and birth defects, kids with seizure disorders, orthopedic problems that ran in families, common and uncommon skin conditions, neuromuscular disorders, deafness, glaucoma and ocular problems, bleeding disorders, mental health and learning problems, social issues, congenital biliary atresia and gastrointestinal problems, teenage pregnancies and menstrual disorders, and many other conditions, including substance abuse and sexually transmitted diseases. One of my patients had a very unusual and rare inborn error of metabolism called *long-chain acyl co-A dehydrogenase deficiency*. More about him later.

All of the skills I had learned during residency were needed and useful. These included circumcisions, laceration repairs, umbilical artery and vein catheterization, chest tube placements, arthrocentesis, percutaneous bladder aspiration, lumbar punctures, intravenous line placements, arterial and venous blood sampling, cryotherapy, bone marrow aspiration, intra-osseous line placement, basic and advanced life support, and placing splints or casts. Certainly the experiences of my residency program prepared me well. However, residency could not put it all in perspective for me until I was essentially alone in providing front-line care for hundreds of patients and their families. Medical training also did not highlight the commitment to hospitals and colleagues and the community advocacy needed to practice in an underserved, somewhat rural area.

Most, perhaps none, of the patients presenting with the illnesses above came in with the diagnosis already made. That was my challenge. In more academic settings or in larger group practices, referring colleagues have often already made a good working diagnosis. That is often not the case for the rural practitioner. That was part of the fun and challenge of employing my diagnostic skills to provide the right therapy at the right time in the right place for my patients.

Perhaps the most difficult aspect of this profession is having to present bad news to patients or to their loved ones. Granted, our medical training tries to desensitize us to be objective. But one never gets use to morbidity and mortality, regardless of significant exposure. Thank goodness, as that would certainly make us feel less empathy. My approach has always been straightforward presentation of the information that supported a diagnosis and patiently awaiting a response and questions. Providing answers to the patient or the caretaker's questions takes priority over elaborate and in-depth discussions. Brief is better, and sharing in the emotions of the moment is helpful. Appropriate details of prognosis and options for treatment need to be presented, but not in any more depth than needed to inform the patient and family members and to answer their questions. Still, it is never easy.

One of the most difficult moments for me was when I diagnosed lymphoma in a teenage girl who presented for a cough to my evening clinic. At first impression, we thought her painful cough was bronchospasm, as she had a history of intermittent asthma. The x-ray findings were a surprise to me, and it was difficult to present my suspicion, later confirmed, that this was lymphoma. Perhaps it was so difficult because her youthful, pleasant smile and appearance reminded me of my teenage daughter, and I thought about how that news would impact me. Perhaps it was knowing the challenges she would face, the morbidity and possible death. Perhaps it was empathy for what the parents would feel, the emotional roller-coaster ride, with such challenges or loss. Perhaps it was some past personal experiences. Whatever it was at the moment, I felt overwhelmed. It was difficult containing my sadness, a quiver in my voice, and tears. Amazingly, they consoled *me* with their positive outlook. Her courage was an inspiration for us as well as her class-mates. The good news is that she survived that cancer and set out upon her own quest, determined to become a pediatric oncologist.

Perhaps there are better jobs, but I can't think of any. Providing medical care to infants, children, and adolescents in such a person-alized setting is incredibly satisfying. The challenges are many, the hours are long, but the impact on my life as well as their lives makes this a life with meaning, worth living.

"I placed a medical record on your desk; you may want to look at it before going home," advised one of my family medicine col-leagues on my first day in the clinic.

The reference was to a patient with an unusual condition, quite rare, called *long chain acyl co-A dehydrogenase deficiency.* In brief, patients with this problem have an inborn error of metabolism that prevents them from oxidizing fats to provide energy. This becomes life-threatening during illnesses that challenge one's ability to com-ply with usual nutritional intake, such as during gastroenteritis. Any fasting can lead to hypoglycemia (low blood sugar) quickly. For this patient, his condition was discovered when he developed hypoglycemia in infancy and had to be resuscitated. Although I knew nothing about this condition at that moment, that would change that night.

If only I had taken the time to review his chart, I thought, as the ED physician called to let me know that a patient's mother was insisting that this well-appearing child be hospitalized. He reported that the patient had vomited only once, that evening, but his mother informed him that her son had a rare medical problem that would lead to his death without quick intravenous treatment with glucose. Upon arrival in the ED, the patient's worried mom thanked me for coming and noted that her family physician was now turning his care over to me. Thankfully, his mom knew what was needed.

The specialist who diagnosed him had given his mother a letter to be handed to any physician needing to treat him. It was a brief summary of his condition, and it provided detailed instructions on how to treat him during illness. A review of the hospital records indicated that this patient had been admitted at least weekly for D10W intravenous fluids until he was able to keep down his oral hyper-alimentation formula. Although he was now in school, his only nutrition was a balanced formula similar to what we used to treat premature infants, but adjusted for weight.

Over the next year, I continued to have to meet him in the ED and to admit him. Although I suggested that we could manage him as an outpatient with intravenous therapy whenever needed, it would be more than a year of building a trusting relationship before his parents would agree. He was admitted by me more than three dozen times in that first year. In several years, however, hospital admissions for him would be rare. The importance of patient-physician rapport in providing better care is exemplified by this case.

Despite all my reading on the subject and communication with his specialist in Philadelphia, there was no reason why he continued to need the diet restricted to formula. However, whenever a food was tried, the patient would vomit, and the fear of him getting hypoglycemic and having to be resuscitated made progress difficult. It was clear that his mother was more dependent on that formula than he was. Several years of discussions and developing a trustful relationship were required before his parents agreed to try to move him toward a more normal diet and to get him off the hyper-alimentation. By the way, that formula cost hundreds of dollars a month ($700+ by my recall). Eventually Medicaid would not cover the cost, so that provided some incentive for the parents to be more aggressive.

Emotionally, this would be traumatic for his parents, especially his mother, who had championed his care so effectively over the years. Multiple attempts failed. Finally, there was only one way to do this, I thought. The patient would need to be hospitalized and monitored closely as we introduced a fat-modified diet and discontinued the formula. As predicted, several hours into his hospitalization, his mom made the nurses call me and insisted that he needed intravenous fluids or he would die. Her fear and panic were obvious. So I went to the hospital several times daily to assess his well-being, principally to reassure his mother that we would not let anything go awry. We monitored his blood sugar closely and ran a progress chart for his mom. It was a week well spent. Our approach was successful. He was weaned off the formula and never had to restart it. There would be times that he needed intravenous glucose to be administered as an outpatient, but those also became rare. It seems that the formula may have been playing a role in his nausea and frequent episodes of vomiting.

There are so many memories that remain vivid, that inspire me, and that provide me a sense of having made a difference in others' lives, directly, indirectly, and in unique ways. The experiences of caring for patients in an underserved area have been educational as well as heart-warming for me. Furthermore, those experiences have helped me to be a more informed and effective mentor for students and resident physicians. They have enabled me to connect with patients and their families in ways that missed opportunities would never have allowed.

Community Advocacy

Never could I have imagined that I would become so overcommitted to the community. Besides the care of my patients in the clinic and hospitals, I felt obligated to provide advocacy for the children of our community.

"Please, dear God, let there be school tomorrow," prayed my daughter at bedtime.

Approximately three years after our move to Philipsburg, the teachers had gone on strike. It was for better wages and benefits, not for better conditions for education. At first, I was neutral, understanding the importance of collective bargaining and believing that this was a last resort for getting an appropriate contract with the school. So, I wrote a letter to the editor and attended some community meetings, encouraging both the teachers' union and the school board to come to terms for the students. Both sides praised my support. However, things went from bad to worse.

The strike was selective. Every morning, parents would have to turn on the radio or television to learn if there would be school that day. This was stressful and heartbreaking for the twenty-five hundred–plus students and their families. Having to make last-minute arrangements for child care and for planning one's day seemed to be an unreasonable and unnecessary burden. A strike that had a duration announced and deadline for action may have been more effective and popular. Any support for the teachers' cause diminished as the strike was prolonged and information got out about how the strike was part of a preplanned strategy statewide (ten-year plan) to gain benefits through arbitration by selecting vulnerable communities that would successfully set precedent for the desired wages and benefits. Some teachers disagreed with the strike and provided me with a copy of the union's strategy.

By January of the school year that started in September, the students were still out of school because of the strike. Graduating seniors were now at risk of not completing the required number of school days on time. Town meetings were getting more confrontational, and the union would not budge on their demands. The school board would not provide a contract. Children, such as my daughter, became distraught. Finally, I took issue with the strike. At town meetings I advocated for the students and denounced the union's strategy. Subsequently, my wife was cornered in the grocery store and told that I better "shut up." The union also reportedly tried to influence my employer to contain my comments or expect an adverse impact statewide by the union and its large membership. Fortunately, my employer's leadership was not intimidated and recognized that I was not professing to speak as a representative of our healthcare organization.

Once again, I wrote a letter to the editor. This time, I provided specific steps that the community could take to encourage the teachers to return to the classroom. The approach included boy-cotting the businesses owned by the teachers and their spouses and protesting outside of the administrative offices of the school. I also addressed the threatening intolerance exhibited by some of the union members and remarked that they could move to China if they did not believe in public discourse and dissent.

The responses were somewhat surprising. People from other areas of the state had been following the strike and called me to thank me for being an advocate for our children's education. Some teachers also thanked me. Others condemned me for not "sticking together" as professionals. Some came to our clinic and asked for transfer of their children's medical records. In one instance, when asked where to, the response was "anywhere, perhaps China." It would be a year or two before most of those disgruntled teachers brought their children back to my practice. Almost all of the other parents coming to the clinic thanked me for my advocacy and wanted to talk about the strike and how to help their children during the interim. My practice seemed to flourish even more.

Shortly afterward, the teachers returned to the school with an interim agreement but still no contract. During my stay there, no other strikes occurred.

If professionals with specific expertise do not advocate for what is appropriate, there can be adverse consequences. Sometimes that advocacy is effective, and sometimes it is not. But it should still be done. That is something I have always believed, and I have not ever been shy about letting my opinion be known. Thus, I assumed the role of advocate for children's education when the school board decided for political reasons to eliminate sexuality education from the school curriculum. Planned Parenthood had been depended upon to present information about puberty and the prevention of unwanted pregnancies and sexually transmitted diseases. There were community members who wanted such information to be removed from the curriculum. Although I made several presentations to the school board about the need to provide, as well as how to provide, education about healthy behaviors and age-appropriate sexuality education from kindergarten through the twelfth grade, as supported by the American Academy of Pediatrics, the advocacy was in vain. Elections to the school board of a majority of members with opposing views allowed a curriculum change. Planned Parenthood services (which did not include abortions) were no longer available, the advice to make sexuality education an appropriate progression from kindergarten through twelfth grades was ignored, and the burden of "sex education" fell to the softball coach in seventh grade, even though he declared himself disinterested and not sufficiently knowledgeable. Although I had no specific data, it did seem that subsequently I was dealing with more risk-taking behaviors, STDs, and unwanted pregnancies in my adolescent patients. That is one argument against local control of educational curricula. In my opinion, knowledge and access to it should never be restricted.

Small-town politics are interesting and often challenging. Community participation, however, is very important and can be personally satisfying. Through trial and error, I learned much about leading effectively. Since I have difficulty saying no, I was often asked to be part of community activities and groups. Examples include having been the president of Rotary during the same year that I was president of the County Medical Society and president of the Philipsburg-Osceola Soccer Association. My participation was also requested on some ad hoc school committees and on the Philipsburg Bicentennial Committee.

Perhaps my greatest community service, outside of healthcare, was my immersion into leadership in community soccer. Our orthopedist had been the president of the soccer association, but when he moved, he asked me to take on that role. He said that he thought my ideas about expectations for athlete and parental behaviors in sports, soccer in particular, were good and much needed to be implemented. That is when soccer took over our family life!

Because I never played soccer, I thought my leadership role required that I gain some expertise about the sport, so I took progressive coaching courses, read diligently about coaching strategies, and eventually earned the highest state coaching license. I combined that knowledge with my understanding of child and adolescent developmental needs and milestones in order to advocate effectively for change and to lead knowledgeably. At one point, both our daughters and our youngest son played soccer, our oldest daughter became certified as a referee, and I coached recreational as well as competitive teams and started a girls' team. Bonnie worked in numerous capacities as team mom and member of the association. Time management had to be creative to get us all to our respective sites on many weekends.

Our soccer association cleared some community land, created

a soccer field there, and built a concession stand. This was quite an accomplishment, considering how embedded football, baseball, and wrestling were, and how most parents were unaware of soccer. Eventually community members became aware of the rules, expectations, and benefits to the child of playing soccer. It was a sport that required player strategies, physical fitness, and commitment and was focused on hitting the ball, not the other players. One of the most difficult challenges was to teach parents the importance of positive sideline cheering and to role model effective and positive attitudes toward the referees and opponents. Expanding their understanding of the differences and benefits of recreational as well as competitive soccer was an ongoing process.

As the community soccer programs developed, it then became a natural progression to get this sport into the high school. Fierce competition from those committed to football and wrestling made that transition difficult. Perseverance pays off. We effectively lobbied the school to embrace soccer as a high school sport. It would be a few years before we got girls' soccer to that level, but we did.

Our first two years in the high school did not go well. I was team physician and could observe close up the problems that would eventually move the athletic director and school board to a position of wanting to discontinue the program. The coach, who had played college soccer and was a professional who everyone thought would be a great role model, disappointed us. He focused on teaching aggressiveness that often took the players' minds off ball strategy and resulted in frequent red cards. His disciplinary measures at practice did not support better ball-handling skills but were primarily physical, making them run around the field until exhausted. Although these were great athletes, their training was not conducive to good ball handling, game strategies, and positive attitudes. The assistant coach was perceived as contributing to the problem. Our team usually had one or two players out for red cards and injuries, and often we played with ten or fewer players. Consequently, we won very few games. The coach's behavior at the games occasionally got him removed from the field and often was embarrassing for the school. His constant yelling at players and referees from the sideline was clearly poor sportsmanship and a distraction for the players.

Once again, I found myself before the school board, but this time with parental support. We argued that the kids and community had worked extremely hard to bring this sport to the school and that what was needed was a new coach, not abandonment of the program. Exasperated, I accepted the board's ultimatum and request that I become head coach for the soccer team or it would be discontinued from the high school. The program would be on probation to become a positive thing for the school or risk being ended. Our hopes to get girls' soccer into the high school were also on the line.

Fortunately, I was able to manage my clinic hours to enable me to run practices and to attend games at the high school. The first weeks as the new coach were challenging. The outgoing coach had "poisoned the water" by emphasizing to the players that I had never played soccer. I countered that scientists who put a man on the moon had also never been astronauts. In addition, I set strict rules for expected behavior and promised to voluntarily pull out any player who got a yellow card for poor sportsmanship, in order to prevent getting red cards and playing one player down. It was my goal to be a good role model, teach the parents to do the same, and educate my players, just as I had been educated at the soccer coach licensing courses I had taken. Thus, our team set goals and put ourselves on a mission to win district championships. I encouraged the use of practices to be times for improved ball-handling skills and to develop team strategies, and I worked to document stats and to enhance the skills of our weakest players while taking our more skilled players to a higher level. Post-game sessions would be held for performance review and to understand the reasons behind our strategies. I even brought in a sports psychologist from Penn State to back up my behavioral management efforts.

It did not surprise me one bit that these same players, who were great athletes, would move from the bottom to the top of the league. They won thirty-four victories in two seasons, won the Mountain League Championship, and earned a place at the District 6, Class AAA championship match, where they lost 2–0 on late goals to Altoona. Their focus on their own performance, what they could control, and what they couldn't and their commitment to team strategies made all the difference. They learned that anger and attempts to hurt their opponents were distractions that took their minds off the game. They now were enjoying the sport, and we secured a place for soccer in the high school and eventually brought girls' soccer in as well. For me, two things happened. First, I learned more about teenagers than ever before. Second, I had an immense feeling of pride, created by these kids' accomplishments and the community support and respect they received and earned.

Family Life as a Small-Town Pediatrician

Certainly, there did not seem to be enough hours in the day or enough days in the week to do all the things that needed to be done. Never before had I been so involved in a community. So, where was there time for family and for other personal interests? Time management was key to getting me through graduate school, medical school, and residency. The same could be said for my life as a small-town pediatrician.

Our house was on top of the hill in Philipsburg, initially

associated with 6.6 acres of land. Later purchases expanded that to seventy-plus acres. The setting was beautiful, with plenty of opportunity to witness beautiful sunrises and sunsets. The prior owner had a horse barn with three dog runs in the lower field and a pole barn for storage in the area behind the house. There was also an established garden, approximately thirty feet by ninety feet, bordered by a couple of dozen full-grown, six-foot high, and equally as wide blueberry bushes that were prolific. The long driveway was lined with beautiful maple trees. Just below that, across from the ranch-style house and midway to the horse barn, there was a small orchard of apple, peach, and cherry trees. The house was dated, in the late '50s and early '60s in style, with shag carpets and a combination of heating sources that included a wood-fired stove, propane gas (a five hundred–gallon tank behind the house), and electric heat. There was a two-car garage, and below that was a tall pine-tree grove. Wildlife including deer, bears, groundhogs, birds, chipmunks, rabbits, and pheasants frequently visited.

As I have done with everywhere we have lived, I remodeled the house to personalize it. There was not one room that did not get changed. Floors, ceilings, walls, windows, and doors were repainted, repaired, replaced, or remodeled. A large deck was added to the entire field side of the house. The pole barn was converted to a *dojo* in order to continue our martial arts. Three golden retrievers, two part of the litter that the first sired, were kept in the barn runs. The rest of the horse barn housed the diesel tractor with front-end loader and back brush hog that was used to keep six acres of pasture groomed. The horse stalls were used to store firewood I cut up and manually split, from an annual delivery of a tri-axle load of fifty to one hundred trees. I also created a jogging path around the property, which later would also be used for cross-country skiing when we would get a fresh snowfall. I also used the other sixty acres and more behind us to ski cross country, enjoying the quiet of the woods, with only the sounds of my heavy breathing and the soft crunching of the snow.

Gardening was one of my favorite activities, and we enjoyed the bountiful harvests of fresh corn, beans, peas, beets, onions, tomatoes, broccoli, squash, zucchini, potatoes, and melons. Bonnie canned surplus tomatoes for winter use and froze surplus blueberries or made them into preserves. There were so many blueberries that some neighbors and relatives helped in the harvest. In addition to the garden near the house, I made an even larger one near the barn to grow the corn, melons, and potatoes. The deer also enjoyed my garden and orchard!

Our kids participated in some of these projects and enjoyed using the tractor. Of course, their help was sometimes voluntary and sometimes conscripted. One memorable reaction was our youngest daughter, Linnea, who used to love helping me to plant the garden. When she was pre-pubertal, things changed, as did her interests.

"Come help me plant the garden."

"No, I don't want to," she said.

"Whatever happened to that sweet little girl who always wanted to help her daddy?"

"That little girl just grew up!" she proclaimed with her hands on her hips and her chin in the air.

Yes, the kids were growing up fast. Their interests became more diverse, and time with their friends became paramount. Imagine our shock when our oldest daughter, Christa, came home from the prom with an engagement ring! Fortunately, she got over that infatuation and successfully pursued her BSN and RN before considering marriage again. The two youngest spent a lot of time in community soccer. Linnea convinced me to start the girls' recreational soccer team that eventually provided a basis for high school.

Her friends were also my patients, and they were conflicted as to whether to call me Coach, Mr. Burke, Dr. Burke, or Daddy. They decided that "Coach Daddy" would be my name. Most of that spirited group had not played soccer previously, but they were one of my favorite teams and provided me with many memories.

Our son, Galen, was on a competitive team that went to Sweden and Denmark, to compete internationally in the Gothia and Dana Cups respectively. While there, we stayed in the Olympic Stadium in Sweden and rented a car to find the town and church wherein my grandparents had been married. In Denmark, we stayed with a family we had previously hosted in our state. Later, he would play on the first Philipsburg-Osceola high school soccer team.

Bob, our oldest son, played soccer when he was younger, in Texas, but his interests changed. As a talented and gifted student, he had been introduced to computers, which back then were quite rudimentary, using the DOS system. During that prolonged teachers' strike, he taught himself computer skills and advanced what would become a lifetime interest for him. He also participated in band in high school and later played in the Blue Band at Penn State, performing one year at the Rose Bowl.

Family-centered activities were at the heart of my nonprofessional time, as was having some time to myself jogging, skiing, gardening, and doing carpentry and painting. I continued to practice my martial arts forms and joined a local club on occasion in a kick-a-thon community fundraiser. Being closer to relatives allowed for more time to visit, and so the kids got to know their cousins, aunts, uncles, and grandparents better. Visiting friends and relatives was always a welcome respite for Bonnie from the chores at home and the demanding hours associated with community soccer and fulfilling all the family roles I could not attend to because of patient and career demands.

Philipsburg was a nice community in which to raise a family, and my pediatric practice was everything and more than what I had envisioned when I set out on my quest to become a physician. After nine years, though, it was time for a change.

CHAPTER 12

A New Mission

What would drive me to move from this community in which we were so engaged? What was missing in my life? Was I leaving a stressful life or looking for more meaning and more challenges? Was it simply impulsive? Was it fate? Was it a combination of these?

Embracing Change

Our oldest daughter, Christa, had just moved back to Texas, to be employed as a nurse at Parkland Hospital in Dallas. We decided to visit her, on a trip to San Antonio for a continuing medical education meeting. After that visit, en route to San Antonio, I stopped in to visit some friends at Scott & White, where I had been employed just out of residency, from 1985 to 1989. Bonnie went shopping. One of the general pediatricians told me about an opening for a medical director in the department, and she encouraged me to apply for it.

"No thanks, I'm happy where I am. But let me look at the position, and maybe I can write off part of this trip as a job search (joking, of course!)."

By the time Bonnie and I met up again, I had given this some thought. Jokingly, I announced that we were moving back. Of course, knowing me quite well, she laughed and said something about not being serious, "Or are you?" A more in-depth, serious discussion ensued. We were happy, but change had come to my practice, the community, and our family. Perhaps it was time to redirect our lives and my career.

Geisinger and Hershey had merged, and that merger brought change. There were changes in the compensation plan and in our practice parameters. No longer would I have local control of my appointment schedule, the clinic hours would be set by the off-site department, and billing would be centralized. Where I admitted patients would now be restricted, and there was no progress in getting local coverage for my patients at night or after hours. My partner took call with the State College group where he lived. Thus, I remained on call 24/7, as our patients were reluctant to travel over the mountain, to a site twenty-five miles away. In my absence, there were many obstacles for my patients to get the care they expected. For over a year, I had been trying to negotiate better coverage for our patients but was unsuccessful. These changes restricted patient access to me and actually made that aspect of my practice easier. But that was not what I wanted. In some ways, it felt like I was on a path toward retirement and less dedicated. I questioned if this was how I wanted to work for the next twenty years. The loss of significant autonomy, and the failure of distant administrators to understand the needs of our community, made me feel like this was no longer my practice.

In thinking about a possible practice change, I created personal mission and vision statements. What did I really want? What was missing? How would I continue to feel the excitement of being someone's doctor? How would I continue to dedicate my life to making a difference in other lives? Did I want to slow down? Did I want to pursue new challenges?

From a career standpoint, this is what I missed. I missed diversity in my patient population. Although I loved my patients, they were primarily indigent Caucasians. I remembered how I enjoyed caring for children of multiple races and cultural backgrounds. I remembered how my life was enriched by cultural diversity. I missed interactions with other pediatricians. I missed attending grand rounds and morbidity and mortality conferences. I missed being a mentor for students and resident physicians. I missed the close relationships that I had with subspecialists and how I learned from them. I missed the feeling that I was an important part of the very large healthcare system that I admired and within which I worked.

Still, the overall nature of my practice satisfaction was positive, and my discontent was not sufficient motivation to leave. However, I had a sense of accomplishment without a clear vision of my future. Certainly, I would need to consider my family's needs. How would change affect them? How would they perceive that change, and would they embrace it?

After some soul-searching, I determined that my future would be a commitment to continue to do my best to provide excellence in patient care and to ensure access to that care. Change would be toward a new mission, not away from the current one. I was still young and had a lot more to offer to this profession. The experiences of the past decade gave me incredibly valuable insights to patients' needs and the delivery of personalized healthcare. Those insights should be passed on to the younger, inexperienced doctors and administrators. It would be important as well to influence the direction of large healthcare institutions.

Long ago, I had decided that it was not within my ability to give 100 percent of my effort to both patient care and research, so

I had chosen patient care as my *raison d'etre*. Thus, once again, I would have to decide how to divide my time. The decision was that I would always devote 75 percent of my efforts to direct patient care, since that is what I loved the most. The remaining time would be dedicated to administrative and teaching roles, as additional ways to influence and affect patient care. Of course, direct patient care would also involve teaching as a preceptor and mentor. This seemed to be a formula for time allocation and career commitment that would sustain my interests, needs, and satisfaction for the duration of my active professional years.

Although there was a lot of soul-searching, it did not just occur during those hours of my visit. For the past year, I had thought through some of this but was not sure when or whether to embrace such changes. Before leaving, though, this direction for my life gained clearer focus. It was sort of like Malcolm Gladwell describes in *Blink*,[43] an insightful moment. Thus, I decided to review the position being offered, assess its fit with my long-term goals, and apply later, after further thought and family discussions.

Bonnie and I had similar thoughts. It was time for a lifestyle change as well. Our two oldest children were now pursuing their careers on their own, our third was in college, and our youngest would soon be entering high school. If we were to move, it would be better done before she entered high school, as that could be more traumatic. Incidentally, a couple of years later, she would write an essay about how the move turned her world upside down but gave her opportunities that she would not have had. Once again, we would be living distant from our relatives, but we could vacation back. Being closer to our firstborn would be a positive. The lure of living in a milder climate, and closer to more expansive shopping,

---

[43] Malcolm Gladwell, *Blink*. (New York: Bach Bay Books/Little, Brown and Company, 2005).

dining, and cultural options, was also a positive. Most importantly, as we got older, we would have ready access to state-of-the-art healthcare at Scott & White, only minutes away. There would be sadness leaving my patients and colleagues, our friends, the community, and our homestead that we had so personalized. But life is all about change—embracing change and leading it.

The Impact of the Move on Our Family

Although the move was made primarily for a change in my career goals, it had an impact on my wife, children, and other relatives. It changed friendships. It changed our lives in different and in better ways. Financially, I was finally, sixteen years post medical school, able to pay off all that debt incurred by such an extended education. There is much more than can be told, but I will provide a look at the long-term impact.

Christa continued to work in Dallas as a nurse, met her future husband, and became a stay-at-home mom to raise their two children. Bob became employed in Maryland in the field of biotechnology after his graduation from Penn State, got married, and continues to live there with his wife and three children. Galen worked while attending the local Temple Community College before changing career directions and earned a bachelor's degree in photography at Brooks Institute in Santa Barbara, where he met his future wife. They have now moved back to Temple and live here with their three children. He is regional manager for a credit union, and she has her own photography business. Linnea continued her interest in soccer, playing on a select team that I coached in the community league here, and then on the varsity team. After high school, she pursued a career in nursing, having met her future husband while at Austin College. He is now a teacher and coach.

She also lives in Temple with her husband and their three children, while working full time as a nurse educator for the NICU at
BaylorScott & White, and pursuing a master's degree in nursing.

Texas thus became a permanent home for us and eventually
three of our children and eight of our grandchildren. Bonnie has
developed numerous new friendships and participates in several
social groups and has enjoyed frequently babysitting the grand-
kids and hosting regular dinners for their families. All of us have
enjoyed the geographical and cultural changes due to the move.

Community advocacy for and education about the needs of the
infant, child, and adolescent have remained part of my personal
mission. Thus, I have given many presentations to community
groups regarding the importance of early literacy promotion on
brain and child development. At one school district, I presented
a lecture and group discussion for teachers and administrators
regarding the effect of poverty on brain development and education. I gave presentations regarding child behavioral management
strategies and attention deficit disorders. For several years I was on
the health advisory committee for the Temple Independent School
District. My outreach efforts helped to promote the administration
of the influenza vaccine through the schools, thereby making our
communities healthier. In addition, I gave numerous interviews for
television and community blogs and a national parenting magazine.

One other community-oriented initiative that I co-chaired was
the development of a weekly column in our local newspaper that
would highlight healthcare and pediatric developmental advice for
the lay public. Pediatricians, generalists, and subspecialists, still
present topics of interest, highlighting what is evidenced-based
advice for care of the pediatric patient. Personally, I contributed
over a dozen articles

Although I worked with the TISD in several ways, it was

disappointing for me to have worked extensively over two years and still not be able to remove spanking (a.k.a., corporal punishment) from that institution as a means of student discipline. This was another example of local control of policy that can adversely affect children and their education. In brief, I chaired a subcommittee on corporal punishment that widely represented the teachers, administrators, parents, students, and members of the school board and the community. After seeking and reviewing the literature on corporal punishment, our committee unanimously recommended to the school board for the removal of this archaic and abusive form of discipline. The school had at least thirty-five other disciplinary measures in place.

Unfortunately, for unknown reasons, the president of the school board decided to table our committee's advice from any further action. Most schools in the nation, as well as in our area, no longer allow corporal punishment. Hopefully someday that will be universal. No other institutions, including the military and prisons, condone corporal punishment as a form of discipline. The American Academy of Pediatrics, as well as medical associations of family practitioners and psychiatrists, concur with national teacher organizations that corporal punishment is dangerous and abusive and has no role in public education.

Beyond Direct Patient Care

As is true of many professions, there are many career choices and options for physicians, to participate in the delivery of healthcare. A major focus of this book, in fact, is to provide a glimpse into what lies beyond the quest to become a physician. It is indeed just a glimpse. The autobiographical portrayal of becoming a general pediatrician differs from what it would be for a pediatric subspecialist,

surgeon, psychiatrist, pathologist, family practitioner, administrator, or other type of physician. What would lie beyond the degree
would be different.

The fear of change is often based on the fear of failure and the
fear that change would not be what one expects. Babe Ruth is cred-
ited with having said, "Don't let the fear of striking out hold you
back." Despite the anxiety of change, I did not fear failure. In fact,
I have always been eager to embrace change, especially after having
compared the positives and negatives. Multiple career changes and
having overcome many barriers to my goals has given me more
confidence than had I not been so challenged. Success through
perseverance was in my DNA. However, I found that change often
did not meet my expectations or was at least different. The game
played would be altered by uncontrollable events. So how would it
be this time? In keeping with the baseball metaphor, would it be a
home run or a strikeout?

My application to rejoin the Pediatric Department at Scott &
White, in a leadership role as medical director, was accepted. Once I
arrived, though, that role was redefined as section chief of community general pediatrics, not division director. The title was changed,
but the expectation that I would be responsible for the day-to-day
operations of our outpatient pediatric practice of about sixteen
providers remained the same. Evidently another pediatrician in
the interim had been hired in the role as division director, primarily dealing with staff development and personnel issues. At least
that is how the role of medical director had been re-characterized.
Concerned that I had misunderstood the job description, I reread
what had been posted. Clearly the change was made after our agreement but not communicated until after my arrival. Nevertheless, I
was excited about getting on with my new mission.

Prior to my arrival, unknown to me, the departmental morale

had been low and was getting worse. Many colleagues complained about inefficiencies of operations, lack of consistent policies, administrative tone deafness, and distrust in leadership. One older colleague who I knew well from my first employment there asked, "Why on earth would you come back to this place?" On balance, he used to have a positive outlook on things. Something had changed. Another colleague, a subspecialist, confided that the departmental leadership had great ideas but did not empower others and would likely work us all to death. Monthly section meetings were shouting matches and essentially venting sessions, much like some of the broader departmental meetings. After experiencing my first raucous section meeting, I provided an agenda for future meetings based on input from colleagues and in advance of the meeting. I also had to set rules of behavior.

Ambulatory pediatrics, later referred to as community pediatrics, was now located in a nice new building that had been designed to have four pods, one dedicated to resident continuity clinic and after hours, and the others to match personalities within the same area and to hope that each would function as a small group practice. However, lab and x-ray were centralized, nursing and other support staff were shared, and after-hours obligations for patient care during evening and weekend clinics was based on the entire group. Clinic absences were also independent of pod staffing. In effect, this was one large group of sixteen providers, including three nurse practitioners who had no role in after hours or resident or medical student teaching. Some of the providers rotated monthly as inpatient attending physicians, but not all. While on hospital duty, their clinic duties were deferred. Some, but not all, served as the attending for the residents' outpatient clinic. Students and residents on rotation with ambulatory pediatrics were inconsistently assigned to multiple providers throughout their assigned month.

Each provider had several pages of personal rules for appointments, and most took no ownership of the practice. *Welcome to leadership!*, I thought.

In order to gain a better understanding of the practice's needs, I met with each provider. In preparation for the meeting, each was to present details of what would be the ideal practice. Where would you like to be located, what appointment hours and rules would please you, what is your preference for after-hours coverage, are you happy with being full-time or part-time, what role(s) do you want in patient care, teaching, research, and administration, what can we do to improve morale, do you have the tools needed to do your job, and what would you change? A half-hour was set aside for each, with a promise to meet again if needed. I created an open-door policy and promised to make the system work for everyone.

Several problems were universally recognized: 1) Everyone felt that the tail wagged the dog, in that patient care was at the convenience of support staff. 2) Most wanted the autonomy of solo practice, despite being in a group practice. 3) No one agreed with the department chair that everyone had to equally participate in patient care, teaching, clinical research projects, and administrative roles on committees. 4) There were many incompatible personalities. 5) The appointment system had too many barriers for patient access, was not optimal for continuity of care, and was not conducive to expectations for teaching. 6) Some providers were not adept at teaching or inpatient care, and most had little interest in clinical research. 7) Most providers felt unappreciated and insufficiently compensated. 8) Most believed that nothing would change.

Those were the major issues, not listed in any attempt at priority. There were many minor issues and requests that were more easily dealt with as a result of the individual meetings. Clearly, there was a need to bring this group together, much like those soccer players, to define our practice goals, and to work as a team on a mission. But where does one start?

Defining the problems was a good first step. Setting group or team priorities would be next. Understanding each player's strengths and weaknesses would be essential. Leveling the workload and getting individual provider buy-in to the practice would be critical. I would strategize with the division director, the department chair, the director of nursing for the clinic, and the department administrator. As leaders, I challenged, we should empower individuals at every level and fairly address the roles and needs of each provider. Happy physicians, I contended, would improve morale and productivity. Best practice strategies would be studied, and I would then aim to implement them in our setting. This included but was not limited to better defining provider roles and expectations, improving communications between providers and support staff, appropriately staffing and providing needed resources, and encouraging the physician's role as team leader. Especially, it would be important to optimally leverage each person's role with defined responsibilities.

In brief, we agreed that developing four independent practice groups would facilitate this. Thus, there would be three senior staff small group practices (a pod of four to five compatible providers) and one teaching team. These would be pods that would take ownership of defined patient panels and take responsibility for practice management accordingly. Perhaps we could develop a budget for each pod that would link productivity with resources and compensation. Policies related to patient care and access would be set universally according to departmental and institutional goals and evidence-based medical practices for quality of patient care and with the patient being front and center. Thus, team-based, patient-centric, high-quality, and personalized care would be our strategy. The concept of "hospitalists" was now in vogue for hospital care of adult patients, and we would strategize as to how to make that work for us. The input of each and every provider would be involved in implementing this, and each team empowered as needed. A more consistent way of staffing after hours, appointing patients for continuity of care with their preferred provider or small group of providers, and teaching for excellence would be priorities.

Of course, the most carefully laid plans may go wrong, as noted by Robert Burns in 1786 in his poem "To a Mouse": "The best laid schemes o' mice an' men (often go awry)."[44] There were many known and unknown reasons why this approach had limited success. Successful changes included the after-hours coverage and appointment system, the creation of a group of dedicated hospitalists without clinic duties, a limited but enthusiastic teaching team, and more compatible teams with a designated physician leader who would hold monthly potluck luncheons to build camaraderie and address issues proactively.

What was never successful was the independent nature of the pods, ironically in part because of the structural nature of the building. More problematic was leadership's focus on cutting costs, centralizing our support services, and rotating staff. The latter gave folks the sense that they were a team in name only, disrupted at will by managers trying to meet acute as well as chronic understaffing. Compensation was not fairly applied or transparent and was often controversial for contrasts between those who taught and those who did not. Resources also were not provided based on need and productivity, as was expected. Positions approved for the generalists sometimes were diverted to the subspecialists or hospital or teaching services. Inconsistency in leadership's behavior, budgetary

---

[44] Robert Burns, "To a Mouse," *Poems, Chiefly in the Scottish Dialect*, Kilmarnock, Scotland, 1786.

gimmicks, and failure to follow through on promises led to a lack of faith in the top administrative levels of the department. In addition, frustration grew over the appointment system being overly managed by administration and not considering the patient flow needs of the pods and need for continuity of patient care with the provider(s) of the patient's choice.

Eventually, micromanagement by the department chair, broken promises, and his undercutting of my authority and that of the division director led me to step down from my administrative role. I resolved to focus on my patient practice, working within the constraints of the system to optimize my availability to patients and my productivity. Also, I continued to work with the students and residents. Despite the creation of a hospitalist group, I was able to continue to see newborns for another couple of years before that changed to a hospital-based strategy as well. Eventually a change in leadership occurred, but it is not my intent to focus on all the details. My apologies if my perspective is not shared by some.

Before the change of leadership occurred, it was clear that there was a move to increase the number of subspecialists, but space was lacking. Our building became prime real estate. The chairman met with me to discuss the possibility of my leading a small group practice at an independent site off campus. This would be an inaugural attempt to take our services to another area of the community, facilitating patient access, with the goal of improving continuity of care and better implementing the small group practice strategy we laid in place years prior. Skeptical, but enthusiastic about the opportunity, I agreed to do so with the condition that I put together a compatible team and set hours, coverage, and appointment templates that would best fit each provider's style of practice. In addition, our support staff would be dedicated to our site, in order to optimize our team's efforts and to give all a sense of practice ownership. He agreed.

Our small group practice was immediately successful, as measured by physician and support staff job satisfaction, patient loyalty, and productivity. This success provided a model that would later produce several independent small group general pediatric practices in Temple, Belton, and Killeen. That network would develop in a few years, after change of departmental chairmen.

There were a few brief interim department chairs, but the last interim chair gained everyone's trust and support and was converted to (more) permanent chairman after a national search a couple of years later. The new chair asked me to become the division director. Our other director had retired earlier. We had a long discussion, after which I agreed. Once burned, twice fearful, so I insisted that a condition of my acceptance would be that I had the requisite authority to match the responsibilities of that position. Success breeds success. Our chairman, within a year, asked me to join him as vice chairman to help set direction, as he realized that a strong Community General Pediatrics program would be needed to sustain the provision of comprehensive pediatric services to the community.

Under new leadership, our Department of Pediatrics began to thrive. Morale improved, we advanced the network of small group pediatric practices, and long-needed subspecialists were added. The stars over the community and the organization aligned such that we were able to go forth with plans and eventually the development and construction of a free-standing children's hospital. This was a twenty-plus-year-old dream come true! In addition, a subspecialty building was added next to the hospital. Again, I would provide the leadership of a small group of general pediatricians within the same building, as support for the subspecialists and the residency program.

Please note that the preceding problems were presented to provide insight to the reader regarding the challenges in delivering healthcare. One goal was to provide insight to the challenges of solo practice, as well as academic group practice. I am sure those problems are not unique to Geisinger or Scott & White, which are among the best healthcare institutions in the country, if not the world. Any problems and my roles were presented in context of my life's story. Any tales or perspectives that placed anyone (including me) in an unflattering light were not intended to do so, but those events were told because they were significant to the challenges faced.

The decision to move from Philipsburg to Temple was the right one. From a career standpoint, I was able to fulfill my desire to impact patient care directly and as a teacher and administrator. This is where I would practice until retirement. In addition to administrative roles as section chief, division director, and vice chairman, I provided direct patient care to a large panel of patients (four thousand-plus) who identified me as their primary care physician. The joy of teaching medical students and resident physicians remained an integral part of that career. The move enabled me to touch the lives of thousands of other patients and families that I will never meet, through the care provided by students and residents I mentored. Having a small but influential role in the success of our children's hospital and network of community general pediatric practices and the delivery of comprehensive services to pediatric patients over a wide area of Texas was another way to touch the lives of thousands of patients and the quality of care they could access. In my role as vice chairman, I also implemented policies that set standard expectations of physicians in the department and standardized the approach of pediatricians and family practitioners throughout our thirty-two-plus county area of service to the preventive care of the pediatric child at well-child checkups.

From a personal perspective, the change in direction and the move gave me more time to experience other aspects of life. A day after the birth of our first grandchild, I was diagnosed with melanoma, a skin cancer that has an extremely poor prognosis. Fortunately, the excellent care I received at Scott & White enabled early detection and surgical cure. That event put my life goals in a new perspective. Life is short. Thus, I vowed at that point to spend more time with family and to travel, as those are areas of my life that often had been placed second to medicine, my other love. That experience has enriched my life's journey in a blessed way for which I will always be grateful. The serendipity of circumstances could have been different.

One of the main reasons I chose general pediatrics as a career, as noted before, was to provide preventive care and help provide for the optimal development of children. Upon rejoining Scott & White in 1998, I was introduced to a new program started there in the prior year, called *Reach Out and Read (ROR)*.[45] Because of my interest in and advocacy for this early literacy promotion program, I was asked to be the medical director for it that very year. I continued in that role until retirement.

ROR is an international program begun in 1989 in Boston[46] that encourages physicians to provide a new book at well-child checkups from six months of age through five years, as a way to encourage parents to be their child's first teacher. A verbal or written prescription from the child's provider is given to the parents and

---

[45] www.reachoutandread.org
[46] Needlman, R., Klass, P., and Zuckerman, B., 2002, "Reach out and get your patients to read," *Contemporary Pediatrics* 19: 51–69.

other caretakers of that patient to read out loud, sharing a book and therefore a nurturing experience with that child daily. The goal is to stimulate the child's interest in books and a lifetime love for reading. Literacy begins to emerge concurrently with language and at a time when the brain is developing the capacity to learn, long before exposure to the educational system. Studies support the efficacy of this program.[47] The early promotion of literacy in this way enhances receptive and expressive language, encourages family orientation to reading, stimulates the child's interest in learning, and improves readiness for school. That improved readiness leads to a more likely successful educational experience and greater success in life.

My advocacy included being the medical director, ensuring funding for the program, and educating other providers, medical students and residents, administrators, parents, community groups, and teachers about the value of this program over the better part of two decades. The impact of this is incalculable, but intuitively it is one of my most important contributions to the optimal development of children, beyond that provided through other parental and patient education, therapy, and preventive health strategies, such as promoting immunizations and healthy lifestyles.

In the couple of years before my retirement, Scott & White merged with Baylor Health to become BaylorScott & White, the largest nonprofit healthcare system in Texas. Its structure and approach to community health is being hailed as a national model for the delivery of healthcare, with emphasis on keeping people and communities well through providing medical homes, education, and better proactive disease-management strategies.

---

[47] Needlman, R., Toker, K., Dreyer, B., Klass, P., Mendelsohn, A., 2005, "Effectiveness of a primary care intervention to support reading aloud: a multicenter evaluation," *Ambulatory Pediatrics* 5: 209–15.

It is an exciting time to be in healthcare, and many positive changes are coming. There will be many challenges related to the delivery of that care, some challenges related to documentation and regulatory demands, and other challenges not yet recognized. As a nation, hopefully we will eventually provide essential healthcare for everyone. That can be done. Although a major challenge lies in how that is financed and delivered, we first need the political will to do so. Clearly then, the best strategy will focus, like pediatricians have always advocated, on prevention.

Retirement

I used to laugh every time I heard folks older than me remark, "It just seems like that was yesterday," when the event was decades ago. Unfortunately, time waits for no one. It is true that the older one gets, the faster that time seems to go. Recognizing that life is short, and wanting to pursue a long-held desire to be an author, I retired at age sixty-six in 2015, also with the hope to spend more time with family and to travel. The greatest advantage of retirement is that unstructured time that gives flexibility to one's days. However, after exactly one year of retirement, I agreed to return to provide urgent care for pediatric patients on an as-needed basis. That need would be determined by the Pediatric Department and my availability. Of course, I will remain a full-time pediatrician for our wonderful grandchildren. Their parents made sure of that by buying me a personal, portable otoscope and ophthalmoscope upon retirement. My stethoscope also refuses to let me go.

Insight

The quest to become a physician is taken up by many. The motivations vary, and the resources available to, and the success of, the "knight-errant" also vary. The foundation for whom we become lies not just in our DNA, and not just in the expression of those genes but also in the experiences that are ours from the day of birth. The role of fate is not as clearly documentable. The roles of parents, siblings, and all those with whom we interact are to provide experiences that will influence us and opportunities that will affect our success. How that occurs also varies and is not fully measurable. However, the effects of one's decisions are meaningful, and the success of any quest is dependent thereupon. Moreover, recognizing what lies beyond the quest, and how the success of the quest impacts one's later contributions to this life, is just as important. Becoming a physician, allegorically finding the holy grail after a long quest, is more about what one does in that role for the patient and humankind in general.

If the reader has come away with a better sense of: how children's activities drive their brain development; how everyone in a family and community impacts that development; how change is part of life and needs to be embraced; how decisions we make help to drive our success; how the events out of our control can be tempered by our responses; how the path our quest follows is often not straight; the challenges of medical education; the healthcare needs of patients; the roles of research, evidence, experience, and reason in personalizing and optimizing healthcare; how varied careers and change enrich our lives; and how we all need to be a part of something bigger than ourselves, that something beyond our quest, then the autobiography of this *not-so-famous pediatrician* will have served its purpose.

ACKNOWLEDGMENTS

Undoubtedly, there would have been no tale to tell if it were not for my soulmate and family, so, Bonnie, thank you for the life we have shared! Thanks for the encouragement to tell the story, and thanks for being my sounding board during the entire process of writing. Thanks to our children, Christa, Bob, Galen, and Linnea, for a lifetime of joy and inspiration. Your advice during certain phases of this process was insightful. To my brothers all, your impact on my life has been immeasurable. You will always have my love and gratitude. My life would also not have been complete without my children's spouses and grandchildren. Lindy May Burke, thanks for your professional author's photograph.

Inspiration has also come to me from our extended family, my teachers, colleagues, students, and those thousands of children and their families for allowing me to share in their lives. Thank you so much.

Truly there are others who have impacted my life, and therefore many other lives, in important ways both directly and indirectly. I thank each of you for those experiences.

Finally, I would like to thank everyone at Archway Publishing for their assistance, guidance, and professionalism.